The Bahamas from Slavery to Servitude, 1783-1933

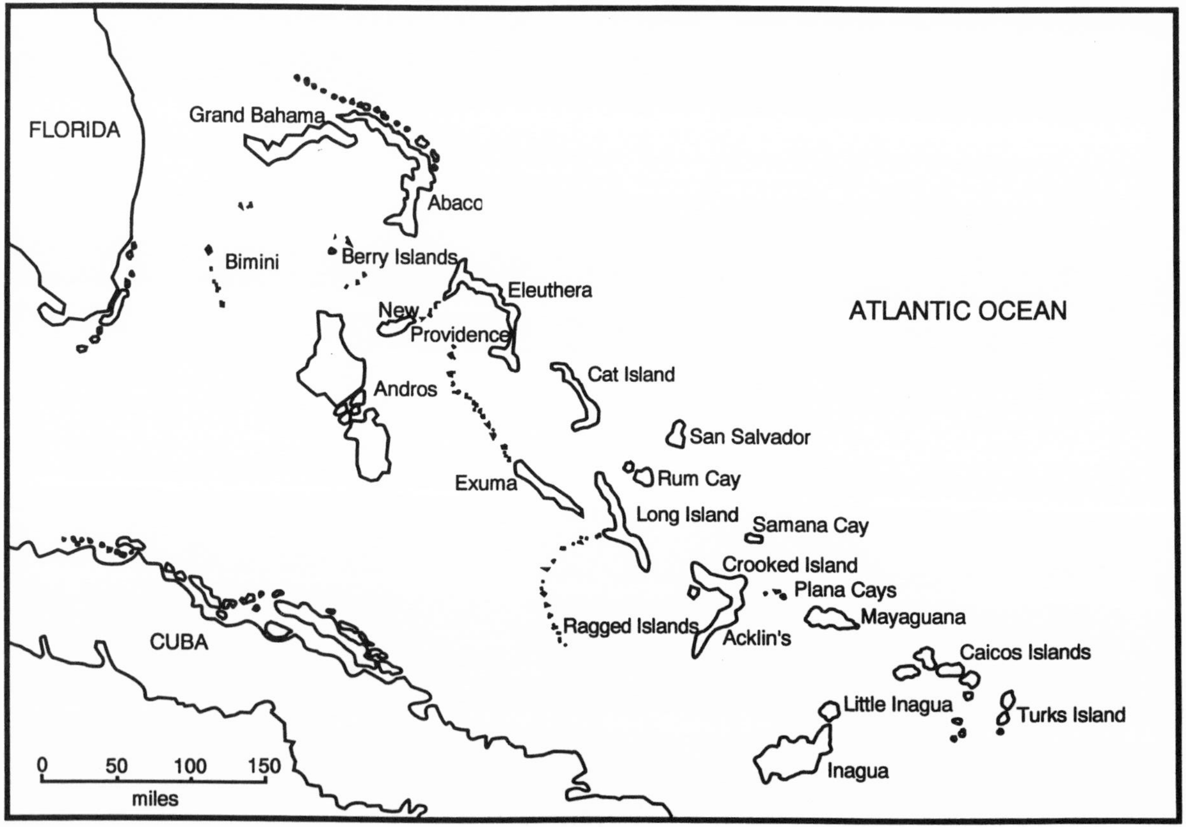

FLORIDA
Grand Bahama
Abaco
Bimini
Berry Islands
Eleuthera
ATLANTIC OCEAN
New
Providence
Cat Island
Andros
San Salvador
Exuma
Rum Cay
Long Island
Samana Cay
Crooked Island
Plana Cays
Mayaguana
Ragged Islands
Acklin's
CUBA
Caicos Islands
Little Inagua
Turks Island
Inagua
0
50
100
150
miles

The Bahamas

THE BAHAMAS FROM SLAVERY TO SERVITUDE, 1783-1933

Howard Johnson

University Press of Florida
Gainesville/Tallahassee/Tampa/Boca Raton
Pensacola/Orlando/Miami/Jacksonville

01 00 99 98 97 96 6 5 4 3 2 1

Library of Congress Cataloging-in-Publication Data

Johnson, Howard, 1945–
The Bahamas from slavery to servitude, 1783–1933 / Howard Johnson.
p. cm.
Includes bibliographical references and index.
ISBN 0-8130-1494-8 (alk. paper)
1. Slavery—Bahamas—History. 2. Plantation life—Bahamas—History. 3. Truck system—Bahamas—History. 4. Slaves—Emancipation—Bahamas—History. 5. Bahamas—Economic conditions. I. Title.
HT1119.B34J34 1996
306.3'62'097296—dc 20 96-26829

The University Press of Florida is the scholarly publishing agency for the State University System of Florida, comprised of Florida A & M University, Florida Atlantic University, Florida International University, Florida State University, University of Central Florida, University of Florida, University of North Florida, University of South Florida, and University of West Florida.

University Press of Florida
15 Northwest 15th Street
Gainesville, FL 32611

For Joyce

Contents

Tables

Acknowledgments

During the twelve-year period of my involvement in Bahamian history, I have incurred several debts in connection with my research and writing. I should like once again to thank Gail Saunders, who first encouraged my interest in Bahamian history by recruiting me to speak on a Bahamian subject at the monthly meeting of the Bahamas Historical Society in March 1983. Her role in directing perhaps the best-managed archives department in the Caribbean has been equally important to my research activities. John M. Trainor suggested as the topic for that initial lecture the truck system in the Bahamas.

Both the Department of Archives and the Nassau Public Library have provided crucial support and assistance over the years. I wish to thank especially Sherriley Voiley-Strachan, Patrice Williams, Jolton Johnson, and David Wood of the Department of Archives, themselves historians of the Bahamas, who have been unfailingly helpful in offering suggestions about sources and sending me research materials since I left the Bahamas. I wish also to acknowledge the vital contribution of Gail Brittingham, who patiently typed several versions of the manuscript.

I have benefited from the constructive criticism of friends during the period of my interest in Bahamian history. Barry Higman provided useful criticisms of my work on the credit and truck systems and, by his own work on the Bahamas, alerted me to the existence of the self-hire system. Roderick A. McDonald and Peter Dalleo generously read parts of the manuscript and offered helpful comments. Mary Turner has helped to refine my ideas on the disintegration of slavery in the Bahamas both by her own pathbreaking work on the process of slave bargaining and negotiation in Jamaica and through detailed editorial comments on a paper that I presented at the 1991 conference "From Chattel to Wage Slavery." My wife, Joyce, has demonstrated great forbearance as I have worked on this project. She continues to read critically everything that I write.

* * *

Chapters 3 to 9 of this book incorporate material from previously published essays. I should like to thank the following copyright holders for permission to adapt material from those publications. Frank Cass and Co. Ltd, London, granted permission to reprint material from "The Share System in the Bahamas in the Nineteenth and Early Twentieth Centuries," *Slavery and Abolition* 5, no. 2 (September 1984): 141–53; "'Safeguarding Our Traders': The Beginnings of Immigration Restrictions in the Bahamas, 1925–33," *Immigrants and Minorities* 5, no. 1 (March 1986): 5–27; "Social Control and the Colonial State: The Reorganization of the Police Force in the Bahamas, 1888–1893," *Slavery and Abolition* 7, no. 1 (May 1986): 46–58; "The Liberated Africans in the Bahamas, 1811–60," *Immigrants and Minorities* 7, no. 1 (March 1988): 16–40; and "The Emergence of a Peasantry in the Bahamas During Slavery," *Slavery and Abolition* 10, no. 2 (September 1989): 172–86. The Institute of Social and Economic Research, University of the West Indies, Mona, Kingston, Jamaica, granted permission to reprint material from "Labour Systems in Postemancipation Bahamas," *Social and Economic Studies* 37, nos. 1 and 2 (March–June 1988): 181–201. Cambridge University Press gave permission to use material from "'A Modified Form of Slavery': The Credit and Truck Systems in the Bahamas in the Nineteenth and Early Twentieth Centuries," *Comparative Studies in Society and History* 28, no. 4 (October 1986): 729–53. Sections of "Bahamian Labor Migration to Florida in the Late Nineteenth and Early Twentieth Centuries," *International Migration Review* 22, no. 1 (Spring 1988): 84–103, are reprinted with the permission of the Center for Migration Studies of New York, Inc.

Introduction

Historical writing on the Bahamas is primarily a twentieth-century phenomenon. Until the first decade of this century, Bahamian history was discussed either as a part of the general histories of the British West Indies or mentioned briefly in travelers' accounts. James H. Stark had published *History of and Guide to the Bahama Islands* in 1891, but it was a popular historical account intended for visitors to the colony. James M. Wright's "History of the Bahama Islands," published in 1905, was the first scholarly treatment of the colony's history. This study, which focused narrowly on the last phase of slavery and the early postemancipation years, was the earliest extended treatment of the black experience in the Bahamian context.

In the forty years following the appearance of Wright's monograph, the modest historical literature on the Bahamas centered on the early period of white colonization and on the Loyalist influx of the late eighteenth century. Wilbur H. Siebert's *The Legacy of the American Revolution to the British West Indies and the Bahamas,* published in 1913, discussed the early years of the American Loyalists in the colony as an aspect of United States history rather than as a contribution to an autonomous Bahamian history. White Bahamians, who were important participants in this early phase of historical writing, directed their attention to the history of their forebears in what was often an exercise in filial piety. In 1914, for example, A. T. Bethell published privately *The Early Settlers of the Bahamas,* which was primarily a source book on white settlement up to the Loyalist era. Until the early 1950s, no general history of the Bahamas was published. This is not surprising, for British and British imperial history continued to dominate the history curricula of Bahamian schools at the elementary and secondary levels. In that decade, three editions of A. Deans Peggs's *A Short History of the Bahamas* were published locally. The decade of the 1960s was marked by the publication, in 1962, of the first extended and comprehensive general history of the Bahamas, written by Michael Craton, who had served as a history teacher in the colony during the 1950s. This pioneering volume, which quickly established itself as the main text on Bahamian history, has been published in three editions—the most recent being the revised and expanded 1986 edition.

By the late 1970s, the historical literature on the Bahamas was changing under the influence of new historiographical trends and political events in the Bahamas. The "new" social history, which emerged as a significant intellectual trend in Europe and the United States in the 1960s and 1970s, shifted the focus of interest from elites to ordinary people. In 1967 a political party representing the black majority assumed control of the colony's government; it led the country to independence in 1973. One consequence of these developments was to direct scholarly attention to the black population, which had hitherto been largely ignored in historical writing. This new approach was evident in the work of Craton and Gail Saunders, who published demographic studies of Bahamian slavery. In his article "Hobbesian or Panglossian? The Two Extremes of Slave Conditions in the British Caribbean, 1783 to 1834," which appeared in 1978, Craton compared the impact of working conditions on slave populations of estates in Jamaica and the Bahamas. In 1985 Gail Saunders's *Slavery in the Bahamas, 1648–1838* was published.

The 1980s saw both continuity and change in the nature of the published literature on the Bahamian past. The bicentenary of the Loyalist arrival in the Bahamas in 1783 was commemorated by the publication of Sandra Riley's *Homeward Bound: A History of the Bahama Islands to 1850, with a Definitive Study of Abaco in the American Loyalist Period.* This book, which examined the experiences of white Loyalists, returned to an earlier tradition of historical writing on the Bahamas. Gail Saunders's *Bahamian Loyalists and Their Slaves,* which also appeared in the bicentennial year, reflected recent historiographical trends in its attention to both white Loyalists and the slaves and freedpersons who were a part of this wave of migration.

The 1980s also witnessed a surge of research interest in and publications on Bahamian history. In 1981, for example, Colin A. Hughes published *Race and Politics in the Bahamas,* which examined the transition from white political hegemony to black rule in the years after 1953. This interest was stimulated in part by the activities of the Bahamas Historical Society, founded in 1959, whose monthly meetings served as a forum for the discussion of current research in Bahamian history. The society's journal provided an outlet for amateur historians and increasingly for academic historians working on aspects of Bahamian history. The imminence of the quincentenary of Columbus's landfall in the Bahamas also promoted research among archaeologists on the pre-Columbian past. These varied research activities were complemented by the publications of the Department of Archives, which were organized around the annual exhibition.

Despite the steady accretion of the published material on Bahamian history, the political economy of the colony in the postemancipation years remained largely unexamined. An awareness of this major lacuna in Bahamian historiography prompted my interest in research on Bahamian history. My first research project focused on the truck system, which nineteenth-century observers like L. D. Powles had identified as a major method of white mercantile control of the black laboring population. Craton had mentioned the existence of this system (in relation to the sponging industry) in his general history but had described rather than analyzed its origins and operation. Detailed research on the truck system revealed the existence of a sharecropping system that had previously escaped the notice of historians of the Bahamas. My initial interest in the truck system thus resulted in additional research on the evolution and operation of the varied labor systems that coexisted in postemancipation Bahamas and the transition from slavery to freedom. My research interests also extended to other aspects of control by a white minority, which involved an examination of policing and immigration policy. My findings from this research were published in a series of nine independent but interrelated essays that, with the addition of a chapter on the self-hire system during slavery, subsequently appeared in 1991 as *The Bahamas in Slavery and Freedom.*

This book is an extensively revised text, reflecting the integration of material based on detailed new research and the amplification of earlier discussions and analyses. The chapters have been thoroughly reorganized, and a stronger interpretive thrust, suggested by the new title, provides a greater cohesion. Chapter 1, on the Bahamian economy to 1815, is entirely new and extends my earlier discussion of the slavery era. Chapters 2 and 3 have been revised to demonstrate that developments in the urban and rural contexts, where the relationship between masters and slaves changed during the last three decades of slavery, were linked to the disintegration of the short-lived plantation economy. In the remaining chapters I have incorporated additional information and made changes to the text in varying degrees. Chapter 5, for example, is a conflation of two separate chapters in the 1991 publication in which the earlier analyses have been expanded. The final chapter in the 1991 book has been excluded, and a conclusion has been added.

This book is an examination of the methods by which a white mercantile oligarchy perpetuated its social and economic control from slavery into the twentieth century in one of the "citadels of the Caribbean *ancien régime.*"[1]

This exercise of power depended on the operation of exploitative labor systems that often originated during slavery. Other patterns of dominance are also considered. Case studies of policy on immigration and policing demonstrate how the colonial state acted as the executive arm of a small mercantile class. For the lower classes, the main escape from this machinery of class slavery by the late nineteenth and early twentieth centuries was external migration.

The first chapter of this study examines how the physical environment shaped a history of settlement and economic activities in the Bahamas that diverged from the plantation economy and society of most British Caribbean colonies. Before the plantation period of the late eighteenth century, the economic activities of the early settlers were primarily extractive in nature—depending on an exploitation of existing resources. Through an examination of contemporary newspaper sources, the chapter provides an extended (and unprecedented) discussion of the diverse ways in which slave and free colored labor was organized in the urban and plantation contexts, where systems of slave hiring, formal slave apprenticeship, and indentured servitude operated. This chapter argues that the decline of cotton as an export staple and the emergence of a surplus slave labor force precipitated a restructuring of social and labor relationships between slaves and their owners that prefigured postemancipation labor systems.

The next two chapters describe the transformation of labor relationships in Nassau and on the Out Island plantations after 1800. Chapter 2 discusses the origins and development of the self-hire system in Nassau. It argues that slaves who worked on this system, often for a wage, gradually replaced a coercive relationship with their owners with one based on informal contractual terms. The changing status of slaves on self-hire to an incipient (and increasingly assertive) proletariat was acknowledged in a legal ruling in 1832 by the colony's solicitor general, who decided that the slave owners' nonpayment of wages to their slaves should be punished as a breach of contract rather than as a criminal offense under slave laws. Chapter 3 considers the impact of a decaying plantation economy on the social relations of production on Out Island estates. It shows that on plantations where export-oriented production virtually ceased after 1800, protopeasant activities were (unlike those of the Caribbean sugar colonies) more than an "interstitial" development. Contrary to the prevailing scholarly orthodoxy, the chapter also demonstrates that a peasantry emerged during slavery within the framework of the slave plantation.

The redefinition of social and economic relationships between slaves and their masters, which resulted in greater slave autonomy, intersected with the introduction of liberated Africans between 1811 and 1860 who worked initially on long-term indentures. Chapter 4 analyzes the operation of this system of unfree labor, which was harsher than legal slavery in the Bahamas. Although this system, described by Governor William Colebrooke as a "kind of modified slavery," was discontinued in 1838, it was reintroduced in 1860 in a form that constituted an officially approved truck system.

Chapter 5 treats the development of labor tenancy and share systems as part of the general trend toward the redefinition of productive relationships in the years before 1838. These precapitalist modes of organizing labor were more widely adopted after 1838 and coexisted with wage labor. This chapter describes the origins and nature of labor tenancy and sharecropping arrangements in a wider discussion of the diverse regimes that were used to recruit, organize, and control labor in the postemancipation years.

The development by the 1860s of a world market for commodities like salt, pineapples, and sponges created incentives and pressure to increase supplies for export and to stabilize the labor force on which output depended. Chapter 6 demonstrates that this was achieved through the introduction of a coercive element (through the credit and truck systems) into the existing precapitalist forms of production and employment. In the Bahamas, the transition from slavery to other forms of labor control after 1838 was effected by an agrocommercial bourgeoisie that combined the roles of employer, landlord, and entrepreneur with the role of supplier of production and consumption loans.

Chapter 7 examines the question of social control—more particularly of policing—in postemancipation society, in which the state acted as a guarantor of the existing social and economic order. It focuses mainly on the context in which systems of social control were adopted and analyzes the motives of those groups that advocated their establishment. The discussion centers on the arrangements made for policing the black population in Nassau after the withdrawal of the West India Regiment that had been stationed in the colony during slavery.

Chapter 8 extends the analysis of the white oligarchy's use of state power. It discusses how the merchant class used its control of the "crucial levers" of political power in the 1920s and 1930s to shape immigration policy and other legislation designed to limit economic competition from trading minorities. It traces the participation of the minorities in the colony's economy, the hostile responses to their commercial incursions, and the reassertion of local control with the enactment of restrictive legislation.

The final chapter examines the labor migration to Florida in the late nineteenth and early twentieth centuries, with the decline of major agricultural staples. The movement to Florida was in part a form of "protest migration"—one aspect of the wider resistance of the subordinate classes to the existing systems of economic control. This discussion also involves an assessment of the effects of labor migration on the family and Out Island agriculture and the impact of remittances on economic development in the Bahamas. One consequence of labor migration was to increase the colony's dependence on imported foodstuffs and further entrench the urban mercantile group as middlemen in the import-export trade.

This book fills a major gap in the historical literature on the Bahamas by analyzing the nineteenth- and twentieth-century foundations of the white mercantile oligarchy, whose dominance Gordon K. Lewis and Colin A. Hughes have described so perceptively for the mid–twentieth century. It is an analysis that integrates a discussion of the economic and political activities of the Nassau-based ruling class with a detailed examination of the black majority's experience of work on the Out Islands.

Although this study emphasizes the postemancipation years, it is equally important as an analysis of the last phase of slavery. Its treatment of Loyalist slavery differs from that of Craton and Saunders in *Islanders in the Stream,* in which, employing cliometric techniques, they concentrate on the demographic experience of the slave population on the Out Island plantations. My study, by contrast, reconstructs the patterns of work of the slave population in both rural and urban settings through a close scrutiny of contemporary newspapers. It thus discusses at length the systems of slave hire, apprenticeship, and indenture (used in connection with free labor), of which Craton and Saunders seem largely unaware. The study also provides a more dynamic view of slavery, for (as I argue) the institution of bondage evolved in response to changing economic conditions after 1800.

This book also qualifies as a contribution to the historiography of slavery in the Americas, the transition from slavery to freedom, and the debate about "systems of domination after slavery" in the British Caribbean, which O. Nigel Bolland revitalized with the publication of his seminal 1981 essay. In my study the Bahamian experience has been consciously fitted into the wider comparative framework of the British Caribbean and the Americas. Until recently, the Bahamas was excluded from the general historical literature on the British Caribbean mainly because it represented a divergent pattern of social and economic development, failing to conform to the "model of pure plantation economy" and society with which the region is usually associated.[2] The evidence from the Bahamas indicates that, as Bolland has suggested for Belize and other areas of the British Caribbean, slavery and freedom were not polar opposites. The Bahamas differed from the rest of the Caribbean, however, since slaves there, whether as wage earners or protopeasants, enjoyed considerable autonomy before emancipation. It was in the postemancipation years that Nassau merchants developed a coercive mode of labor control with the integration of the colony into the capitalist world economy by the mid–nineteenth century.

Chapter One

THE BAHAMIAN ECONOMY TO 1815

The Bahamian archipelago consists of approximately 700 islands and 2,000 cays extending from the coast of Florida to Haiti. Although the total territorial area of land and sea covered by the Bahamas is approximately 100,000 square miles, the total land area has been calculated at only 5,350 square miles. Most of the islands in this chain are small, the largest being Andros (2,300 square miles), Inagua (599), Grand Bahama (530), and Abaco (395). These islands are low-lying—the highest point, in Cat Island, measuring just 206 feet above sea level—and are made up of coralline limestone. In fact, the islands and cays are located on a shallow bank of limestone, with more than 200 charted submarine reefs.

Throughout the Bahamas the soil is extremely thin and patchy and usually deposited in pockets in the limestone rock. In a geographical study of the Bahamas, Neil E. Sealey has pointed out that many places have sparse and stunted vegetation and virtually no soil. These areas include the southeastern islands and cays, which are either too dry or too exposed for a thick cover of vegetation to develop on them. Sealey has divided the soils of the Bahamas into three main categories. The first is organic or "black" soil, which is typical of the forested areas of the northern and central Bahamas. Second are the residual soils commonly referred to as "red" or "pineapple" soils. Finally, there is sedimentary soil, a mixture of sand and humus that Sealey describes as common in areas where there are sand dunes. Bahamian soils tend to be stony and lacking in nutrients.

The Bahamas, located in the subtropical zone, experiences none of the extremes of temperature. Temperatures rarely fall below 50°F, largely because of the warming Florida Current (the Gulf Stream), and seldom rise above 90°F because of the cooling influence of the northeast trade winds. The Bahamian climate, however, can be temporarily disrupted by cold fronts from the North American continent in winter and tropical storms and hurricanes during summer. Summer is the wet season, largely as a result of the northeast trade winds. In the northwestern islands rainfall is moderate, rising to an annual average of 53.3 inches in West End, Grand Bahama; but the southeastern islands are dry. In Matthew Town, Inagua, for example, the annual rainfall is 27.5 inches. On these islands rainfall either runs off into the sea or filters through the porous limestone to form underground lakes. Since the islands have no rivers or streams, the sources of accessible fresh water on most of them are limited.[1]

The topography and climate of the Bahamas have been important influences on the country's history of settlement and economic activities. William F. Keegan has argued that the islands must have provided an attractive alternative to the Greater Antilles for the Tainos who colonized the Bahamian archipelago between A.D. 600 and 1200. As Keegan has observed, "Although production in these small limestone islands could not be intensified to the levels possible in the larger volcanic islands of the Great Antilles, the initial consideration would have been their potential productivity with regard to the colonists' economy." Manioc, for example, which was a staple of the Taino diet, thrives in relatively poor soils, and the dry season in the southern Bahamas might, as Keegan has suggested, have promoted increased yields. The pre-Columbian environment of the Bahamas also provided abundant "marine and terrestrial animal resources" like the queen conch, monk seals, green turtles, hutia, and rock iguana, which prompted initial colonization and population expansion throughout the archipelago by the Tainos and their descendants the Lucayans.[2]

European perceptions of the Bahamian environment differed markedly from those of the Taino colonizers who had evaluated the archipelago in terms of obtaining food. The Spanish who made contact with the Bahamas and the Lucayans in October 1492 were primarily interested in discovering new sources of precious metals (gold and silver). After Christopher Columbus's initial landfall on Gunahaní (which he renamed San Salvador), his progress through the island chain was devoted to the unsuccessful search for the city of gold that the Lucayans had mentioned. The quest for gold eventually led the explorers to the island of Hispaniola, where they established a small settlement on the north coast. Spanish interest shifted from the Bahamas to Hispaniola, which became the principal Spanish colony in the Caribbean, a base for further exploration of the region, and a source of placer gold. With its fertile land, Hispaniola was also better suited than the Bahamas to the production of food for Spanish settlers and commercial crops for the European markets.

The Bahamas and its indigenous population gained a fleeting importance as a temporary solution to the labor crisis experienced by Spanish colonists in Hispaniola in the first decade of the sixteenth century. The combined effects of the wars of conquest, along with overwork, malnutrition, and exposure to European diseases, had sharply reduced the number of Indians, who had been forced to render labor services to Spanish settlers under a system known as the *repartimiento*. In 1509 Nicolás de Ovando, governor of Hispaniola, received royal approval for importing Indians from the neighboring islands and in that year organized slave-raiding expeditions to the Bahamas. Lucayans were exported to Hispaniola, but because of their reputation as skilled divers, they were also sent to work in the pearl fisheries near the island of Cubagua, off the north coast of Venezuela. By 1520 the Lucayan population, estimated at 80,000 at the time of contact with the Spaniards, had virtually disappeared.[3] By then the Bahamas had lost its importance. Spanish interest in the Americas had been redirected from the Caribbean to the mainland, and all but the islands of the Greater Antilles were neglected. Although Spain never effectively occupied the Bahamas, its claim to the territory was not formally given up until 1783, by the terms of the Treaty of Versailles.

Permanent European settlement of the Bahamas was to wait for more than 150 years after the initial Spanish intrusion, with the arrival of immigrants from Bermuda in the years after 1647. There is evidence that, before that date, the French had twice attempted to settle the Bahama Islands. An attempt by René de Laudonnière in 1565 to establish a colony in Abaco failed. In 1633 Cardinal Richelieu granted four of the islands of the Bahamas to Guillaume de Caen, a Huguenot, but plans for settlement collapsed when only French Catholics were allowed to colonize them. The earliest English claim to the Bahamas was made in 1629 with the grant by Charles I to Sir Robert Heath, his attorney general, of territories in the Americas located between northern latitudes 31° to 36°—an area that included the Bahamas and the mainland territory of Carolina. Heath, however, made no attempt to settle the islands because of the struggle between Crown and Parliament in England, which culminated in civil war in 1642.[4]

The earliest Bermudian immigrants to the Bahamas were Puritans and republicans who were attracted by the possibility of religious and political freedom in a new colony. They were also interested in increased economic opportunities because, by the 1640s, Bermuda was overpopulated, and the chances for upward social and economic mobility there were severely limited. These concerns were reflected in the Articles and Orders of the Company of Eleutherian Adventurers of July 1647, which were intended to provide a blueprint for the new venture. In the spring of 1648, a group of seventy Bermudians left for the Bahamas under the auspices of the Company of Eleutherian Adventurers and settled in northern Eleuthera. In the following year, the original settlers were joined by sixty Bermudian Puritans and republicans who had been expelled from the island after news was received of the execution of Charles I. The majority of the Eleutherian immigrants eventually returned to their home colony between 1652 and 1656, when conditions improved for Puritans and republicans once the English Commonwealth government exercised control there. Those who remained formed new settlements on two islands off Northern Eleuthera, Harbour Island and St. George's Cay (Spanish Wells). The number of settlers was increased periodically by the influx of whites, slaves, free blacks, and coloreds who were deported from Bermuda as socially undesirable.[5]

In 1666 a group of Bermudians who had been sailing through Bahamian waters searching for Spanish wrecks and ambergris settled on the island of New Providence. These immigrants were eventually joined by other Bermudians who were financially assisted by two of their compatriots, John Darrell and Hugh Wentworth, in the process of relocation. Michael Craton and Gail Saunders have estimated that there were 1,000 settlers in the Bahamas by 1670, two-thirds of whom were white. In that year Darrell claimed that there were "near 500 inhabitants" in New Providence and "about 20 families of Barmudians" residing on Eleuthera, Harbour Island, and Spanish Wells.[6]

As early as 1670, the pattern of economic activities in the Bahamas diverged from that of most English Caribbean territories where the plantation system geared to the production of agricultural staples already predominated. In creating the frontier society of the Bahamas, the Bermudian settlers duplicated the strategies for survival that they had used in their homeland. The early emphasis on seagoing activities was as much a continuation of the Bermudian way of life as it was a response to the physical environment of the new setting. In the Bahamas (as in Bermuda) the settlers fished and searched for turtles, whales, seals, and ambergris (an essential ingredient of perfume), which was usually washed up on the beaches. In some of the drier southern islands like Crooked Island and Exuma, the early immigrants also produced salt, which they exported to markets in the Caribbean and on the North American mainland. Woodcutting was another important economic activity of this early period of colonization. This involved the exploitation of the forest resources of the islands of the archipelago for the construction of ships and furniture, as dyewoods, and for their reputed medicinal qualities. Agriculture was engaged in only for subsistence. The pioneer settlers preferred (as John Darrell noted in 1672) "to run a-coasting in shallops which is a lazy course of life and leaveth none but old men, women and children to plant."[7]

The economic activities of the early settlers were extractive, involving an exploitation of existing resources. The nature of the Bahamian economy (combining elements of hunting and gathering) was described by Mark Catesby after his visit to the islands in 1725–26:

> The barrenness of these rocky islands, and the little soil they contain, employs not many hands in its culture; therefore the greater part of the inhabitants get their living other ways, *viz:* the more enterprising in building ships, which they lade with salt at Exuma, and Crooked Island, and carry it to Jamaica, and to the French at Hispaniola. They also supply Carolina with salt, turtle, oranges, lemons, etc. but the greater number of the Bahamians content themselves with fishing, striking of turtle, hunting guanas, cutting brasiletto wood, Ilathera bark, and that of wild cinnamon or winter's bark, for these purposes they are continually roving from one island to another, on which shores they are frequently enriched with lumps of ambergris, which was formerly found more plentiful on the shores of these islands.[8]

The most significant maritime activity of the early settlers was "wrecking"—salvaging ships (and their cargoes) wrecked on the reefs and shoals surrounding the islands. Since the Bahamas was on the main shipping route to and from the Caribbean, shipwrecks were frequent, and wrecking proved lucrative. Writing in 1708, John Oldmixon noted the tendency of wreckers to appropriate all salvageable materials from the wreckage: "As for Wrecks, the People of *Providence, Harbour-Island* and *Eleuthera,* dealt in them as it is said the good Men of *Sussex* do: All that came ashore was Prize, and if a Sailor had, by better Luck than the rest, got ashore as well as his Wreck, he was not sure of getting off again as well. This perhaps is Scandal, but it is most notorious, that the Inhabitants looked upon every Thing they could get out of a Cast-away Ship as their own, and were not at any Trouble to enquire after the Owners."[9]

In 1670 the Bahamas was regranted to six of the Lords Proprietors of Carolina. There is evidence to suggest that the twenty-six signatories of the Articles of the Eleutherian Adventurers in 1647 had claimed a shared proprietorship during the period of the Commonwealth. That claim, however, must have been canceled by the restoration of Charles II to the throne in 1660. The Crown and its ministers assumed that the grant would lead to investment by the patent holders, the recruitment of settlers, the production of agricultural staples, and the growth of trade with the metropolis. In fact, the Proprietors had estimated that £633,000 would be needed to defray the cost of recruiting, transporting, and providing subsistence for a group of 1,000 white settlers and for defence and public works. It was anticipated that this initial investment would prove profitable once cotton, tobacco, and indigo plantations were established. These projections were based on John Darrell's 1670 report that New Providence had produced "good cotton and tobacco, Suggar Cains," and "Indico Weed."[10]

In the years following the grant, the Lords Proprietors failed to invest, as promised, in the establishment of plantations and the recruitment of settlers or to provide crucial support for the governors they appointed to administer and develop the islands. Governor John Wentworth complained in 1675 that he had received no money from the Proprietors in two years and had thus been forced to rely on Governor Lynch of Jamaica to supply basic foodstuffs. The failure of the planned experiment in staple production was due in part to the reluctance of the earlier settlers to change their means of making a livelihood. Governor Charles Chillingworth's efforts "to persuade the people to plant provisions and clear the ground for cattle and planting tobacco, indigo and especially cotton" were strongly opposed and might have been partly responsible for his forcible expulsion to Jamaica by the colonists.[11] In the opening decade of the eighteenth century, the Bahamas remained marginal to the wider imperial economy. Writing in 1708 in his *History of the Isle of Providence,* John Oldmixon observed:

> This Island [New Providence] is chief of those called the *Bahama Islands,* and notwithstanding that Character is so inconsiderable in itself, that it had been well if it had never been discovered; for all the Advantage the Inhabitants can pretend it is to *England* or the other Colonies is, that it lies convenient for *Wrecks;* by which they mean to save such as are driven ashore there, and for Ships forced thither by Stress of Weather: And it being some Hundreds of Miles out of any Ship's regular Course, to or from any of our Colonies and *England,* it is certain we had never lost any Thing by it had it never been heard of.[12]

In a context of endemic warfare between the European powers in the Caribbean in the late seventeenth and early eighteenth centuries, the Bahamas served as a base from which privateers harassed enemy shipping and plundered European coastal settlements. These activities (which attracted new settlers and temporary sojourners) provoked reprisals against the Bahamian settlements. In 1684 the Spanish devastated Charles Town (later renamed Nassau) on New Providence and the settlement on Northern Eleuthera, dispersing settlers to the colonies of Jamaica and Massachusetts. In 1703 and 1706 the French and the Spanish jointly sacked the inadequately fortified town of Nassau. The 1703 invasion prompted some settlers to relocate to Carolina, Virginia, and the New England colonies.

After the end of the War of the Spanish Succession (1702–13), the Bahamas emerged as a major base of piracy, which was essentially the continuation into peacetime of privateering activities. Piracy provided employment for ships and their crews that had previously been involved in privateering. The target of the pirates' attacks was the steadily increasing but as yet inadequately protected trade associated with the establishment of new colonies. The geographical character of the Bahamas, with cays and islands beyond the control of a Nassau-based government, made it an ideal site for pirates to shelter and lie in wait in. The presence of the pirate community benefited some sections of Bahamian society. Residents of Nassau provided pirates with necessary services and supplies. Merchants, for example, profited from the sale or barter of provisions at inflated prices, receiving in exchange stolen cargoes, plate, or cash. Piracy was also another form of marine employment for Bahamians who would otherwise have been involved in wrecking or privateering. In addition, several governors appointed by the Lords Proprietors accepted bribes and a share of the plunder for their tacit support of piracy. Opposition to the pirates, however, developed among the colonists, who by 1717 were outnumbered by them. They were anxious to have law and order restored and a measure of security guaranteed for their lives and property. Representations from the colonists and, more important, appeals from governors of mainland and West Indian colonies, whose trade was threatened by piracy, resulted in the appointment of the first royal governor, Captain Woodes Rogers, to the Bahamas in 1718. The Crown assumed civil and military responsibilities for the Bahamas, but the Lords Proprietors retained their rights to distribute land and collect quit rents and royalties, which they leased to a company in which Rogers was a major shareholder.

In 1718 Woodes Rogers's pressing concerns were to expel the pirates from the Bahamas, to establish an effective administration in Nassau, and to promote economic growth and trade. A more long-term goal was to secure the British claim to the entire archipelago, especially against the threat posed by the Spanish, who regarded the outlying central and southern islands as their own. By 1725 the expulsion of the pirates was complete, order had been restored, and the Spanish threat had receded. The problem of diversifying the narrowly based maritime economy of the Bahamas, however, persisted despite the efforts of Rogers and his successor, George Phenney. Rogers, like his proprietary predecessors, encountered an unwillingness on the part of Nassauvians to cultivate the land except for a basic subsistence. In May 1719 he complained, "They thus live, poorly and indolently with a seeming content, and pray for wrecks and pirates." During his term of office, Phenney encouraged the establishment of plantations in New Providence. In 1721, 295 slaves were imported from Guinea and distributed among a small number of plantations on which cotton, sugar, indigo, and ground provisions were cultivated. These official efforts had no immediate impact on the pace of economic growth. The Bahamas remained unimportant as a producer of export staples and a market for metropolitan goods. In 1723, for example, the Bahamas traded primarily with other British colonies on the mainland and in the West Indies. These exchanges usually involved barter rather than cash transactions. In that same year the value of British imports into the Bahamas amounted to only £2,320.

Both Rogers and Phenney took the view that economic growth and the emergence of a landowning class were retarded by the fact that settlers had no security of tenure on the land they occupied. Without the assurance of secure titles, they believed, settlers would not be encouraged to exert themselves, nor would immigrants be attracted to the colony. They argued that this problem would be remedied by the establishment of a legislative assembly capable of enacting legislation to protect freehold tenure. In 1729 a legislative assembly was set up and quickly passed a series of laws that included measures for establishing clear title to land and for encouraging economic activities. A law entitled "An Act for Settling Claims and the Payment of Quit Rents" set up the machinery for verifying land claims, making surveys, and recording sales and transfers of land. Other acts were passed "for the Encouragement of Strangers and Foreigners Settling in these Islands," "to Encourage the Planting of Cotton on these Islands," and "to Encourage the stocking of Keys and Islands with Cattle and to punish Such as destroy the same." Two laws were clearly intended to stimulate shipbuilding by forbidding the export to any North American colony of timber suitable for the construction of vessels and forbidding the destruction of timber trees by fire.

The incentives provided by the 1729 legislation to stimulate economic growth did little, in the long term, to change the well-established pattern of economic activities. In 1730 Woodes Rogers complained to the Board of Trade about the slow pace of progress despite his efforts to encourage sugar and cotton production and shipbuilding. He also noted the failure in attracting large numbers of immigrants to the colony. This is not surprising because the Bahamas, unlike the sugar colonies, offered few economic opportunities for permanent settlers to acquire wealth. In February 1722 the Bahamian population numbered only 989 persons, and 67 percent of that population was concentrated on New Providence. Blacks formed 28 percent of the total population. By 1731 the population had increased to 1,388 persons, of whom 75.1 percent resided in New Providence. The census listed 453 persons or 32.6 percent as "Negroes"—a category used for slaves.

In the mid–eighteenth century, the settled economic activities that the two earliest royal governors had encouraged came into direct competition with those generated by maritime conflict. European wars, which spilled over into the Caribbean, lasted for most of the period between 1739 and 1763 and revived privateering based in Nassau. Local ship owners became involved in the lucrative business of privateering and recruited Bahamian sailors to man their vessels. Land-based colonists also prospered because they provided a wide range of services to the free-spending privateers. Agriculture, as Governor John Tinker noted in 1748, was neglected, "especially in these Times when a Common Seaman, nay a Negroe Slave, shall step on board a Privateer and in a Six week Cruise return often with a Booty of a hundred pound Sterling to his share." Privateering had spinoff effects for other sectors of the economy because it stimulated local shipbuilding and the consumption of British goods. Between 1731 and 1748 the number of locally built or locally owned ships increased sharply from 14 to 52, and the annual value of British imports in 1748 was estimated at £30,000—twelve times the 1723 figure.[13]

Privateering created wartime prosperity in the Bahamas, but the routine peacetime economic activities at mid-century were unchanged from those of the early settlers. Peter Henry Bruce observed, after a four-year residence in the Bahamas between 1741 and 1745, that the Bahamians "neither sow nor plant more than is necessary for maintaining their own families; whereby one of the most fertile parts of our West Indies is neglected for want of cultivation. They depend on their cargoes of salt, mahogany plank, dying wood, tortoises, fruit, etc. which they sell to great advantage; and likewise upon the shipwrecks, which happen frequently upon those extensive banks; all which make them careless in improving the natural produce of that fertile country which, were it once peopled, would soon be in a flourishing situation."[14]

After a four-month visit to New Providence in 1783, Johann David Schoepf described a colony that was in the process of breaking away from a pattern of economic stasis. He noted that the inhabitants preferred extractive economic activities to arduous agricultural pursuits and thus relied primarily on woodcutting, "wracking," turtling, and fishing and on privateering during wartime. Schoepf also pointed, however, to the beginnings of commercial agricultural activities that have usually been associated with the resettlement of American Loyalists in the Bahamas. By 1783, for example, Bahamian colonists had successfully experimented with cotton cultivation and found it well suited to local conditions. As Schoepf commented on these early efforts in cotton production, "the culture of this shrub is extending, not so much on Providence as on the other islands; experience having proved that this crop is one of the best and surest rewards of the planter's toil. It grows at all seasons, is not so dependent on rain as other plants, and takes a quick and strong hold of the rocky soil."[15] Schoepf's observations on the role of the "old" inhabitants in introducing commercial cotton culture were corroborated by the Loyalist Joseph Eve in an editorial comment in the *Bahama Gazette* in 1800. Eve identified Abraham Pratt as the "first Individual who carried Cotton Planting to any extent in this Colony, and evinced the Bahama Islands, were capable to afford success to the Planter, as well as to Wreckers and Privateersmen." According to Eve, Pratt had left New Providence in debt in 1777 to settle with his family and a few slaves on Long Island. Within six years he "had made a handsome independence as well as paying off his debts by Cotton Planting." In fact, Eve believed that Pratt's widely publicized success in cotton production was mainly responsible for "peopling this Colony with the greater part of its present respectable Inhabitants."[16]

In his survey of economic activities in the Bahamas, Schoepf also mentioned the existence of an established export trade in pineapples to North America and Europe. On the London market, the fruit fetched between four and eight shillings sterling each, depending on size and appearance. By 1783 there were Bahamian colonists who recognized that the plantation production of certain agricultural commodities with slave labor could be profitable. As Schoepf observed, "From these several products and the work of the negroes those who own plantations draw considerable returns. The statement is made that only from pineapples, yams, lemons, and coffee, a plantation (large to be sure) has yielded a profit in one year of 2,300 pieces of eight."[17] The evidence from both Schoepf and Eve indicates that by 1783 Bahamian colonists had responded to the external demands for commodities like cotton and pineapples and had already extended their agricultural production beyond subsistence needs.

The trend toward the production of agricultural export staples accelerated with the influx of the American Loyalists into the colony between 1783 and 1785. Most of the Loyalists were refugees from Georgia and South Carolina who arrived in the Bahamas (accompanied by their slaves) via the British colony of East Florida. Others came directly from New York. The Loyalists from East Florida reluctantly relocated to the Bahamas after the British government returned the territory to Spain by the terms of the Treaty of Versailles in 1783.[18] In East Florida, planters from South Carolina and Georgia had attempted to recreate the plantation economy of the lowcountry (based on the production of rice and indigo) and were unwilling to move to a colony where the agricultural prospects were so unpromising.[19] In 1783 a "committee of prospective settlers" had reported, after a visit to New Providence, that the soil was rocky and there were "no tracts of land contiguous where any considerable number of negroes could be employed." Later that year, an official report by the engineer John Wilson admitted that the islands of the archipelago were rocky, but he called attention to three types of soil that were well suited to the cultivation of cotton, vegetables, and Guinea corn respectively.[20] In his report on the island of Exuma, Wilson noted: "There are cotton trees now growing . . . which were planted by a Mr La Rush who died eighteen years ago. Although the trees have been entirely neglected since his death, being now intermixed with weeds, shrubs and bushes, which have spontaneously sprung up amongst them, yet they flourish in a surprising manner and yield a great quantity of cotton every year."[21]

It has been estimated that in the period between 1783 and 1790, approximately 1,600 whites and 5,700 slaves and free blacks from the United States settled permanently in the Bahamas. These migrants trebled the colony's population and increased the proportion of slaves and free blacks from one-half to three-quarters of the total. The Loyalists from East Florida (with their slaves) entered the Bahamas through New Providence. This group consisted of 300 white families, more than 100 of whom owned 10 or more slaves. The main inducement to migrate to the Bahamas was the British government's promise in 1785 to grant land to settlers free of charges and quit rents (nominal rents paid annually to secure continuous tenure) for a period of ten years on a headright basis. A grant of forty acres was allocated to each white head of household and twenty acres for each dependent (a category that included slaves). More than half of those white migrants remained in New Providence, while the rest, accompanied by two-thirds of the incoming slaves, settled in southern and southeastern islands and began the large-scale commercial production of cotton. Smaller groups of Loyalists and free blacks, departing from New York and St. Augustine, Florida, and numbering about 1,650 persons, established settlements on the northern island of Abaco. One consequence of the influx of American Loyalists was to increase the number of permanently settled islands in the Bahamas from three to twelve.

The establishment of a system of land grants in 1785 precipitated a rush to claim unoccupied lands in New Providence and the outlying islands. These grants were made from land bought by the Crown from the Lords Proprietors on an ad hoc basis after 1784 or acquired with the purchase of the proprietary rights to the Bahamas for £12,000 in 1787. A. T. Bethell estimated that between 1784 and 1789, 114 grants, totaling 42,829 acres, were made to Loyalists. The evidence indicates that there were other groups that benefited from land grants during those years. Although special concessions (such as the waiving of quit rents for a ten-year period) were made to Loyalist refugees who applied for grants, "old" inhabitants were eligible for the basic land grant.[22] Moreover, the terms of the land-grant policy did not exclude other individuals who chose to settle in the Bahamas from receiving grants. The early success of the cotton industry in the Bahamas attracted planters (with their slaves) from other areas of the British Caribbean who might also have acquired land through the land grant system. Writing after a visit to Crooked Island in 1803, Daniel McKinnen observed, "In advancing east we passed through several deserted plantations, particularly a neighbourhood of planters from Grenada, who had removed, with many of their negroes, from that colony, and vested their fortunes in the deceitful speculation of planting cotton."[23]

In the years after 1783, many Loyalist refugees established cotton plantations primarily on south and southeastern islands like Exuma, Long Island, Crooked Island, and Acklins. By November 1785, 124 tons of cotton had been produced on the 2,476 acres under cultivation. Between 1785 and 1788 the area planted in cotton increased to 8,000 acres.[24] This enthusiasm for cotton production was stimulated (as Joseph Eve suggested) by the success of Abraham Pratt. Equally important factors in the decision to plant cotton, however, were developments on the world market that coincided with the arrival of Loyalists in the Bahamas. In Britain, the textile inventions of the late eighteenth century had led to a sudden increase in market demand for cotton. As Lewis C. Gray noted, British imports of cotton that averaged fewer than 7 million pounds between 1776 and 1780 grew to more than 23 million by 1787. This increase in demand for cotton was accompanied by higher prices per pound.[25]

The favorable prospects for the cotton industry and the availability of land attracted Loyalist planters as well as merchants, lawyers, and government officials (based in Nassau) to cotton production. It was not unusual for individual merchants and merchant houses to own several cotton plantations on the Out Islands. In 1789, for example, the list of proprietors in the southern district of Long Island included the merchants Hugh Dean and Robert Rumer and the merchant houses of Denniston and Taylor, Begbie and Turnbull, and Forbes and Stevens. One of the leading proprietors of cotton plantations during this period was the merchant James Moss, who owned twelve plantations on Crooked Island and Long Key.[26]

Mercantile involvement in the cotton industry also included the provision of estate supplies, slaves, transportation facilities, and credit services.

In the early years of Loyalist settlement, it was a common practice for merchants to barter imported merchandise to cash-poor planters for cotton and varieties of wood that had been cut down in the process of clearing the land for planting. In October 1784, for example, the firm of John Petty & Company advertised the arrival of goods from London that would be "sold wholesale or retail on most reasonable terms for Cash, Bills of Exchange or Country Produce." The advertisement further noted, "Cotton, Mahogany, and Dye Woods will be taken in payment at Market Price."[27] As cotton production expanded, some Nassau merchants organized the shipment of cotton overseas and acted as the intermediaries for the metropolitan merchants to whom the cargoes were consigned for sale. The following advertisement by the firm of Panton, Leslie, and Company clearly illustrates aspects of the merchant's role in the Bahamian economy at the height of the cotton boom:

> The Subscribers beg leave to inform their Friends on Exuma, and the Islands adjacent, that it is their Determination to send the ship *Hero* (now daily expected from London) to Load at the Port of Exuma for London; and that they will be obliged to such Planters and Merchants as chuse to ship Cotton, for a Preference of Freight.
>
> PANTON, LESLIE, and Co.
>
> N.B. To Planters who chuse to ship their Crops upon their own Account and Risk, they will give Bills at 30 Days Sight, for Half the Market Value, on Bills of Lading being signed, and on consigning the same for sale to their Correspondents in London.
>
> Nassau, June 27, 1789[28]

Some merchants became involved in the slave trade, importing slaves directly from the West African coast or from other West Indian colonies. The terms on which these merchants made slaves available to the planters were not uniform. An advertisement by William and James Moss in the *Bahama Gazette* of 28–31 August 1792, announcing the sale of 210 slaves recently arrived from the Windward coast of Africa, specified that they could be purchased "for CASH, COTTON, or approved BILLS OF EXCHANGE." Other merchants sold slaves on credit terms, as a notice placed by John Petty and Denniston and Taylor in the *Bahama Gazette*, 27–30 April 1790, indicates: "All Persons indebted for NEGROES, imported by the Subscribers in the Ship Sherborne Castle, Capt Preston, in August, 1788, are hereby informed, that unless Payment is made before the 15th Day of June next, their Account and Bonds will be indiscriminately put in Suit."

The most important economic function of the merchants during the years of large-scale cotton production was to provide planters with operating capital. This was a role they assumed since there were no formal financial institutions in the colony to supply the planters' need for short- and medium-term credit. Loans advanced by the merchants were secured by cotton consigned to them for sale or by slaves, who constituted the major assets of a planter class without cash reserves. The nature of these credit arrangements is suggested by an advertisement placed by Hugh Dean of the merchant house of Dean, Bain, and Company in the *Bahama Gazette* in April 1791. He mentioned that "in Junction with his Partners . . . [he] will advance 50 per cent on the Value of any Cargoes or Property that might be consigned to his House."[29] Although the leading merchant houses made loans from their own capital resources, many were linked to British commercial houses that advanced them credit in return for steady supplies of cotton. The following advertisement by Thomas Thorpe and Company in 1815 indicates that a network of credit often extended from metropolitan merchants to the planters in the Out Islands, with the local merchants as the intermediaries: "The Subscribers having established a first rate connexion with a Cotton Merchant in Manchester, are desirous of receiving Cotton from Planters, or others, to be consigned there for Sale on their account; on the valuation of which liberal advances will be made or the proceeds vested in merchandize."[30]

In historical writing on the Bahamas, it has sometimes been assumed that the Loyalist planters from Georgia and South Carolina who settled in the colony were "experienced cotton raisers" who wished "to recreate the cotton-based economy they had known in the southern colonies."[31] The evidence indicates, however, that they were generally part of a coastal elite who were primarily involved in the production of rice and indigo and had no sustained experience of cotton culture on a plantation basis. Cotton did not become a commercial staple in that region until the 1790s although it had been cultivated throughout the South during the colonial era mainly for domestic use. As relations between the colonies and Britain deteriorated, culminating in war, cotton cultivation significantly increased, and the manufacture of cotton textiles began as American colonists reduced their dependence on British textiles. Joyce E. Chaplin has argued that cotton production provided planters with an alternative way of using their land and slave labor force while the European markets for rice and cotton were closed.[32]

The Loyalist planters who entered the Bahamas were committed to "the view that slaves and plantation agriculture were essential ingredients of economic success."[33] It was their dubious achievement to establish plantation slavery on a firm footing by extending cotton cultivation. Plantation slavery was introduced to the Bahamas in 1721 when a cargo of slaves was imported to provide a labor force for a number of newly established plantations. Craton and Saunders have speculated that 188 slaves mentioned in the 1731 census as living in eight units of more than ten were gangs employed on plantations that produced cotton, sugar, indigo, or large-scale provisions.[34] By 1783 only a small number of slaves were engaged in agricultural production, although the major economic activities of the colony depended on slave labor. As Schoepf remarked, "One is puzzled to see most of the white inhabitants of Providence living well and yet going about in idleness; but they live by the sweat of their slaves."[35]

In devising a method of organizing the labor force for cotton production in New Providence and the outlying islands, the Loyalist planters turned to the task system that had long been "the predominant method of labor management" in the lowcountry.[36] The transference of slave management techniques from rice and indigo to cotton culture in the Bahamas was perhaps most striking in the case of drawing, weeding, and pruning, for which the slaves were "tasked" rather than organized in gangs, as they were in other British Caribbean colonies.[37] Writing in January 1790 on cotton culture in the Bahamas, a Grenadian cotton planter observed, "The method of tasking the Slaves at the time for drawing, weeding and pruning is wrong; as the Overseer ought to have the Gang together, each Slave to have his own row, that he may be able to examine with ease the work as he goes along. When they are dispersed and cannot be kept in view, you may have doubled work by being obliged to do it over again; remembering at the same time that your Slaves know as little of this work as your Overseer, so that will take some time before they can be trained to it."[38] Although the task system was most widely used on the cotton plantations, slaves were organized into gangs for specific chores like planting and harvesting.[39]

At the height of the boom in cotton production, plantation slaves often labored under the supervision of owners who resided on the estates. This was especially true of the small slaveholding units that predominated in the Bahamas until the abolition of slavery. According to Saunders, almost 75 percent of Bahamian slaves lived in units of fifty or fewer in 1834.[40] Overseers were, however, generally employed by merchants and professional men resident in Nassau to manage their plantations in different locations.[41] The demand for overseers was perhaps greatest in the early years of Loyalist settlement, when the expansion of the cotton frontier was underway. Between July 1789 and May 1790, for example, Nathaniel Hall, a planter who was based at Mount Pleasant in Great Exuma, advertised for three overseers to undertake cotton production on other plantations he owned in the Exumas. Applicants for positions as overseers were usually required to be sober, respectable, experienced in slave management, and expert in cotton culture. Overseers were paid either by wages, about which the advertisements are vague, or by sharing in the product of the estates. In his advertisements for two overseers in May 1790, Nathaniel Hall specified, "A Person possessed of a few Negroes to plant, on shares, will be preferred by either of the above Properties."[42]

By the early years of the nineteenth century, it was not unusual to find slaves exercising managerial functions on the farms and plantations of the Bahamas. Slave drivers were often employed on the colony's larger plantations, although they were not as vital to plantation management as in the sugar colonies.[43] As the cotton industry declined, however, absentee proprietors who were unable or unwilling to pay overseers on a regular basis relied increasingly on trusted slaves (often drivers) resident on their estates to assume the supervisory role. In the early 1800s, for example, an overseer for the Rolle plantations in Exuma resided in Rolleville but left the business of management to a field headman at each of the six plantations.[44] James Moss made a similar arrangement for the management of his plantations in Crooked Island and a farm that he owned in New Providence, near Nassau. In 1809 Colonel John Douglass acted as his agent in Crooked Island, but his slave drivers were responsible for implementing his decisions on each plantation. In New Providence, Moss's small farm was left in charge of a slave named Paul.[45]

The dependence on slave management skills on Bahamian plantations was evident in 1798 when a runaway notice pointed out that on Long Island, three or four plantations in the vicinity of Mount Morris, owned by Jno. Morris, had "no White Person residing upon them, as the Law directs."[46] That practice contravened a deficiency law of 1797 stipulating that there should be 1 resident white male, age sixteen to sixty, for every 30 slaves on Out-Island settlements.[47] In 1800 the House of Assembly once again addressed the problem of the declining white presence on the plantations (in part a reflection of a planter exodus) when it enacted legislation for "laying a Tax on all Plantations, not having resident Owner, Agent or Overseer." As the text of the legislation indicates, landowners left slaves to manage their plantations more often by choice than by default: "It is enacted that from and immediately after the first day of May, 1800, every Owner of any settled Plantations within these Islands, having Negro or other slaves thereon, and not being resident on such Plantation himself or herself, or not having employed a Resident thereon, at least one White Overseer or Manager, every such Plantation shall be liable to a fine of Five Pounds for every Negro so employed on any such Plantation or Plantations."[48]

The expansion of cotton production and the routine maintenance of plantations in the Out Islands in the closing years of the eighteenth century and first decade of the nineteenth depended on slaves owned by individual proprietors and on hired slave labor. In this period, it was a well-established practice for proprietors to advertise in the local newspapers for slave hirelings to meet their labor demands. The following advertisement, which appeared in the *Bahama Gazette* in January 1789, was typical:[49]

WANTED IMMEDIATELY ON HIRE FOR TWELVE MONTHS

A Few able FIELD SLAVES seasoned to the Country.—They will be employed on a COTTON PLANTATION on an Island to Windward. Six Months Wages will be paid in ADVANCE, and good treatment given.

It is difficult to determine from the advertisements which category of proprietor relied on hired slave labor. The advertisements did not always mention the names of the proprietors, for the printers of the newspapers often acted as the intermediary in the hiring process. The evidence suggests, however, that landowners who employed hired slaves on a regular basis were sometimes Nassau merchants who owned few slaves and preferred to hire them rather than invest heavily in labor purchases. It is also likely that the proprietors who hired slaves included those who had exhausted their capital in establishing the plantations and could not afford to add to their permanent labor force. Hired slaves (invariably field hands) were thus used to augment the planters' core labor force at the times of peak labor demand, such as harvest.

Slaves who were hired in New Providence for work on Out Island plantations were usually engaged for periods ranging from six months to a year. There is no evidence to indicate the standard rental that was paid to owners for their slaves or the other terms of employment. By 1806, however, the terms were sufficiently standardized for an advertisement to mention that slaves would be hired "at the customary price" and "receive the usual allowance of provisions."[50] The most specific information about the nature of the financial arrangements between the planters and the slave owners is provided by an advertisement placed by the merchant Thomas Forbes in the *Bahama Gazette* in 1790:[51]

WANTED IMMEDIATELY

From ten to fifteen good taskable Hands, for six months, from the 10th to the 15th of next month, or sooner if offered, for which the Subscriber will give at the rate of eight pounds sterling each for the six months. They

> are to be worked in Exuma, but the Subscriber will stand the risk and expence of sending up and bringing them back to their place of abode, if required.

There is nothing to suggest that this proposed arrangement was atypical.

With the expansion of cotton production, slavery in the Bahamas became disproportionately rural, though it remained important as a labor system in the urban economy. As the center of exchange and distribution of commodities from its economic hinterland and from the external economies with which it had trading links, Nassau provided its slave population with a wide range of employment opportunities. In the urban context, slaves performed both the lowest levels of menial services and the highly skilled tasks that were often associated with the commercial economy. The majority of the male slaves worked as casual laborers, but a significant proportion labored as carpenters, joiners, caulkers, coopers, sailmakers, sailors, pilots, blacksmiths, wheelwrights, stonemasons, stonecutters, cabinetmakers, sawyers, bakers, butchers, tailors, hairdressers, butlers, and shoemakers. Female slaves generally worked at jobs that were extensions of their traditional responsibilities as women—as cooks, washers, and ironers in urban domestic households. Slave women rarely received formal training for the tasks they were required to undertake.

The evidence from newspaper advertisements for runaways and slaves for hire or for sale indicates that male slaves in Nassau often served a formal apprenticeship with master tradesmen. Artisans who wished to expand their business often bought slaves, whom they subsequently trained in "the art and mysteries" of their trade to serve as their assistants. This practice was reflected in the 1808 sale notice for a young slave who was advertised as "a remarkable good house servant, very intelligent and speaks English well; his abilities are such as may insure the purchaser that he will very shortly become perfect master of any trade he may be put to." The artisan trades in which slaves were formally trained were varied, as the advertisements of the period illustrate. In 1795 the *Bahama Gazette* advertised the sale of a "Negro Man, who has been regularly bred, a Blacksmith, and is a good Workman—together with a Set of Blacksmith's Tools complete." A runaway notice in 1807 called attention to the flight of "a young Negro Man named Isaac . . . a ship carpenter by trade, . . . who served his apprenticeship with young Don Cox." In the following year, a "mulatto boy" of eighteen or so who had served "six years apprenticeship to the taylor's trade" was advertised for sale.[52]

In the Bahamas there were two basic patterns of urban slave employment: the direct ownership and employment of slaves, and slave hiring in which the ownership and management of slave labor were separated. Although many urban slaves worked for their owners in the household or on the property, the practice of hiring out slaves or allowing them to hire their own time was widespread among urban slaveholders. Slave hiring flourished with the economic expansion that followed on the arrival of the Loyalists. There was an increased demand for labor from both individuals who owned no slaves and slave owners needing additional labor on a short-term basis. In fact, slave hiring was a temporary arrangement that was often better suited to the fluctuating demands of the urban employer than slave ownership.[53]

In Nassau, slave owners with surplus labor hired out their slaves. In 1785, for example, David Zubly, Jnr, a recently arrived Loyalist, advertised the opening of his school in Nassau and the availability of "a Negro Carpenter, some Wenches and Labourers, to hire by the Day or Week."[54] Another source of slaves for hire was those slaveholders who could not provide the necessary supervision for their slaves. Among this group were those slave owners who left the colony for an extended period. In a notice of October 1796, announcing his intention "to be some Time absent from this Country," Nathaniel Hall stated that he had "several valuable NEGROES to dispose of, or hire out; amongst whom are Carpenters, a complete Cooper, a good Man Cook and Gardener, and several House Servants; to all of whom he shall give Tickets, to make their own Choice of Masters."[55] There were also slave owners who maintained jobbing gangs for hire in New Providence and the Out Islands, as the following runaway advertisement, placed by G. Bunch in the *Bahama Gazette* of 27 June–1 July 1800, indicates: "RUN AWAY from the Subscriber's Plantation, on or about nine miles to the westward of the town of Nassau, six Negroes, formerly the property of John Petty, Esq. deceased; viz; *Leader,* the driver; *Franck, George, Billy, Juba, Hamlet,* and his wife. . . . At the time of absenting themselves, they were hired to Mr Thos. Outten."

Slaves were also hired out to provide income for beneficiaries of estates.[56] An examination of surviving wills indicates that executors were sometimes directed to hire out slaves to defray debts and maintain dependent heirs, especially women and minors. A pre-Loyalist example of such a will was that of Edward Turner of New Providence in 1769, which stated, in part, "I hereby empower them [the executors] to employ the said negroes in their or other persons service till such time as their earnings will be sufficient to reimburse my said father-in-law's funeral expenses." Elizabeth Edgecombe's will of March 1807 made provisions for her grandson: "My negro man Pom to be placed out to service for the term of seven years in order that the wages of the said Pom . . . [will] support and educate Alexander Edgecombe the reputed child of my son John Edgecombe." John Lusher's will of 1824 directed that his mother be given "during her lifetime and no longer the earnings and emoluments arising from the share and labour of my negro man slave known by the name of Ben."[57] Women who acquired slaves by inheritance or purchase sometimes chose to support themselves from the revenue generated by hiring them out.

Provisions made in wills for hiring out slaves were sometimes intended to benefit the slaves involved. Several wills stipulated that slave hirelings should share in the wages they earned in order to cover the costs of manumission.[58] Will Smith of Grand Key, Turks Island, directed "that my negro property be kept together and employed to provide for the payment of all my just debts . . . afterwards their earnings to be paid to my mother, sisters and brothers . . . furthermore to purchase their own freedom from slavery." In 1818 the will of Samuel Mackey provided for "the man Cork to have half the wages or to say half freedom under the direction of the Executors . . . say one half of what he works for." John Lowe's provision for his slave Brim in his 1824 will was more generous: "It is my will that my servant Brim (for his faithfulness to me) be allowed or indulged to bring wages until he pays his value which I limit at one hundred pounds Bahama currency."[59]

In the urban setting, slaves who were hired out by their owners were employed primarily as laborers on construction projects or as household servants.[60] Public bodies that owned no permanent slave labor force were largely dependent on the slave-hiring system to supply their labor needs. In July 1796, for example, the trustees of the Public Lot and Buildings advertised their interest in hiring "Twenty Stout Negro Men" whom they promised to employ for a minimum of six months. In August 1800 the commissioners of the town district of New Providence placed a similar advertisement for slave laborers in the *Bahama Gazette:*

> WANTED
>
> Two horses and carts, and twenty negroes furnished with the necessary implements of labour for the purpose of working on the streets in the town district.[61]

The demand for the services of slaves as laborers in construction did not originate only from the public sector. Private individuals often advertised in the colony's newspapers for slaves with skills in building walls and cutting stones. The evidence also indicates that Joseph Eve, the Loyalist inventor, used hired slave labor in the manufacture of his cotton gins in the late 1790s.[62]

Many urban slaves who worked on the slave-hiring system were employed as household servants, for urban dwellers generally preferred to hire rather than buy domestic slaves. An advertisement for a household servant that appeared in the *Royal Gazette* of 15 July 1807 was typical: "Wanted to Hire—For 12 months—A NEGRO Wench, Who is a good cook, washer and ironer." Household chores were not, however, performed exclusively by females. Newspaper advertisements often mentioned a preference for male cooks, and in 1788 Thomas Forbes boasted of a slave he offered for hire on a twelve-month basis that he was "as complete an House Servant and Waiting Man as any in the Country."[63] Further evidence of male performance of domestic tasks is provided by an advertisement in the *Bahama Gazette* of 27 January 1814, which stated, "For hire, two Negro Men, the one a good Cook and house Servant, and the other capable of attending in the house or for any other domestic employment." Outside the urban household, there were other employment opportunities for male and female slaves who could cook and clean. In July 1797, for example, one Mr. Henderson announced the opening of a coffeehouse and tavern and advertised for slave assistants: "Wanted on Hire, Two Negro Women, a good Cook, and House Wench. Good Wages will be given for such as can be well recommended." In that same month there was also an advertisement for "a Handy Negro Man to assist in a Bake House." Some jobs, however, were gender-specific, among them wet nursing. In 1798 an advertisement for wet-nursing services stated: "WANTED on HIRE immediately a WET NURSE—Good Wages and kind Treatment will be given."[64]

However they were employed, slaves who labored on the hiring system were income-generating assets for their owners. They provided additional revenue for slaveholders with more slaves than they required for their own labor needs and a steady income for those who maintained jobbing gangs for hire. The profitability of the ownership of slave artisans, for example, was acknowledged in the tax that was levied on the owners of such slaves for the year 1800. Owners were assessed the sum of eight shillings for "the poll of every male slave, being an artificer actually employed in and about the business of some trade, in the island of New Providence."[65] The hiring system also allowed slave owners to reassign their slaves (particularly male slaves) to the available jobs as labor market conditions changed. This practice was evident in the case of the runaway slave Jack Clark, who was described in 1793 as "well known about this Town, where he has occasionally worked out as a Jobbing Carpenter, Wall Builder, or Labourer."[66]

Slave hiring made the institution of slavery more profitable to the Bahamian slave owners but yielded minimal economic benefits for their slaves. Wages for individual slaves were paid directly to slaveholders, who usually arranged for their slaves' employment. From those earnings, slaves generally received a sum that paid only for their food (when it was not provided by their hirer) and clothing. It was, perhaps, this failure to benefit materially from their labor (in a context in which slaves on the self-hire system were paid wages) that led some slaves on hire to take wage-paying jobs without the consent of their owners or hirers. In a notice placed in the *Bahama Gazette* of 5–8 August 1800, Joseph Eve called attention to one such case: "Some Person or Persons have lately hired, without the Subscribers consent or knowledge a *Black Mason* named *Daniel* belonging to *John Kelsall,* Esquire, and engaged by him to the Subscriber for certain time, this Notice is therefore to forewarn all Persons of the danger of such practices, as he is determined to prosecute any Person who employs any Slave who is engaged to him without their owners or his consent."

In Nassau the self-hire system (as the discussion in chapter 2 will demonstrate) provided slaves with the greatest scope for autonomy within the limits imposed by the institution of slavery. There is, however, evidence that urban slaves who worked under the direct supervision of their owners were able to influence their working conditions. A perusal of runaway advertisements suggests that running away was sometimes a mechanism of labor bargaining used by slaves to improve their terms of employment.[67] The advertisements indicate that some slaveholders were anxious to placate their runaway slaves—a concern that probably extended to removing the cause of their disaffection. In 1792 William Wylly made this promise to his runaway slave John, who had maintained "a Field and Hut near Buen Retiro": "If he returns of his own Accord in the Course of Ten Days from this Date, he will be forgiven." Alexander Wildgoos, a mason, also offered comparable terms to his slave John in 1795: "Should he voluntarily return before the End of the ensuing Week, and offer any tolerable Excuse for absenting himself, he will be forgiven."[68]

The measure of control that slaves exercised over their conditions of employment was reflected in the willingness of some masters to accede to requests for a change in ownership.[69] In 1784, for example, the Loyalist John Russell, owner of a shipyard on Hog Island, advertised the flight of six of his slaves, three of whom had been "bred to the ship carpenter's trade." In his advertisement, he gave this assurance: "The runaways shall have a free pardon, and the liberty of chusing another master, if they return." In September 1789, a female slave who was a good washer and ironer was offered for sale by John Ferguson "for no other Reason, than her being unwilling to go with the Subscriber's Family to Abaco." In 1795 an advertisement for the sale of "a NEGRO Woman that understands Washing and Ironing in the most compleat Manner" explained that "the only reason of her being offered for Sale is that she appears to be discontented in her present Situation."[70]

Slaves were sometimes involved in selecting their new owners. In 1796, for example, Nathaniel Hall, advertising the availability of several of his slaves for sale or hire, declared that he would give tickets to all of them "to make their own Choice of Masters."[71] By 1815 the practice of allowing slaves to seek out prospective masters was widespread, as William Wylly noted: "Gangs of Slaves intended for Sale in these Islands are generally brought to Nassau and sold at Auction, they are however/as the Examinant believes in all instances/allowed to go about Town, previous to the day of Sale, in order to look out for Masters of their own choosing."[72]

The success of some urban slaves in shaping the contours of their own working world is partly explained by the high incidence of *marronnage,* or slave flight, in the early years of Loyalist settlement. So pervasive was marronnage that as early as 1786 Bahamian slave owners were organizing themselves to cope with the problem. In November and December of that year, for example, the Loyalist merchant Thomas Forbes advertised in the *Bahama Gazette:* "Those Persons who have out Runaway Negroes, in this Island, may hear of terms proposed for catching them."[73] In these circumstances, slave owners reluctant to risk the permanent loss of their slaves (especially skilled artisans) at a time of economic expansion were inclined to make concessions to them. Their advertisements promising leniency to returning runaways reflected, at the micro level, the amnesty that successive governors guaranteed to maroons, or slave runaways, who surrendered to any of the colony's justices of the peace. The Earl of Dunmore's proclamation of June 1790, which admitted the adverse impact of large-scale marronnage on the slave economy and society, was typical:

> WHEREAS, it has been represented to me in Council, that a considerable Body of Negroes are collected together in the interior Parts of this Island, who have for some Time past absented themselves from their Owners or Employers, and have committed Felonies and other Crimes to the great Detriment of the Community: AND WHEREAS it is found expedient to extend His Majesty's Mercy towards the said Delinquents: I DO THEREFORE by and with the Advice of His Majesty's Honourable Council, hereby offer His Majesty's most gracious free Pardon to each and every of the said Negroes under the above Description, who shall surrender themselves to any of His Majesty's Justices of the Peace, on the said Island of New Providence, on or before Thursday the first Day of July next.[74]

Slaves performed most organized labor in the urban economy, but they did not totally dominate the labor market. Free persons of color (a term inclusive of free browns and free blacks) who were concentrated in Nassau and its environs competed directly with slaves in most categories of employment.[75] Male free coloreds, for example, worked as artisans, using skills and tools they had in many cases acquired as slaves. Some free artisans owned slaves whom they employed in their own businesses or hired out to clients. By 1796 this practice was sufficiently established and lucrative for the colonial government to impose a tax on free colored artisans. Robert Thomson, the colony's deputy receiver general and treasurer, inserted the following notice in the *Bahama Gazette* of 28 June–1 July of that year: "Those Persons who have been assessed for Taxes as Retailers of Spirituous Liquors, Free People of Colour being Artificers, and Owners of Slave Artificers, are requested to pay their respective Taxes on or before the 25th of *July* next, otherwise Warrants will be indiscriminately issued against them." The Chief Justice's comments in March 1980 on the free coloreds as a group indicate that they formed a large part of the colony's "labour aristocracy": "In this class of persons are to be found many expert and skilful handicrafts and mechanics, honest and industrious in their several callings."[76]

The majority of free coloreds probably had no craft skills and were thus forced to fend for themselves in a context in which there was competition for casual employment. This competition was intensified after 1800 with the influx of surplus slaves from decaying Out Island plantations and liberated Africans. Like their slave counterparts, free colored males were employed in a wide range of menial jobs in most sectors of the town's economy. The working world of free colored females was, by contrast, largely defined by domestic service, like that of female slaves. Newspaper advertisements suggest that there were employers who preferred the labor services of free persons of color. An advertisement by William Gamble in 1793 for laborers on a public works project was directed to free persons of color: "WANTED, twenty able bodied PEOPLE OF COLOUR, to work on the New Road to the South Side.—Generous Wages, and good Provisions will be given." In 1813 a prospective employer advertised for the services of "a Free Woman of color; to take charge of the Upper Servant in a family on an other island; and a Free Man of color, as a gentleman's servant; preferable if versed in cookery and the management of horses."[77]

Some free coloreds were employed under a system of indentured servitude. There is no evidence that such a system operated in the Bahamas before 1783. In that year, as Sandra Riley has noted, recently manumitted blacks who embarked in New York for Abaco were indentured to some of the white Loyalist refugees whom they accompanied. The reasons for indenturing free blacks and the terms of their indenture are unknown.[78] The indenturing of free blacks had, however, a contemporary parallel. In Pennsylvania, after the enactment of the Gradual Abolition Law of 1780, a system of indenture for former slaves "created a substitute form of labor that in some ways was more efficient than perpetual servitude."[79] The American Loyalists migrating to Abaco were probably anxious to guarantee labor services for themselves in an unfamiliar environment and turned to a system of unfree labor that predated chattel slavery as the predominant labor system in the British-American colonies.

In the years after 1783, indentured servitude provided employers with an institutional alternative to slavery as a method of commanding and controlling labor. It is difficult to gauge the extent to which the system of indenture was adopted because references to its existence appeared primarily in advertisements concerning runaways in the colony's newspapers. Those advertisements indicate that the system was used to bind both free nonwhites and whites to regular employment in the rural setting but more frequently in the urban one.[80] In July 1789 Peter Wemyss of Nassau placed an advertisement in the *Bahama Gazette* that stated: "WHEREAS *John Scott,* a free NEGRO Man, a Seaman, and *Curaçao Tom,* also a free Negro Man, by Trade a Carpenter, both indented Servants to the Subscriber, have lately absented themselves from him: This is therefore to give Notice to all Persons, not to employ or carry either of them off this Island, on Pain of being prosecuted for the same." The evidence suggests that the system of indenture was used most frequently for domestic servants. In 1794, for example, William Mitchell, who described himself as "A Free Negro" of "Negro Town, New Providence," advertised for the return of "a Negro Girl named *Margaret,* about 13 years old, olive Complexion, an indentured servant to the Subscriber." William Wylly, in 1796, offered a reward of twenty shillings for the return of "an indented Black Servant, called *Dick Smith,* a Private in Captain *Thomson's* coloured Company, and well known about this Town," who had left his service. In 1806 William Gathorn advertised the fact that "a Free Mulatto Wench called Betty Newman, who is under Articles of Indenture to him, until the 14th Day of August, 1808" had absconded.[81]

Employment opportunities in Nassau for slaves and free coloreds in the years after 1783 were, as previously noted, directly linked to the performance of the cotton industry. This industry had declined drastically in market significance by the end of the first decade of the nineteenth century. In the early years of Loyalist settlement, the prospects for cotton production had seemed excellent. By 1785 the initial misgivings of the refugees about the viability of agricultural production had been dispelled, as an editorial in the *Bahama Gazette* of 2 July of that year noted: "The prejudices entertained against these Islands are wearing off apace; few persons on the spot now doubting of an industrious attentive Planter here meeting with a produce that will amply reward his labour." This mood of optimism continued into the early 1790s as the area under cotton cultivation was extended and cotton exports soared. In 1785 cotton exports amounted to 124 tons, with 2,476 acres under cultivation, but by 1790 had increased to 442 tons from approximately 12,000 acres.[82] These developments led to a sharp rise in the value of arable land and prosperity for the planter class.[83] As "A Planter" remarked in 1794, "very many [Loyalist planters] have acquired competence and some wealth, who had very little reason to expect either."[84]

The expansion of cotton production was accompanied by the adoption of new techniques for processing the crop. Planters were increasingly aware that the market value of cotton depended on the quality of the fiber and the method of ginning employed. In March 1791 a "Gentleman in London," in a letter to a Bahamian merchant house, attributed the lower prices paid for Bahamian cotton to the fact that it was generally poorly cleaned: "I have been at great Pains to find out the Reason of Bahama Cotton not selling so high as that of Grenada, and I am convinced it is nothing else, than the latter is better cleaned."[85] In these circumstances, Bahamian planters welcomed in 1790 the introduction of a cotton gin, invented by Joseph Eve, which promised to raise productivity and improve the quality of the cotton processed.[86] Within a few years of its introduction, Eve's gin was widely used by cotton planters throughout the Bahamas. It was estimated that almost two hundred of his cotton gins were in use in the colony by 1795.[87] Among the planting class, the machine quickly gained a reputation for increasing the production of ginned cotton and sharply reducing labor costs, partly because it made the handpicking of cotton (after ginning and prior to packing) unnecessary.[88]

Despite early optimism, cotton planters had cause for concern by the end of the 1780s. In 1788 the chenille caterpillar made its first appearance on the colony's cotton plantations and destroyed most of that year's crop. The chenille also attacked food crops like Guinea and Indian corn, potatoes, and pumpkins and increased both the cost of slave maintenance and planter reliance on external sources of food supplies.[89] In 1790 swarms of red bugs damaged the cotton crop "by staining and otherwise injuring the Cotton."[90] The effect of insect pests was partly responsible for the slump in cotton exports to 3,000 pounds in 1794 and 1,800 pounds in 1797. Between 1798 and 1800 no cotton was exported.[91] Cotton production was also adversely affected by hurricanes in 1794, 1795, and 1798.

By the late 1790s the cotton industry was experiencing a crisis in production. Although insect pests and hurricanes were partly responsible for precipitating this crisis, Joseph Eve suggested in 1800 that these obscured other problems like the inadequacy of Bahamian soils: "The instability of the soil . . . was sufficient of itself to have blasted every hope even in absence of all other impediments."[92] Initially the virgin soils yielded promising crops, but they became progressively exhausted. The failure of most Bahamian planters to apply manure to the soil undoubtedly hastened the process of exhaustion. This practice reflected both the unavailability of manure on plantations that generally stocked no cattle and the planter perspective on land as a resource to be exploited and "consumed."[93] When the soils in one locality were exhausted, cotton planters tended to establish new plantations in other islands.[94]

The crisis in the cotton industry was also the long-term consequence of the planters' inexperience. The planter class was comprised either of individuals without previous experience in agriculture or those (as mentioned earlier) with no expertise in large-scale cotton production. Most planters were, moreover, unaccustomed to agricultural production in a subtropical environment. One of the earliest mistakes planters made in cotton production was to clear the land for the establishment of extensive fields, often "without leaving a margin or scarcely a tree to intercept the dry parching current of the atmosphere." As Eve explained in 1800, the planters from "the marshy Sea Coast of the Southern States of America," where humidity was a problem, transferred their agricultural techniques to the Bahamas without taking into account the local climatic conditions.[95] There was also no uniform method of cultivating cotton, and experiments showed that practices employed in the tropical British Caribbean were sometimes unsuitable for the Bahamas.[96]

The erratic performance of the cotton industry and the sustained slide in exports by the late 1790s forced planters to adopt measures for increasing productivity. These included the search for a seed variety suited to Bahamian conditions. Loyalist planters at first cultivated Persia or Georgia cotton but later experimented with the Anguilla and Bourbon varieties.[97] In 1806 the Agricultural Society of the Bahamas was actively promoting the cultivation of Bourbon cotton as the solution to the problems of the cotton industry.[98] In 1798 the House of Assembly passed the Bug Act, which made provision for the control of insect pests in Cat Island. In the following year similar legislation was enacted for Long Island, the Exumas, Watlings' Island, and Crooked Island. However, as "A Cotton Planter" noted in 1799, the commissioners who were appointed to protect the plantations against the depredations of the red bug were "authorized *to employ Negroes,* if necessary, for the purpose, *but have no money to pay either the one or the other.*"[99]

Despite the planters' efforts to increase cotton production, the downward trend in exports continued into the early years of the nineteenth century. Between 1800 and 1805, there were three years in which no cotton was exported, and in the other years annual exports did not exceed 1,500 pounds.[100] Bryan Edwards claimed that Bahamian cotton exports increased to 602 tons in 1810.[101] By that stage, however, many planters had either abandoned their estates and left for New Providence or the United States or shifted from cotton production to the cultivation of foodstuffs for the domestic market. Although cotton was cultivated on a small scale as late as the 1830s, the commercial industry barely survived the eighteenth century.

The impact of a declining industry on the economic fortunes of the planter class was evident by the late 1790s. By 1799 the series of harvest failures had left many planters seriously indebted, and the abandonment of plantations had begun. In a letter to the editor of the *Bahama Gazette* in April of that year, "A Cotton Planter" described the state of the cotton industry and warned of the consequences of another poor harvest: "Our Planters in general are much in debt. The loss of the last Crop has occasioned several Plantations to be abandoned; and the failure of the next . . . will probably bring one-half of our Negroes to the hammer, and reduce to nothing the now sinking value of our hands. As a planting Colony, our all is at stake."[102] In the early 1800s, as predicted, many planters were forced to sell their slaves and other property to satisfy the claims of their creditors.[103] Other planters migrated to islands in the archipelago where the soil remained fertile. As Eve remarked in 1800 of Cat Island, "there are several [planters] returning to it who left it when the rage was in favour of Long Island."[104] This process of resettlement within the Bahamas was facilitated by the reopening of the grant office in 1802 to make additional grants of land to interested planters. There was, however, a significant number of Loyalist planters who emigrated to Georgia and other Southern states in this period. In 1803 Thomas Brown (one of the colony's leading proprietors) estimated that more than 3,000 Loyalists had emigrated to southern Georgia.[105] On some islands the cotton fields quickly reverted to wilderness as planters abandoned their estates. This was the situation described by the British traveler Daniel McKinnen after a visit to Crooked Island in 1803: "I beheld some extensive fields originally planted with cotton, but which from the failure of crops were now abandoned, and had become covered with a luxuriant growth of indigenous shrubs and plants. . . . I found the plantations on Crooked Island for the most part deserted; and the proprietors whom I visited were generally in a state of despondence, in an agricultural point of view, as to the future."[106]

Commercial agriculture in the Out Islands did not end with the decline of the cotton-based plantation economy. On the surviving plantations, landowners shifted from cultivating cotton to producing provisions and raising stock for the domestic market in an attempt to stabilize their income and provide employment for the slave labor force. This transition from cotton to provisions is best documented in the case of the Crooked Island plantations of James Moss. In December 1809 Moss gave Colonel Douglass, the resident manager, instructions on the crop mix and the deployment of the labor force for each plantation in the ensuing year. The Marine Farm was to be used "to plant provisions of all species, grass and to receive the stock I have fitting for sale." On Cape Mount and Sea View plantations, the manager was instructed to "plant provisions in the best fields." Moss also made it clear that he was moving away from cotton production: "As soon as the Cotton is taken in, I wish every tree rooted up, and when the fields are weeded to be burnt, and then planted with corn—no more Cotton to be planted on these places until better times." Similar instructions were given for the Fairfield plantation: "to plant provisions as above and as soon as the cotton is taken in to root it up, burn it off after the fields are weeded, and plant them with Indian corn—Guinea corn peas & c." The new importance of the production of provisions in the economic calculations of erstwhile cotton planters was reflected in Moss's instructions as they related to the three Perseverance plantations: "to plant provisions of all kinds in the best fields, when the cotton crop is over. . . . I expect Renty [a slave driver] will make provisions to supply all my wants and a quantity for sale *as I give up planting Cotton, I rely on it to pay expences* [emphasis added]." The True Blue plantation was the only one where Moss expected to continue cotton production in conjunction with corn cultivation: "Having a good gang at *True Blue,* I shall continue to plant Cotton and Corn there and wish, as many new fields cut down . . . both for Cotton and Corn."[107]

The trend toward the cultivation of provisions for the local market was promoted by two laws enacted by a legislature dominated by Loyalist merchant-planters. In 1811 a law was passed that provided a bounty for locally produced corn that exceeded the subsistence needs of each plantation. Planters who produced a minimum of 100 bushels of Indian or Guinea corn of "good and wholesome" quality for sale in New Providence were paid a bounty of one shilling and sixpence per bushel. This legislation, as the preamble indicates, was prompted by a recognition of the need for self-sufficiency in basic foodstuffs, especially in a time of economic decline: "It will tend much to the advantage and prosperity of these Islands, if a quantity of Indian and Guinea Corn, sufficient for the supply of the Inhabitants thereof, can be raised within the same."[108] In 1813 a law was enacted "to oblige Planters to plant a certain quantity of Provisions to each taskable Negro."[109]

Given this new emphasis on agricultural production for local consumption, it is not surprising that a provision plantation was established by 1813 at Fresh Creek in Andros, the island closest to New Providence.[110]

In the wake of the decline of the cotton industry, the search for a profitable export staple resulted in the expansion of salt production. As noted earlier, salt had been an item of export from the earliest years of European settlement in the Bahamas. With the coming of the Loyalists, there were individuals like Duncan and Archibald Taylor of Ragged Island who engaged exclusively in salt raking.[111] During the years of the cotton boom, however, salt raking was generally regarded as an ancillary activity to cotton production. On those cotton-producing islands where salinas existed, planters usually moved their gangs of slaves to the salt ponds in the summer months after the completion of cotton picking in the spring. The complementary nature of salt and cotton production on some plantations is indicated by the sale advertisement for the Hermitage Estate on Little Exuma in 1806: "It has the farther advantage of laying adjacent to the great Salt Pond of Little Exuma, and generally rakes about 15,000 bushels of Salt, annually with its own hands without detriment to the Crop."[112] By that date, salt raking was already assuming primary importance with some planters. In a letter to Bahamian planters in February of that year, urging them to experiment with Bourbon cotton, William Wylly acknowledged salt production as "an object of almost equal importance."[113] In the first decade of the nineteenth century, some colonists were beginning to occupy islands that were suitable only for salt raking. In 1803 McKinnen mentioned the settlement of Inagua: "The new settlers are invited to *Henega* principally by the salt-ponds, to which object the inhabitants of the Bahama Islands have this year (1803) very generally turned their attention." He also mentioned the migration of some Crooked Island planters to the extensive salt ponds of Long Key.[114] In December 1809 James Moss had only recently completed drafting his "principal people" on his Crooked Island plantations for his establishment on Long Key.[115]

The salt industry developed in the early years of the nineteenth century with the encouragement of the colonial government. The recognition of salt's potential as an export staple and a source of revenue had led to government regulation of salt raking even before the arrival of the Loyalists. In 1781 Governor John Maxwell passed an order-in-council to establish the guidelines for leasing the colony's salinas that remained the property of the Crown. Salt commissioners, with responsibility for enforcing the regulations, keeping records of the rakers and salt production, and collecting taxes and duties, were appointed by the governor for each island or group of islands where salt ponds existed. In 1789 the provisions of the order formed the basis of an act for regulating salt raking that was later periodically revised. In 1802 a committee of the Bahamian legislature, which was appointed to inquire into the state of the salt industry, reported that the colony's salt ponds could produce (at the lowest estimate) 3 million bushels or 100,000 tons annually. The members of the committee calculated that the transportation of that harvest to overseas markets would require 498 vessels of approximately 200 tons. They were, however, aware that the colony's shipping was inadequate for that task and that the salt industry would remain "neglected and unproductive" unless some provisions of the imperial legislation that confined colonial trade to British ships were waived. In 1803 a salt act was passed that stipulated that foreign vessels could obtain salt directly from the areas of production rather than trade through Nassau. In the short term, Bahamian salt production did not meet the 1802 projection, but it surpassed that of cotton in value by 1800. Within the first decade of the nineteenth century, salt was established as a commodity on which the colony's economy would increasingly depend.[116]

The decay of the plantation economy and the search for alternative ways of making a living also refocused attention on wrecking. Although the cotton mania had initially overshadowed wrecking, the latter had remained a vital economic activity in the islands of the colony that had been settled earliest, and it had become increasingly important in areas like Abaco and its cays, which were unsuited to cotton production. An observation of John Melish, an American visitor to the Bahamas during the War of 1812, draws attention to the renewed economic importance of wrecking in the early nineteenth century: "The white inhabitants are of two classes, called *residents* and *wreckers*. The residents are chiefly loyalists and their descendants who emigrated from the southern states of America, at the close of the war. The wreckers are those persons and their slaves, who are employed in rescuing Shipwrecked vessels, and their crews and cargoes, from the waves."[117] An editorial of 3 April 1819 in the *Bahama Gazette,* prompted by the United States purchase of Florida from Spain, assessed the importance of wrecking to the Bahamian economy. It noted that a fleet of small craft amounting to about "25 sail" and crews of about 250 men were involved in wrecking and pointed out that both the crews and the owners of wrecking vessels "derived a comfortable support for their families" and the colony "a considerable revenue therefrom." The editorial warned that should the United States prohibit wrecking off the Florida coast, Bahamian wreckers would be forced to migrate to Florida since they had no other skills. It further suggested that there were no other economic activities in which the wrecking vessels could be employed, "especially in the present distressed state of the colony, when nearly one half of its population have already moved from it, or determined to do so."

By 1815 the Loyalist dream of establishing a plantation economy in the Bahamas had faded. Writing in 1812, William Wylly (himself a survivor of the experiment with cotton cultivation) described the state of commercial agriculture in the Bahamas thus: "We are indeed rather *Farmers and Graziers* than West Indian Plantations In so much that the greater part of every Plantation is generally employed as Pasture, or planted with provisions, And our Out Islands produce more corn than they consume."[118] The strategies employed by planters to maintain their estates as viable business concerns could not, however, provide full employment for their slave labor force. Stock raising was, for example, a labor-extensive activity that involved a relatively small number of the total slave population. Without an agricultural export staple to keep slaves occupied at "maximum intensity of labour," the problem of slave underemployment emerged on the decayed plantations of the Out Islands.[119] This problem was exacerbated by the high levels of slave fertility and the introduction of liberated Africans (or recaptives) into the colony from 1811 onward.[120]

The economic depression that followed on the collapse of the cotton industry had important long-term social and economic consequences. The first of these was the gradual withdrawal of a large number of planters from the Out Islands to reside in Nassau. This action was often accompanied by a retreat from direct production on their plantations. More important, however, was the fact that sharply falling profits on the operation of the plantations and a surplus labor force resulted in a process of restructuring of the relationships between slaves and their owners (in both rural and urban settings) that prefigured the labor arrangements of the postemancipation years.[121]

Chapter Two

THE SELF-HIRE SYSTEM AND THE TRANSITION TO CONTRACTUAL RELATIONS IN NASSAU

The transformation of labor relationships between masters and slaves, which was precipitated by the collapse of cotton production, was most marked in the case of slaves who labored on the self-hire system in Nassau. By 1834 this relationship had clearly shifted from a coercive to a contractual one in a process of "slow and extended abolition."[1] The operation of a self-hire system encompassed both urban and maritime economic activities and involved, in the last two decades of slavery, both slaves and liberated Africans who labored under indenture.

In the Bahamas, the system of self-hire was firmly established by the late eighteenth century. Writing in 1783, Johann David Schoepf remarked on the existence of a self-hire system on the island of New Providence: "Even the blacks here take part in the general contentment. . . . Many of them are free, or if they are slaves, by paying a small weekly sum they are left undisturbed in the employment of what they earn by other work. Some of them own houses and plantations, and others are even put in command of small vessels."[2] As Schoepf's statement indicates, there was little to distinguish slaves on the self-hire system from freedpersons in the Bahamian context. They exercised substantial control over their lives and labor and accumulated property while they were themselves chattels.

The emergence of a self-hire system by 1783 is explained by the nature of the economy and the character of slavery in the Bahamas. Unlike most of the other British Caribbean colonies of this period, the Bahamas produced none of the labor-intensive tropical staples that required a closely supervised workforce and kept the slaves steadily employed. Up to this point, Bahamian economic activities were primarily extractive and mainly for subsistence. Without an export staple to determine the work rhythm of the slave population, slave owners undoubtedly experienced difficulty in employing their labor force productively. In that situation they allowed their slaves to seek their own employment in return for a sum, mutually agreed upon, that was paid to them at regular intervals. By that arrangement, labor services that were due to the slave owners were commuted into cash payments. This practice had clear parallels with the *obrok* system in Russia, by which serfs made cash payments to their masters.[3] For the slave owners, the self-hire system provided a steady cash income from slaves who assumed responsibility for their own maintenance. For the slaves, the system presented an opportunity to remove themselves from their owners' surveillance and enjoy a status that fell somewhere between chattel slavery and freedom. Self-hire often involved two levels of contractual relations for the slaves, the first with their owners and the second with employers to whom they provided labor services for a negotiated wage.

Prior to the arrival of the American Loyalists, slaves who worked on the self-hire system often exploited the resources of unoccupied land in New Providence for a living. By 1783 both whites and blacks (slave and free) had established certain customary rights to unclaimed land in New Providence. These included the right to fell trees for timber, gather wood, cut grass, and quarry stones. Schoepf noted the existence of these use rights: "Every man can fell wood as it pleases him and wherever he finds it; and this is a considerable source of gain to most of the families here resident, who keep their negroes constantly employed in this way, and send them hither and yon on the business."[4] That slaves shared in these rights is confirmed by a 1799 advertisement placed in the *Bahama Gazette* by the Loyalist Robert Cunningham, which stated that it had "long been a Practice with Numbers of Negroes who are allowed to work out on this island, to cut Wood off Lands not the Property of their Owners, which they sell to raise money to pay their Wages."[5] This practice indicates that slaves on self-hire did not necessarily depend on waged employment but often derived an income from sources outside the wage labor market.

The arrival of the American Loyalists in the colony after 1783 had far-reaching consequences for the Bahamian labor market. The immigrants expanded cotton production on a plantation basis and extended commercial agriculture to islands in the archipelago that had been hitherto unsettled. These developments created a demand for labor and opportunities for slave owners to rent out their surplus slaves to investors in cotton plantations who preferred to hire gangs of slaves on a long-term basis rather than purchase them.[6] The establishment of large-scale cotton production did not, however, result in the total redistribution of the available labor force from the main population center to the outlying islands. Associated with the cotton boom was the development of Nassau as the service port for the plantation hinterland. Commercial activity also expanded with the opening of

Nassau as a free port after 1787 for trade with the Spanish and French colonies, which led to an increased demand for slaves to labor as porters and stevedores and to work in the skilled trades associated with the maritime economy.[7]

In the urban context, slaves working on the self-hire system remained a major source of labor in the years immediately following the arrival of the Loyalists. Michael Craton has argued that the American refugees regarded Bahamian blacks as having enjoyed "too much practical license" and were thus intent on tightening controls over the slave population.[8] They continued, however, to recognize the long-established autonomy of slaves on the self-hire system. The slave code of 1796 stipulated, for example, that slaves should not travel about without a ticket from their owner, employer, or overseer stating the time of their departure, their destination, and expected time of return to their usual place of residence. Slaves who provided food, fodder, and fuel to the urban community were the only exceptions to that regulation.[9]

Although some of the customary rights of slaves on self-hire were retained, others were circumscribed. Throughout New Providence, Loyalist immigrants were granted extensive acreage. These land grants constituted an enclosure movement in which slaves who had earlier earned a living from unallocated land were increasingly denied access to their means of subsistence.[10] New grantees sometimes placed notices in the colony's newspapers asserting their ownership of the land and threatening legal action against trespassers. Some proprietors, like Isaac Baillou, supplied incoming vessels with wood for fuel and stone for ballast and thus competed directly with the slaves.[11] As early as 1784 John McKenzie gave notice, in an advertisement in the *Bahama Gazette,* that "no Person or Persons, *White* or *Black,* are to cut Wood or burn Lime above the new Road, on the piece of land situated between Mr. *Perpaul's* and Mr. *Lairy's.*" In May 1791 one issue of the *Bahama Gazette* had two notices from Loyalist proprietors. The first of these, placed by Robert Cunningham, referred to slaves who cut wood on his land behind Fort Charlotte and warned their owners that "unless they desist immediately from such Practice, they will be prosecuted with the Rigour of the Law." The second advertisement, by the Earl of Dunmore, concerned his property on Hog Island (the cay that forms the harbor of New Providence), which colonists had regarded as common land since the early period of European settlement:

> Notice is Hereby Given, That the Earl of Dunmore is now Proprietor of the Whole of Hog Island, except thirty Acres belonging to Mr Russel the

> Ship Builder. His Lordship having been informed that some People have Stock on the Island, and that others cut Wood, Grass, & c. This is to desire that the former will remove their Stock before the 1st of June, and that the latter will desist immediately from cutting Wood, & c. Persons offending may be assured of being proceeded against as the Law directs.[12]

The appearance of similar notices in subsequent years suggests that some slaves continued to support themselves by the sale of wood, grass, and ballast.[13] There must, however, have been others who were forced to seek wage employment to survive.

By the late 1790s, slaves on self-hire controlled important areas of the urban economy. In 1799, for example, the grand jury complained that slave middlemen were monopolizing the supply of fruits, ground provisions, and vegetables in Nassau and forcing up prices by intercepting shipments of produce from the American mainland and Eleuthera. Itinerant slave traders hawked these goods around the town rather than sell them in the public market: "We present the Practice adopted by Negroes, of monopolizing all Fruits[,] Roots and Vegetables on board Vessels from America, and the Plantation Boats from Eleuthera, & c., whereby these articles are prevented from coming in to the public Market, to the injury of the Inhabitants in general, and contrary to the laws in that case made and provided."[14] The publication of an extract from the Slave Act (pertaining to the penalties for engrossing and forestalling foodstuffs) by the acting magistrate in the *Bahama Gazette* in the following year indicates that the practice continued despite the complaints of white consumers.[15]

In 1799 the members of the grand jury also expressed resentment of the fact that slaves on self-hire were successfully dictating wage levels in their negotiations with employers. They were, moreover, concerned that these high wages gave slaves disposable income that was spent on leisure-time activities like drinking alcohol and gambling: "We present as a very great Grievance, the present irregular Mode of hiring out Negroes to daily labor, whereby great Impositions are made, by their extorting unreasonable Wages, and keeping the greatest Part of the same to themselves, which furnishes them with the Means of indulging in every kind of Dissipation; and we recommend this Grievance to the consideration of the Legislature, that proper Rates and Regulations may be adopted."[16] In a period when expanding economic activities placed pressure on the available labor supply, slaves on the self-hire system (aware of the market value of their services) had sharply increased the wages they demanded from prospective employers. It is probable that the grand jury's recommendation that legislative action be taken to regulate wages rates was inspired by a similar measure enacted by Georgia's House of Assembly in the 1760s.[17]

The collapse of the cotton-based plantation system after 1800 created once again a surplus of slave labor in the colony. With the decline in cotton production, slave owners on the Out Islands experienced difficulty in finding profitable employment for their labor force. In his evidence before a select committee of the House of Assembly on the proposal for a general registry of slaves in 1815, Theodore George Alexander, editor of the *Royal Gazette,* expressed a more widely held view on the state of the colony's labor market: "That I verily believe from the number of Negroes now on these Islands, there is no sort of encouragement for, or advantage to be gained by the Introduction of African Slaves, as in consequence of the exhausted state of the Lands, there is not employment enough for those at present upon them: Nearly whole Islands which were formerly under cultivation in Plantations of Cotton, being at present capable of little else than raising cattle and Sheep."[18] Some slave owners, among them James Moss, sold more than 3,000 of their slaves in the British Caribbean sugar colonies between 1808 and 1825 before the imperial government ended this intercolonial traffic.[19] Despite these slave exports, the problem of surplus labor persisted.

Slave owners often adjusted to the stagnating agricultural economy and the concomitant reduced demand for slave labor by transferring their underutilized slaves to Nassau, where there were employment opportunities for both skilled and unskilled labor on the hiring-out and self-hire systems. By the closing decade of slavery, slaves on the self-hire system dominated the urban scene. Although the Slave Registration returns for 1834 mentioned few examples of slaves on self-hire, the qualitative evidence indicates that it was entrenched in the urban and maritime economy. In April 1830, Governor Sir James Carmichael Smyth commented, "At Nassau almost all the mechanics, & even the seafaring people are slaves, who pay a fixed sum to their owners, & make what they can by their labour."[20] During the Apprenticeship between 1834 and 1838, Charles Penny, special justice in the Turks Islands, made similar observations about the labor market in Nassau: "In Nassau, a large proportion [of slaves] being non-praedials and a great number working for themselves, and only paying wages to their owners."[21]

By 1816 the system of self-hire had been extended to include liberated Africans who served an indenture in New Providence. According to the collector of customs, Alexander Murray, the system was introduced at the request of the recaptives themselves. In a letter to Earl Bathurst in August 1816, seeking approval for permitting such an arrangement, Murray asked, "Whether I have been acting right/in granting Various Applications which have been made to me by Apprentices; with the approbation of their Masters or Mistresses, to be allowed to work & carry in a certain proportion of their Wages[,] in having given my approbation to the measure not only as gratifying to the Apprentice in the mean time—but as giving them such habits of Industry as would accustom them to provide for themselves, at the end of the term of their Apprenticeships—and insensibly lead them to the habits of freedom."[22] The African apprentices pressed for self-hire because it allowed them to earn a wage. The colonists to whom they were indentured endorsed a proposal that offered the prospect of regular cash payments in lieu of labor services.

In Nassau, as in Rio de Janeiro, the categories of slaves who worked on self-hire were extensive.[23] Skilled artisans were among the earliest participants in the system and continued to form a significant proportion of those who hired their own time until the end of the slavery era. As Carmichael Smyth remarked in 1832, "it has long been a custom in this Colony to permit the more intelligent of the Slaves, & more particularly Artificers, to find employment for themselves & to pay to their owners either the whole or such a proportion of what they may gain as may be agreed upon between the Parties."[24] Most slaves who eventually labored under that arrangement were, however, no more than unskilled casual laborers who turned their hands to a variety of tasks to eke out a living. This adaptability was, in part, a reflection of the situation on the small-scale plantations of the colony, where occupational boundaries were comparatively fluid. The multiple tasks that slaves generally undertook on most Bahamian plantations were described in a message to the governor from the House of Assembly in 1823:

> A crop of cotton, or provisions being raised, or a few small cargoes of cedar or dye woods cut from the woods, the slaves are frequently sent, for the season, to rake and manufacture salt at the ponds; from thence they are, in due time, called back to the fields, the provision grounds, or the orchards or gardens, where fruits are raised for exportation. The produce was next to be taken to market; and a portion of the same gang become sailors for the occasion, and at other times through the year, fishermen, wreckers . . . and even domestic servants, to attend to the business of their master's house, his cattle and other stock, for use, or for consumption or sale. Thus, with all the varieties of season and casualty, the nature of the Bahamian negro's occupation changes.[25]

Self-hire was not confined to land-based activities, for slave mariners constituted a majority of those who worked under that system. In March 1830 Carmichael Smyth observed, "The greater part of the slave population here are seafaring people. The crews in the wrecking vessels are in a great measure composed of slaves—these people are paid in shares, & they almost all invariably work out their freedom."[26] Slaves worked on droghing vessels (schooners used for cargo) that plied between the outlying islands and New Providence; on wrecking, turtling, and fishing boats; and on the ships that linked the Bahamas with the neighboring Caribbean islands and the North American coastline.

An advertisement placed by slave owner George Johnston in the *Bahama Gazette* of 25 November–2 December 1786 indicates the far-ranging voyages in which slaves sometimes participated and their importance to the colony's maritime economic activities:

> WHEREAS the Subscriber is well informed that his Schooner MAYFLOWER, commanded by SOLOMON WITHERLY, was, in the latter end of July last, while on a turtling voyage in the neighbourhood of Cape Cartouch, seized by a Spanish Guarda Costa, from Campeachy; and that the master and crew made their escape, and have gone for the British Settlements in the Bay of Honduras: He earnestly requests that every British subject, or other person, to whom the said master or crew, or any of them, may make application for assistance to get hither, that they will grant it to them, and the Subscriber will cheerfully re-imburse every expence they may be at in so doing.
>
> Besides the master, there were on board the said Schooner, *William Kemp,* a white man, and the following Negroes, viz. *Cesar,* belonging to *Robert Hunt,* Esq; *Isaac,* belonging to Mr. *John Warner; Sam, Ben, Jemmy,* and *Jack,* the property of
>
> GEORGE JOHNSTON

In the various maritime occupations, as William Wylly claimed with some exaggeration in 1815, slaves worked on the same terms as white crewmen: "Our Black Seamen are perhaps *equal to any in the World,* our Island Vessels are principally manned by them; and many of our Droghers, Turtlers and Fishing Vessels are commanded by them; they are generally allowed certain proportions of the Profits of each Cruize or Voyage and there is no difference between their treatment and that of our White Seamen."[27] An 1828 official report indicated, however, that the terms of compensation for slaves and liberated Africans who worked as sailors were usually less generous than Wylly suggested: "The vessels to which they are attached are usually engaged in Fishing and Wrecking. In addition to the food provided for the people on board an abundance of Fish may, at all times, be caught.

When occasional Wrecks come in the way the Africans, in common with the rest of the Crew who may be in Slave Condition, generally receive some small gratuity out of the Salvage awarded."[28]

Female slaves on the self-hire system were employed primarily as domestics and itinerant vendors. There were, for example, opportunities for employment as house servants, cooks, and laundresses in private households. Occasionally they worked as seamstresses. A market for slaves on self-hire also existed in public institutions that required labor services but did not wish to assume the wide-ranging statutory obligations of slave owners. In 1799, for example, Alexander Begbie, commissary to the West India Regiment stationed in Nassau, advertised for slave women to serve as nurses and washers at the hospital at Fort Charlotte.[29]

The practice of using slaves in the itinerant retail trade was established in New Providence before the arrival of the American Loyalists. In fact, they were so well established that the Consolidated Slave Act of 1796 expressly forbade the employment of slaves to retail dry goods, primarily because they competed directly with Loyalist merchants.[30] In 1795 the grand jurors complained about the activities of slave and free colored vendors who sometimes peddled their own goods:

> We present, as a Grievance of a very heinous Nature, and often complained of heretofore, the Number of Slaves and other People of Colour, who are employed by their several Owners and Employers in vending in Baskets, Trunks, & c. Dry Goods of all Kinds, which is not only contrary to Law, but an Injury to the fair and industrious Trader; keeps alive a ruinous Extravagance in the Purchase, and operates to encourage Robbery and Theft by affording specious and safe Opportunity of selling Stolen Goods under the Sanction of their respective Owners and Employers Names and Licence.[31]

A notice issued by the colony's high constable in December 1804 indicated, however, that the legislative restrictions had proven ineffective: "Notice is Hereby Given, to all such persons who have heretofore permitted their Slaves to retail Dry Goods, & c. about the streets, that the subscriber intends in future to put the above clause [in the Slave Act] rigidly in force against all delinquents."[32] Despite those stated intentions, female slaves continued to hawk merchandise about Nassau.[33]

With the exception of the skilled trades, liberated Africans found similar types of employment on the self-hire system. In fact, the 1828 report of a committee appointed to examine "the state and condition" of the liberated Africans provides detailed information from the recaptives' own testimony about the operation of the system in the major categories of employment. In her evidence to the committee, Encom, a domestic, reported that "she was first employed by her Holder as a domestic Servant since which she has been allowed to work out, paying her Holder two dollars a Month wages. Is at present living with a Sergeant at the 2nd W. I. Regt. who is her Husband. That she washes [for] one of the Companies for which she earns eight dollars a month." In his testimony, Boomba, a sailor, described the changing terms of his arrangement with his holder: "That he is intended to Mrs Anne Saunders of New Providence and has been entirely employed as a Seaman on board of different Vessels. Has occasionally gone Wrecking. At one time he received a deserving share of Fifty Dollars—for himself, and since smaller Sums. Has also been employed as a Seaman on board of Merchant Vessels on wages at Twenty two dollars a month out of which he was allowed by his Mistress two dollars a month for himself to purchase clothes. That he can always procure employment and good wages as a Sailor." Like many slaves, Pabu was transferred by his holder from an Out Island plantation to New Providence, where he worked on the self-hire system "during the first two years on a Plantation of his Holders as a Laborer, and received Seven Quarts of Corn a week, and two Suits of Clothes a year. Since then he has been working out on Wages, and pays his Holder Twelve shillings a week and finds his own food. Is working as a Stone Cutter and Wall builder and received three shillings a day, out of which he is allowed by his Holder a shilling a day."[34]

Although the self-hire system was commonly referred to as "working out on wages," it involved a diversity of labor relations that included wage relations as well as share relations and self-employment. Both skilled and unskilled laborers were paid wages, but mariners were usually given a share from the voyages in which they participated—an arrangement that Steve J. Stern has described as "a right of fractional appropriation in the *product* of the work performed."[35] It is not clear how the system of itinerant vending was organized, but it is likely that female slaves were required by their owners to return a stipulated sum and that earnings in excess of that amount went to the seller.[36] The grand jurors in 1795 also noted that slave vendors often sold a selection of dry goods on their own account. In some cases (like those of the woodcutters mentioned earlier) participants in the self-hire system worked neither for a wage nor for a share but depended on informal and often irregular sources of income.

Wage rates for slaves who labored on self-hire reflected skill levels and the type of work performed. In 1828, when the committee on the liberated Africans provided data on wage rates, slave mechanics were the most highly paid. The slave mechanic was paid the same daily wage as a "Mechanic of colour"—6 shillings 3½ pence sterling. From those earnings he was allowed to keep a weekly minimum of 5 shillings 5 pence for food and clothing. The average monthly income of a sailor, exclusive of food that was provided for him on board the vessel, was approximately 10 dollars. Domestics who were fed and clothed by their employers averaged 5 dollars per month, and laborers were paid an average daily rate of 1 shilling 7½ pence sterling.[37] After discharging their contractual obligations to their owners, some slaves (particularly those who lacked special skills) probably had little disposable income. A significant number, however, earned enough money to indulge in leisure-time activities like drinking and gambling on a regular basis and to purchase inexpensive consumer items.[38]

Many slaves accumulated enough savings to buy their own freedom. The process of manumission was facilitated by falling slave prices in the opening years of the nineteenth century and the replacement of a manumission fee of 90 pounds (introduced in 1784) by a nominal registration fee in 1827.[39] So widespread was the practice of slaves' purchasing their freedom that Carmichael Smyth (referring to slave mariners) predicted in 1830 that "if the system which at present exists is suffered to continue, they will by degrees all become free without exciting any shock or convulsion in their little community."[40] B. W. Higman has noted that the Bahamas had the highest manumission rate in the British Caribbean in the period 1808–34. The manumissions per 1,000 slaves were 3.1 in 1808, 4.5 in 1820, and .4 in 1834.[41]

The self-hire system eased the transition from slavery to freedom because it not only allowed some slaves to purchase their freedom but also gave those who continued to work on it substantial control over their lives while they remained chattels. Away from the direct supervision of their owners, slaves bargained with potential employers for wages; managed their money; and arranged for their own food, clothing, and accommodation.[42] An advertisement inserted by John Leslie in the *Bahama Gazette* of 14–18 March 1800 for the return of his fugitive slave Charles demonstrates the scope for self-governance that the self-hire system offered some slaves: "Ran Away from the Subscriber, a few days ago, a Negro Man named *CHARLES*, Butcher by Trade, and is well known in Town.—As he may have concerns of his own in the Market, the public are cautioned against having any further dealings with him."

The prospect of earning a wage prompted some slaves to hire themselves out without their owners' prior approval. Advertisements by owners warning prospective employers against hiring their slaves without permission were a common feature of the colony's newspapers in the last four decades of slavery. In 1795, for example, Maria Woods warned "all Persons against employing or hiring her Negro Wench named *Jane*" without her consent. In 1808 Alexander Wildgoos complained "that several of my Negro slaves, have at various times been employed without my leave, and used for that purpose materials belonging to me." In 1831 Thomas Atwell cautioned persons "not to employ Jacob Gibson, a slave, by trade a Ship Carpenter, without written permission from the Subscriber."[43]

Some urban slaves ran away but remained in Nassau in a bid to earn a cash income without having to make payments to their owners. The evidence from runaway advertisements suggests that fugitive slaves encountered little difficulty in finding employment. In July 1796, for example, John Morris advertised for the return of his slave Nancy, who, he admitted, "being a tolerable Washer and Ironer, she may employ herself in that Way during the Time she can absent herself." In an August 1800 advertisement for the return of his slave Trusty, William Bradford, M.D., noted that "it is suppose[d] he works daily about the town." Joseph Moxey, advertising the flight of his slave Jack in November 1800, mentioned that he had "reason to believe that the said Negro is harbored and employed." In these advertisements, slave owners routinely threatened to bring legal proceedings against persons who employed their runaway slaves.[44] Although slave owners seldom knew who illicitly hired their slaves, the grand jurors in February 1790 identified a prominent Loyalist as an offender: "We present *Alexander Harrald* for harboring and employing Runaway Slaves, upon the information of Isaac Baillou."[45]

The quasi-freedom that slaves on self-hire enjoyed was disturbed only if they failed to pay their owners the prearranged sum from their wages or ran afoul of the law. Although slave owners acquiesced in the development of a measure of autonomy for their slaves, they continued to exercise their powers of coercion from time to time. The main targets of their disciplinary measures were those slaves who failed to make the fixed payments. As the following advertisement, which appeared in 1799, indicates, slaves were sometimes imprisoned for such offences: "Broke out of Gaol, a Negro Man, the Property of the Subscriber named *Dick,* a ship carpenter by Trade, a smart looking young Fellow, African born, speaks remarkably good English, has no Country Marks. He was put into Gaol for not paying his wages regularly. *Twenty Dollars* Reward will be paid on said Runaway's being delivered to Timothy Cox, Ship Carpenter." Dick was clearly a habitual offender; Timothy Cox advertised the following month for his return when he ran away after receiving his wages: "Run away on Monday last, immediately after having received his Wages for four Days Hire, from Mr Ritchie which he carried off, a Negro Man called *Dick* belonging to the Subscriber, a Ship Carpenter by Trade and well known about Town. He frequently saunters about the Western Suburbs, and there is Reason to suspect he is occasionally employed there." Dick's reluctance to "pay wages" was not an isolated case, as a 1794 advertisement by Elisha Swain suggests: "All persons are hereby forewarned from hiring or paying any Wages to a Negro Fellow named *Chatham Darre,* (a Carpenter) without Leave from the Subscriber."[46]

Nonpayment of wages by slaves on self-hire was widespread by the 1830s. The offenders were not only those who wished to evade payment but also those slaves who (anxious to work on the self-hire system) agreed to pay their owners more than they could regularly earn. The punishment meted out to those slaves, as Carmichael Smyth noted in 1832, continued to be confinement in the workhouse:

> Almost every Slave is anxious to enjoy this species of Liberty [the self-hire system] & will readily promise & undertake to pay more than, at times, he may be able to acquire. Many of them have a sort of account current with their owners; & in hopes of better times get deeper in debt every month. There are of course also some dishonest and dissolute Slaves who will spend whatever they may gain & state to their owners that they have not been able to get work. The day of reckoning is however sure to arrive at last, & I have had occasion to observe, in the weekly returns, Slaves repeatedly confined in the Work-House & punished for "not paying wages."

This practice was discontinued after Carmichael Smyth's intervention. He took the view that since this punishment was inflicted "without the intervention of any Magistrate and at the will & by the command of one of the Parties to an agreement who thus became a Judge in his own case," such an action was "contrary to every Principle of Equity." He regarded the slaves' nonpayment of wages as a civil rather than a criminal offense: "It occurr'd to me that if the Master gave up his legal right to the labour of his Slave to the Slave for a certain weekly or monthly sum such a transaction must be viewed as a bargain between two Individuals. It was a voluntary not a compulsory act on the part of the Master; & if he did not receive the complete benefit he expected, it was always in his power to resume his rights & to recall his Slaves to his daily labour." The colony's solicitor general concurred in this view and gave an official opinion stating that the "non-payment of wages was similar to any non-fulfillment of any agreement & was not a crime or offence which could be punished at the command of the master by a flogging." This opinion was eventually forwarded to the superintendent of the workhouse, who was instructed to comply with the ruling.[47] This ruling is significant because it marked a further stage in the substitution of a relationship based on contract for one based on coercion. The first stage was the commutation of labor obligations into a cash payment.

The nonpayment of wages by slaves on the self-hire system continued to be a source of controversy even after the solicitor general's ruling. In August 1836 Special Justice Thomas Winder noted that it was a matter about which former slave owners complained: "If the records of Complaints made to all Magistrates in the Colony were carefully inquired into, it would be found that nearly all of them who have been made by the agents of non-resident Proprietors, or by Persons who having no profitable employment for their Apprentices at home have turned them out to seek their living in order to avoid the expence of food and clothing expecting them to pay wages although there is no agreement entered into legally requiring them to do so."[48] It is clear that with the threat of the workhouse removed, many slaves on self-hire no longer paid "wages" to their owners; they functioned essentially as free wage labourers before full emancipation.

Slave owners had also attempted to reassert control over slaves on self-hire by legislation first enacted in December 1800. The legislation "for regulating the hire of Slaves, Carts, Waggons and Drays" stipulated that proprietors who allowed their slaves "to hire themselves to work, either on board of vessels, or on the shore, as porters or labourers," should register the names of the slaves with the police office and obtain a copper badge that each slave was required to wear on his jacket or frock "in a conspicuous manner." The law further stated that persons who hired slaves without such a badge would be liable to a fine of 5 pounds for each slave employed and would also have to pay double their wages to their owners.[49]

Those provisions were prompted by two main considerations, the first of which was to distinguish slaves on self-hire, who operated virtually as freed persons, both from other slaves and from the rapidly growing free population. In the same session of the House of Assembly a law was enacted that stipulated that free persons of color had to be registered and given a certificate and must provide themselves with a silver medal bearing their engraved initials, the certificate number, and the word "Free." The legislation stated that the medal had to be "worn at all times thereafter by such free person of color, at his or her breast, exposed to public view, in order that they may be generally known and distinguished from slaves."[50] The potential for confusion is demonstrated by the case of Peg Morgan, a runaway slave who hired "herself about town as a washer saying she had liberty to work out and pay wages."[51] The second motivation behind the laws was to help slave owners monitor the movement of their slaves and make it more difficult for them to evade payment of wages. There is no evidence indicating whether those laws were effectively enforced.

By the late eighteenth century, a self-hire system emerged in New Providence, where the absence of an agricultural export staple meant that the slave labor force was not kept continuously at work. This system survived the short-lived cotton boom, during which there was some redistribution of the workforce to the cotton-producing islands. With the decline of cotton production, many slave owners (anxious to rationalize their surplus labor force) turned to the self-hire system. Its major attraction for slave owners, many of whom had withdrawn from direct production, was that it produced a steady cash income from their human property and shifted maintenance costs to the slaves themselves. Under this system, slaves exercised considerable freedom of movement and action, which ran counter to their legal status. In the process of seeking employment, they bargained for wages and agreed on informal contractual terms with their employers.[52] Since they decided how some of their earnings should be spent, slaves on self-hire participated in the market economy as both earners of income and consumers. In the Bahamas, where the system was probably more widespread than elsewhere in the British Caribbean, slaves worked on arrangements that foreshadowed the postemancipation labor systems. Like the development of a "protopeasantry," the emergence of self-hire during slavery was "an inherently contradictory development."[53] If there were slaves who, as Sidney W. Mintz has demonstrated, were in important respects like peasants before they became free, there were also slaves in the Bahamian context who were like wage laborers while still chattels.

Chapter Three

THE RESTRUCTURING OF AGRARIAN RELATIONS AFTER 1800

The protoproletarianization of a significant number of urban slaves in the years after the collapse of cotton production was paralleled on the Out Island plantations by the gradual transformation of a field labor force into a protopeasantry.[1] Unlike the case in other territories in the Americas where the development of a protopeasantry constituted a "peasant breach" in vibrant sugar economies, in the Bahamas protopeasants emerged on decayed plantations where a primarily absentee proprietorship struggled to maintain agricultural production above subsistence levels.[2] Without the strictly regulated work regimen associated with export-oriented production or the monopoly of arable land this generally involved, "the transition from 'protopeasant' to true peasant," as Michael Craton has suggested, "was probably more advanced in Exuma and similar Bahamian islands than anywhere in the British colonies."[3] On those plantations, the liberated Africans also formed the core of a free peasantry in the Bahamas before emancipation.[4]

On the island of New Providence, both a protopeasantry and a peasantry had emerged by the late eighteenth century. In 1767 legislation that regulated the social and economic activities of "Negroes, Mulattoes and Indians" referred to the fact that "it had hitherto been customary for slaves to make plantations for themselves on lands not the property of their several owners." In that context, the term "plantations" clearly referred to the cultivation of small plots for the slaves' subsistence as well as for sale. The provisions of the law suggest that the main objective of the legislators (who were usually slave owners) was to bring these economic activities under their direct control rather than to end them: "Be it enacted that . . . no slave shall clear or plant any land for him or herself but such as shall be the property of his or her owner." Another provision of the 1767 legislation indicates that slaves in New Providence were involved in marketing as well as production: "And whereas many evil-minded and covetous people of these islands make a practice of trading with Negro and other slaves. To prevent which be it enacted that . . . no person or persons shall presume to trade with any Negro or other slave either in buying, selling or bartering without the leave or consent of the owner of such Negro."[5] By 1783 both slaves and free blacks operated as small producers and traders. As Johann David Schoepf observed in that year: "Some of them own houses and plantations."[6]

The development of a protopeasantry by 1767 was facilitated by the availability, to slaves, of unoccupied land in New Providence (a fact acknowledged in the slave law of that year); the nature of the labor demands made on the slave population before large-scale cotton production; and the marked reluctance of white colonists to plant their own food crops. As noted earlier, Bahamian slaves existed in an economic environment in which wrecking and the harvesting of several varieties of wood for export were significant activities, but there was no major export staple whose production kept them steadily at work. Contemporary travelers' accounts also indicate that the white settlers did not exert themselves beyond subsistence needs. Writing after a stay in the Bahamas in the 1740s, Peter Henry Bruce commented, "In short, it is their own fault if the inhabitants want any of the necessaries of life: they have horses, cows, sheep, goats, hogs, and all sorts of poultry, and have grass all the year round; but they neither sow nor plant more than is necessary for maintaining their own families."[7] Schoepf's comments approximately forty years later were little different from those of Bruce: "The so-called planters work, all told, perhaps not more than two, at most three months in the year. They fell some wood, catch fish, sell what they raise—drink up their gains and dance away the time, for not even the hottest weather can keep them from this diversion. They are amiable, courteous, and according to their circumstances hospitable—but of severe work they know nothing and do not want to know anything."[8] In this context, slaves had both the time (outside the usual demands on their labor) and space to cultivate their own "plantations" and a market for their surplus among the easygoing white population.

In the early years of the establishment of cotton plantations on the south and southeastern islands, slave food production for their own subsistence and the internal economy was not as important as it later became. Slave labor was initially directed to clearing the land and producing the cotton crop for the export market, and planters thus preferred to rely on external sources for slave rations.[9] In an editorial comment of October 1789 in the *Bahama Gazette*, John Wells noted planters' dependence on imported food and the drain on economic resources this involved: "In the event of an increased population—and everything indicates a rapid increase—other articles besides Cotton will merit the attention of the Bahama Planters. Those Islands most unfavourable for Cotton, will produce Guinea Corn and other tropical ground provisions in abundance; and it certainly would be more to the general advantage to have our Negroes fed from Grain raised in our own Islands, than to send our specie, as is now done, for Indian Corn to the American States."[10] Five years later the situation on slave provisioning remained virtually unchanged, as a letter from "A Planter" in March 1794 indicated: "We all want to make a great crop, to get rich at once, and leave the d—d country. It is seldom considered that when such crops are made, they are applied to the purchase of pork at 30 dollars the barrel, corn at 12s the bushel, and other articles in proportion."[11] There is, however, evidence that some plantation slaves as early as 1789 were allocated land to raise their own food. A runaway advertisement in June of that year, inserted by the mercantile partnership of Forbes and Stevens, referred to "Negro Fields" on their Long Island plantation.[12] It is possible that, in the new setting, American slaves had insisted on the reinstatement of customary rights to provision grounds that they had enjoyed on the rice plantations of the Carolina and Georgia lowcountry.[13]

The development of a protopeasantry was encouraged by the Consolidated Slave Act of 1796, which, in addition to specifying the rations that should be given to individual slaves, stipulated that they should also be allocated a "sufficient quantity of Land" for their own use.[14] This concession was an aspect of a policy of "legislative amelioration" of slave conditions that was adopted in the Bahamas, as elsewhere in the British Caribbean, as a defense against the metropolitan campaign for the abolition of the slave trade.[15] The collapse of the cotton-based plantation system after 1800 had two main implications for the expansion of protopeasant activities. First, slaves were left with more time for productive labor on their own provision grounds since there was no crop of comparable commercial importance to replace cotton.[16] Second, without a profitable export staple, slave owners encountered difficulty in maintaining a steadily increasing and underemployed labor force. Thus they were willing to shift the burden of slave maintenance to the provision grounds.

Perhaps the most important factor in the expansion of protopeasant activities in the stagnating agricultural economy of the Bahamas was the way the labor of the slaves was organized. Throughout the Bahamas, slaves who were employed in agricultural activities worked primarily on the task system.[17] As noted in chapter 1, Loyalist planters adapted the task system, used in rice culture in the coastal region of South Carolina and Georgia, to the Bahamian context. The lowcountry paradigm was evident in two features of the task system as it operated in the Bahamas. First, slaves were assigned tasks, usually on a daily basis, that took their individual physical strength into account.[18] Second, the fields where task labor was used were divided into plots that ranged in size from a quarter of an acre to one acre. In the rice fields, the plots were marked off by the trunks and ditches of the irrigation system, but in the Bahamian cotton fields these areas were defined by "permanent stations."[19] By 1823 the task system had been so long entrenched that some slave owners observed that it had been the principal mode of organizing slave labor "within the memory of the oldest of us."[20] At the beginning of the nineteenth century, the task system was well suited to a context in which (as in the outlying islands) proprietors were often absentee and supervision of the slave labor force was at best perfunctory.

One consequence of the task system was that it provided slaves daily time outside the plantation routine to devote to leisure-time activities or the cultivation of their provision grounds. This was in marked contrast to the situation in Antigua, where, as David Barry Gaspar has noted, the "free time" of the slave labor force (which was organized on the gang system) was concentrated mainly at the end of the week.[21] On his visit to the Bahama Islands in 1803, Daniel McKinnen remarked on the operation of the task system that the slaves' labor "is allotted to them daily and individually, according to their strength; and if they are so diligent as to have finished it at an early hour, the rest of the day is allowed to them for amusement or their private concerns."[22] In 1812 the collector of customs, Alexander Murray, also described a plantation work routine that allowed slaves a part of the day to labor on their own plots: "They on most of the Plantations with ease complete their task of labor for the day by three or four o'clock in the Even[g] after which they employ themselves in their own grounds."[23] As that statement suggests, by 1812 slaves found it increasingly necessary to supplement the statutory allowances, which impoverished slave owners often supplied erratically, with the proceeds from the cultivation of their provision grounds.[24]

The most detailed description of labor organization on Bahamian plantations is provided by William Wylly in a letter to Zachary Macaulay in 1812. Although Wylly's description of task work refers specifically to cotton production rather than to the cultivation of foodstuffs for the Nassau market (to which many plantations on the Out Islands turned in this period), it establishes the fact that there was general concurrence on what constituted, in Philip D. Morgan's phrase, "the 'basic' task unit."[25] It is also clear that elements of the gang system were used for certain categories of work on the plantations:

> No field labour in any Country where the Plough is not in use, can possibly be lighter than that of our Plantations, and whenever the nature of the work will admit of it, our Negroes are regularly *tasked*. The *tasks* are one fourth of an Acre in extent, they are usually marked out by permanent stations in every field, and two, three, sometimes four Slaves (but in general more than one) are put into each Task, at the discretion of the Driver, according to the actual state of the field. But in seed time and Harvest, when it would hardly be possible to assign set Tasks, they are allowed one Hour at Breakfast, and two Hours at Dinner. It happens too that we have no Canes to grind, no dung to carry out, either by day or by Night, and I verily believe it rarely happens that the setting sun ever leaves a Negroe in our Fields.[26]

On the plantations, the combination of task work and the provision-ground system allowed slaves to cultivate food crops and raise small livestock for sale as well as for their own subsistence. In his letter to Macaulay, Wylly remarked on the pervasiveness of this practice: "Besides the stated allowance of Grain, to which our Plantation Negroes are by Law entitled, they are allowed as much ground as they choose to cultivate, and are universally permitted to raise Hogs and Poultry. Yet it is true to a Proverb that—'*No negroe ever eats his own Fowl or kills his own Pig. They sell them all.*'"[27] On his two cotton plantations in western New Providence, Wylly provided incentives for his slaves to raise poultry and livestock. Regulations drafted for his plantations at Clifton and Tusculum in 1815 stated that each male slave "upon taking his first wife" was entitled to "a sow pig and a pair of dunghill fowls, as a donation from the proprietor." Separate pastures were allocated for the hogs, and each family head was allowed to keep one sow. Wylly also made arrangements for slave cultivation of their own provisions, as the regulations indicate: "Sufficient land is set apart for the use of the people, and half an Acre is annexed to each house, as the property of the occupant for the time being."

In New Providence, as in the Out Islands, proprietors sometimes provided a market for the goods their slaves produced. Wylly, for example, reserved the right to purchase "all hogs, pigs, poultry, and eggs" that his slaves wished to sell at Nassau prices, set by the plantation's driver and two other men selected by the seller.[28] For slaves in New Providence and the adjoining islands, however, Nassau was the principal market for surplus products. On Wylly's estates, slaves were generally allowed to attend the Nassau market on Saturdays if they had "poultry, vegetables, or other articles" for sale. The marketable products of the slave provision grounds included Guinea and Indian corn, yams, potatoes, pumpkins, squashes, peas, beans, benne (sesame), groundnuts, eddoes, plantains, bananas, watermelons, and muskmelons.[29] In Nassau the market was held throughout the week, not only on Sundays as in the sugar colonies. As the members of the House of Assembly explained in 1823: "Sunday markets, such as we understand have crept into use in other colonies, are altogether unknown here. From the effect of the climate on the more perishable meats and vegetables, we must have a daily market, or we could not eat—But on Sundays, the markets, in compliance with a law of long standing, are never suffered to open after nine o'clock in the forenoon."[30]

In Nassau the slaves supplied foodstuffs not only to local residents but also to the crews of incoming ships. In April 1830 Governor Sir James Carmichael Smyth explained the failure of the government savings bank to attract slave deposits by the fact that slaves preferred to invest in poultry and vegetables for resale: "A savings bank is established by Law; but not one farthing has ever been paid into it—What little money is possessed by Slaves, is invariably laid out in fowls & vegetables which they sell again to the Shipping."[31] Carmichael Smyth's comment further establishes the economic importance of urban slaves who acted as middlemen in the distribution rather than the production of provisions. Those slaves who sold their produce in Nassau came into direct economic competition with white farmers who cultivated their holdings with slave labor. In 1815 William Wylly pointed to the existence of "some hundred petty Farmers in these Islands, who supply the Town of Nassau with Poultry, Fruit, Roots &c, the people generally own a few Slaves."[32]

On the more remote islands, the participation of the slave population in the market economy—a characteristic feature of a protopeasantry—was usually intermittent. Droghing vessels manned by slaves linked those islands with Nassau, but this service was irregular. In some islands a local market existed for the products of the slave provision grounds. On the Perseverance plantation in Crooked Island, for example, the slaves were able to sell their surplus provisions to their owner, James Moss, and to other resident proprietors. It was not unusual for Moss to purchase corn from his slaves to be later issued as part of the slave ration. In April 1815 Henry Moss, another planter on that island, noted that he had occasionally purchased provisions from those slaves: "Witness has bought Hogs, Poultry &c from

Defendant's Slaves, and on one occasion a quantity sufficient to maintain 300 Negroes belonging to a Slave ship in distress for the space of three weeks." Those slaves were sometimes able to sell their produce to ships that visited the islands. As Captain Andrew Duncan, master of the ship *Bridgetown,* reported, "Witness bought Pigs, fowls, Eggs, Pumpkins &c from Negroes at Crooked Island for which he paid them about thirty or forty Dollars."[33]

Sometimes this trading went beyond the legitimate channels favored by slaves' owners. There is evidence that slaves in New Providence and the outlying islands often independently established a covert trading network beyond the purview or control of their masters.[34] This was made possible by the geographical isolation of the plantations, the high incidence of planter absenteeism, and the unwillingness of proprietors to employ overseers once cotton production declined. Several advertisements placed in the colony's newspapers by slave owners indicate that plantation slaves formed regular trading links with sailors and others to whom they sold and bartered their produce. In 1810, for example, William Wylly placed a notice in the *Royal Gazette* of 10 February drawing attention to the fact that his slaves regularly bartered their produce with Nassau fishermen for rum: "Whereas the fishermen of this port make it their practice to go on shore at the plantations situate at a distance from Nassau, under pretence of wanting wood and water, but for the real purpose of carrying on an unlawful traffic with our Negroes and supplying them with rum, in exchange for provisions and poultry."

Wylly's complaint was that proscribed alcoholic beverages were made available to slaves. Other proprietors, however, were concerned that slaves stole and sold commodities on which the economic viability of their plantations often depended. In an 1805 advertisement, John Hepbourn accused both the slaves and the overseer of the Bight Plantation on San Salvador of stealing and selling the estate's livestock to the captains and crews of visiting vessels. Theft and illicit trading remained a problem on the colony's surviving plantations in the closing years of slavery. In 1834 Joseph Hunter and A. S. Poitier warned potential trading partners against "dealing with, or receiving by way of barter either Cotton, Corn, Stock, Poultry, or any thing whatsoever from the slaves on any of their plantations, on the Islands of St. Salvador or New Providence."[35] It is possible that these slave owners continued to believe that all the products of their slaves' labor should accrue to them.

The involvement of plantation slaves in independent economic activities gave them disposable if modest incomes and the opportunity to become consumers.[36] On the remote islands and cays of the archipelago, slaves bartered with and purchased goods from individuals with whom they regularly traded. In 1807, for example, John Edgecombe warned "all manners of persons whatever, from buying, selling or bartering with his Negroes, on Bond's Key." Some slaves were even able to buy on credit (on their owners' accounts without authorization), as an advertisement by Mary Stout of Watling's Island in July 1814 indicated: "This is to forewarn all persons whatsoever from giving credit on my account; and against trading with my Negroes on this Island, without a written order from myself."[37] Plantation slaves who lived on New Providence or on neighboring islands probably purchased their goods from urban hucksters whose steadily growing numbers were an index of the expanding consumer market among the slave and nonwhite free population.

The information on the nature of slave purchases is limited. Wylly's notice, cited above, suggests that some plantation slaves bought alcoholic beverages on a regular basis. It is most likely, however, that they spent the bulk of their income on food and clothing to improve on the quantity and quality of those items that were issued to them by law. Slave owners were, for example, required to supply a weekly allowance of one peck of unground Indian or Guinea corn (or other stipulated substitutes) to each slave.[38] A law of 1824 also mandated that slaves be provided with "two suits of proper and sufficient clothing" per annum.[39] The slaves' desire to purchase extra and better-quality clothing led to accusations that hucksters of dry goods were keeping "alive a ruinous Extravagance in the Purchase."[40] Nassau merchants like William and James Moss also imported items such as "Coarse and Negro" shoes specifically for the slave consumer.[41]

In the Bahamas, both plantation and urban slaves became not only participants in a consumer economy but also owners of property. Before 1826 a slave's right to own and dispose of property was recognized in custom, as the slave act of that year stated: "By the usages of the Bahama islands, persons in a state of slavery have hitherto been permitted to acquire and enjoy property, free from the control or interference of their owners." In 1826 this right was established in strict law by legislators who "deemed [it] expedient that such custom should be recognized and established by law." By the provisions of this legislation, slaves were declared competent to hold, inherit, purchase, and dispose of lands, cattle, "implements or utensils of husbandry, or household furniture and other effects."[42] The recognition of the slave's legal right to own property represented one aspect of a significant broadening of "the status of the slave as a *persona* in the eyes of the law," which colonial legislatures initiated in response to the pressures of British humanitarians.[43]

It was in the context of the slave plantation (where provision grounds were allocated to a labor force organized on the task system) that the liberated Africans formed the nucleus of a peasantry. Between 1811 and the end of apprenticeship in 1838, approximately 4,851 Africans were freed in the colony from slavers en route to Cuba that were either wrecked in the area or intercepted by ships of the British Royal Navy as part of the campaign against the slave trade.[44] By the provisions of an Order in Council of March 1808, these recaptives were employed either in the West India Regiment or in the British Navy or were apprenticed to "prudent and humane masters or mistresses" in the colony by the Customs Office. The liberated Africans were initially settled by the collector of customs on the island of New Providence, but the fears of this concentrated African presence, expressed by a section of the white population of Nassau in 1816, led to the wider distribution of the apprentices to employers on the outlying islands.[45]

Wherever the liberated Africans were employed under the apprenticeship system, they performed the same tasks as the slaves; labored under similar conditions; and were, like the slaves, generally given rations rather than wages. In New Providence and the Out Islands, they were employed in fishing, wrecking, cutting wood, raking salt, and agricultural and domestic tasks. In all these areas of employment, the recaptives were treated no better than the slaves alongside whom they worked. This was the conclusion of a committee that was established to examine the "state and condition" of the liberated Africans and reported in 1828: "The general impression, which has resulted from the Examinations taken, is that the African Apprentices, with regard to their comfort and the supply of their wants, were certainly not placed upon a better footing than the Slaves of their Holders. The work the Apprentices had to perform on the Plantation has been purely that which the slaves would have to do and they appear to have been kept to it by the same means."[46] Despite these similarities in the conditions under which both the slaves and the liberated Africans worked, there was one essential difference between the two groups: the labor services of the recaptives were owned for a specified term.[47]

The 1828 report, with its extensive supporting testimony from the recaptives (rendered in reported speech by the committee), provides detailed information on their work routines on the plantations and, by proxy, those of the slaves. It also gives us some insight into the set of circumstances that led to the emergence of a class of free small-scale agriculturists during slavery. The distinguishing feature of the apprentice's daily routine (like that of the slave) was the task system. In fact, the task system was so firmly entrenched on the plantations that the term "task" was commonly used by the apprentices in the Bahamas (as by the slaves in the lowcountry region of South Carolina and Georgia) to refer to both a unit of work and an area of land.[48] On the completion of their daily tasks, the apprentices (like the slaves) were usually free to work on the provision grounds that were allocated to them. The evidence indicates that it was not unusual for apprentices to be allowed as many as three acres of land. The round of activities described by the apprentice Onambu, who was employed on a plantation in Long Island, was perhaps typical: "Is allowed a piece of Ground for himself, which after finishing his Task about twelve o'clock he attends to. Has growing on it Ground Provisions and some Corn. Has a few fowls of his own." There were, however, some apprentices with such limited labor obligations to their employers that they were able to spend most of the day working on their provision grounds. That was the situation described by the apprentice Mesa in his statement reported by the committee: "That he is indented to Mr Charles Bethell of Eleuthera by whom he is employed in agricultural labour. Has no fixed task allowed him but works about three hours in the day for his Holder, and afterwards for himself on a piece of Ground which he is allowed to cultivate for himself. Has Saturday also for that purpose and that the produce of his Ground enables him to clothe and support himself very well."[49]

The African apprentices labored on the plantations under different types of arrangements with their holders. One important influence on these arrangements was the poverty of some employers, who were often unable to supply their apprentices with the basic allowances of food and clothing. The contracts of the apprentices did not specify any minimum allowances, but their holders generally used those prescribed by law for the slaves.[50] It was the usual practice for holders who were unable to supply the full rations of corn per week to permit their apprentices additional time to work on their provision grounds. On that point the 1828 report observed, "There seems to have prevailed a sort of Understanding that six Quarts of Corn should be the weekly allowance and when this fell short one working day has been allowed to the Apprentices for himself [*sic*] for every Two Quarts short of their weekly allowance."[51] In some instances apprentices, by an arrangement that prefigured the labor tenancy system of the immediate postemancipation period, divided the working week equally between their individual plots and their holders' fields.[52] The apprentice Aguara, who worked on a plantation in Eleuthera, described this arrangement to the investigating committee, which reported: "Gets no allowance but is allowed three days in the week for the purpose of maintaining and clothing himself, which he manages to do by selling a part of what his Ground produces that he raises on it Corn[,] Yams[,] Potatoes and other things. The three other days he is employed by his Holder."

The provision grounds were often tended with the help of those persons (whether slave or free) with whom the apprentice cohabited—in short, with family labor. The apprentice Ocba, for example, reported, "Is allowed a piece of Ground for himself and his Wife about three Tasks, and that he has now growing in it Corn, Yams, Squashes, Potatoes and other Provisions." The female apprentice Renneche, in her statement to the investigating committee, said, "Has a Husband . . . who assists her in cultivating a piece of Ground between them, of three Acres and that the produce of it contributes in supporting them and their child a boy about three years old."

From the proceeds of the provision grounds, the African apprentices were usually able to supplement their inadequate rations and satisfy their need for consumer items such as clothing and household articles. In his evidence to the committee, Mocacha indicated that he was able to support his family mainly from the produce of his plot of land: "Has Ground allowed him about Ten Tasks which is planted in Potatoes, Corn, Yams, and Pease. After finishing his Task he attends his own Ground, and is enabled in that way to maintain his Wife . . . and her four children. Has some Hogs and a few fowls. Occasionally sells a Hog for the purpose of buying Corn and a few other things. Says his Master is very good to him 'never meddles with his fields or troubles his Pigs' that he cannot tell a lie upon his Master." Like the slaves, the apprentices marketed their goods primarily in Nassau, but they also had opportunities to sell their produce locally. A group of African apprentices, for example, who worked on a plantation at Man of War Sound, Andros, sold their surplus "to the small Drogging Vessels and Fishing Smacks that constantly pass that way." Orofea, who was based in Exuma, also mentioned that "he sometimes sells a Hog or two at Exuma."

Although the apprentices concentrated on cultivating ground provisions and raising small livestock, there were individuals who produced craft items for sale. The case of the apprentice Freni illustrates the range of economic activities the recaptives pursued on the plantations as well as the problems they sometimes experienced with their holders:

> That he has been employed by his Holder Mr. Alexander Knowles as a Labourer on his Plantation at Long Island. When there was Corn on the plantation he received six Quarts a week, and sometimes he got only from

> three to four Quarts a week. When he received no allowance he was allowed to work for himself, and that he maintained himself by making Baskets and Mats which he sold. Says he has two pieces of Ground in cultivation, one of three Acres and another of an Acre and a half with Yams[,] potatoes[,] corn and Pease. That whenever he finishes his Task rather early, for the purpose of attending to his own Ground, his holder increases his Task the next day. That he once gathered a quantity of Sponges about Ninety five pounds in weight, which he sold for Eighteen Dollars but he only received Four Dollars out of that sum from his Master.

In a few instances, African apprentices led an independent existence on plantations owned by their holders. These individuals engaged in economic activities entirely on their own account. Irdy, for example, was sent by her holder, David Bethell, to a plantation he owned on Andros island. When he removed his slaves shortly afterward to Turks Island, Irdy and another apprentice were allowed to remain on the plantation. Working "entirely for herself," Irdy produced a surplus of ground provisions that she transported to market in a boat that she had bought for that purpose. As a result of her efforts, she was also able to acquire other household items: "Says she has Chairs, Tables, and a good Bed and that she is very comfortable."[53]

The case of Quamina is worth quoting at length because its detailed description of the apprentice's daily routine shows what J. S. Handler has identified as "the essential features by which any peasantry is characterized":[54]

> It would appear that about ten years ago, and about five years after his arrival from Africa, Mr Freeman Johnson allowed him to occupy a part of his property at Andros Island. Thus he has now six acres in Cultivation on which he raises the Common sorts of ground provisions such as Corn, Yams, Pumpkins, Potatoes, peas, water Melons and Sugar Canes. He avails himself of the opportunities which casually offer of sending for Sale to New Providence such Articles as he does not require for consumption in his family. In this way he clears about thirty dollars a year. He generally rises every morning before Six o'Clock, and works two or three hours until he feels disposed for breakfast. After breakfast say about nine or ten o'Clock he goes again into the fields and works continuously until about four, he then goes home to his dinner which his wife has prepared for him, and does not go any more into the field the same day. His Wife is a Slave on an adjoining Property, he has two female Children by her. She assists him on Saturdays. He has a boat on which he occasionally goes a fishing after he has ceased working in his fields, he catches a good deal of fishes, collects Crabs and

> Conchs and occasionally shoots Pigeons and Ducks but he makes these secondary considerations to working in his fields. In bad weather he plaits straw and makes Hats and Baskets which he sells at two and three shillings each. On the present occasion of his coming over from Andros Island to New Providence he has brought with him fifty Sugar Canes, which he has sold for two dollars; one bushel of peas for which he has received twenty shillings or two dollars and a half, he paid two dollars and a quarter for his passage and freight, he has to pay a dollar for his passage back. He intends carrying back some clothes for his daughters and some Rum for himself.[55]

As the discussion above has demonstrated, an African peasantry with access to land rather than ownership of it existed by 1828. By that date too a freehold peasantry had emerged from among those recaptives whose period of indenture had expired. In 1825 the collector of customs, Mr. C. Poitier, purchased from public funds 400 acres of land in New Providence for resale to liberated Africans whose apprenticeships had ended.[56] This scheme, as Poitier admitted in a letter to Governor Sir Lewis Grant, originated with the recaptives themselves: "This purchase originated as a wish expressed to me by some of these people themselves to have land they could call their own. They offered one Dollar per acre for 30 acres but Mr. Findlason [the vendor] would only sell the whole." The land in this settlement, which was known as Head Quarters, was sold in 10-acre lots to the liberated Africans at one dollar per acre. Shortly after the establishment of Head Quarters, Poitier was able to report, "Such is the abundance with which they [the settlers] are surrounded that they are unable to carry their spare provisions to market, and are now procuring Cattle for that purpose."[57]

By the following year, the liberated Africans at Head Quarters had become important suppliers of vegetables to the Nassau market, an area of production in which they competed with free persons of color. As Governor Grant remarked: "The quantities of vegetables which are brought into the market of Nassau from this source have tended considerably to reduce the price. There are a number of free coloured persons in the Bahamas who earn a livelihood by their own labour on a few acres."[58] The settlement at Head Quarters continued to be a source of foodstuffs for the town of Nassau into the early 1830s. In 1832 Governor Carmichael Smyth commented on these economic activities: "The women & the children of the free Africans think nothing of bringing the produce of their little fields & gardens (which are at least seven miles from this Town) upon their heads to the market, & that, most frequently twice a day. They never come to Town without either a basket of vegetables or a great bundle of wood upon their heads."[59]

Although some African peasants enjoyed a measure of prosperity, there is evidence that others could not support themselves from the proceeds of these fields. Like the postemancipation peasantries of the British Caribbean, the African peasants in the Bahamas during the slavery era, with little capital at their disposal, were often forced to combine labor on their own plots with other forms of employment including wage labor.[60] This trend was already discernible to the members of the committee on "the status and condition" of the liberated Africans:

> The Agriculturists among them having no sort of capital nor any aid from Government to commence with, are obligated to employ themselves in some other way to procure the means of supporting themselves while they are bringing their Land into cultivation and also occasionally when it is laid down with seed, until the season arrives when their fields require their more immediate attention. Some go to Sea, some in order to be near their fields work with their Neighbours obtaining maintenance for the portion of labour they give. Some cut Timber and some work on the Roads and gather fire wood. This will be the case more or less every year for the Bahama Husbandry is not to be solely depended upon for furnishing the means of support.[61]

The focus in this chapter on the emergence of the liberated Africans as a peasantry during the slavery era is not to downplay the emergence of a class of creole peasants in the same period. As noted above, there is evidence that there were freedpersons who could be described as peasants as early as 1783 and that by 1826 free persons of color cultivated foodstuffs for sale in Nassau. This trend must have continued with the increased rate of manumissions in the early nineteenth century as former slaves utilized skills they had acquired during their period of enslavement. The concentration in this chapter on the liberated Africans reflects the fact that information about their economic activities is extensive since they were the object of official interest and concern. By contrast, our knowledge of the activities of creole nonwhites as peasants is reconstructed from scattered references in the official sources and from a limited number of travelers' accounts. It is clear, however, that by the time of the abolition of slavery in 1834, the production of foodstuffs for the internal market was an area of economic activity that nonwhites (whether slave or free) had come to dominate. This fact was tacitly acknowledged in legislation of 1837 that made it illegal for persons to hawk or retail certain kinds of goods without a license. Hawkers who wished to sell dry goods (an area traditionally dominated by the white merchant class) had to obtain a license that was granted only after an extensive and complicated process. Those persons who sold foodstuffs and small craft items they produced themselves were exempted.[62]

Caribbean peasants of the immediate postemancipation era, scholars are agreed, had their origins in the plantation-slave system. However, as this discussion has shown, the Bahamas diverged from the general pattern in two important respects. First, the evolution of the Bahamian protopeasantry (unlike those of the sugar colonies) was more than an "interstitial" development on the slave plantation.[63] After 1800, time and space for independent economic activities became increasingly available to slaves on the colony's plantations as proprietors ceased their commitment to export production. Impelled by the need for self-maintenance, slaves established "networks of exchange" and operated effectively as peasants.[64] Second, the slave plantation provided the institutional framework within which not only slaves but also freedpersons produced goods for their own consumption and for sale in the local markets. Liberated Africans serving their period of indenture often worked on plantations where labor was organized on the task system, ample provision grounds were provided, and an impoverished planter class was anxious to shift the onus of maintenance costs to the laborers themselves. Owing to the combination of those factors, the recaptives had a large part of the day to tend their grounds and small stock. Liberated Africans employed in this way were usually able to maintain themselves and market their surplus. On Bahamian plantations in the last years of slavery, "slaves who were in some ways like peasants before they became free" thus coexisted with free laborers (in many respects treated like slaves) who were already peasants.[65]

Chapter Four

BETWEEN SLAVERY AND FREEDOM

The Liberated Africans and Unfree Labor

The redefinition of social and economic relationships between slaves and their owners after 1800 intersected with the introduction of liberated Africans into the colony. Although legally free, the liberated Africans experienced in the Bahamas, as in Cuba and Brazil, a form of unfree labor that was, in important respects, harsher than the legal slavery that was then undergoing a slow dissolution.[1] This chapter focuses on two aspects of the experience of these immigrants between 1811 and 1860: their reception in the host society and the operation of a system of indentured labor that had earlier been used mainly in connection with the colony's free persons of color.[2]

The settlement of the liberated Africans in the Bahamas was the direct result of British efforts to suppress the transatlantic slave trade. In 1807 Britain made participation in the slave trade illegal for its subjects. Until the end of the Napoleonic Wars, British efforts had mainly involved stationing ships of the Royal Navy on the slave trading routes to intercept any vessels (British or foreign) suspected of transporting slaves. Such ships, with their cargoes, were brought to the nearest British port, where the captain and crew were tried before a vice admiralty court. If they were successfully prosecuted, the slaves were liberated. With the return of peace in 1815, these naval activities were restricted to British ships. The British government subsequently persuaded the major maritime powers in Europe to abolish the slave trade and agree to a series of bilateral treaties that, in effect, permitted the British Navy to search their ships for slaves. Courts of mixed commission were established in West Africa, the Caribbean, and Latin America to adjudicate on ships seized on suspicion of trading in slaves. Slaves on board ships condemned for engaging in the slave trade were freed.[3]

Despite these efforts, the transatlantic slave trade was not effectively suppressed until the close of the 1860s. Although the Spanish government agreed to prohibit the slave trade north of the equator in 1817 and south of the line after May 1820, these agreements did little to slow the trade to the Spanish colony of Cuba, where the rapid expansion of the sugar industry sharply increased the demand for slave labor. According to Philip Curtin, approximately 550,000 slaves were imported into Cuba.[4] Slavers bound for Cuba were intercepted by ships of the British Navy, but the number of slaves seized and liberated was small in comparison with the number successfully imported into that colony. As the most active participant in the search and seizure of slave ships, Britain was responsible for disposing of groups of African recaptives who could not normally be repatriated. Those Africans liberated in the Caribbean were settled in colonies like British Guiana, Trinidad, Jamaica, and the Bahamas.[5]

The transference of liberated Africans to the plantation colonies in the 1840s and 1850s was regarded as a possible solution to the labor problems experienced especially by British Guiana and Trinidad.[6] The primary reason for settling liberated Africans in the Bahamas, however, was the colony's position on the main shipping route used by slavers between the African coast and Cuba. The Bahama Islands, as one colonial official aptly remarked in 1811, were "the Turnpike Road to the market of Cuba."[7] In a similar comment, the Legislative Council and the House of Assembly, in a joint petition to the king in council in the same year, accurately predicted the role of the colony as a "reception depot" for liberated Africans: "As the Bahamas are situated immediately on the high Road between the African Coast and the only Places where the Slave Trade can now find a Market in the West Indies, there appears but too much reason to apprehend that a very large portion of such Vessels as may be hereafter selected, on this side of the Atlantic, unlawfully engaged in that traffic, will also be brought hither."[8] Between 1811 and 1860 approximately 6,000 Africans were landed in the Bahamas from 26 slave vessels, flying either the Spanish or Portuguese flag, which had been captured by British ships or were wrecked on the rocks and reefs surrounding the islands.[9] Once liberated, the Africans were, as noted in chapter 3, employed either in the West Indian Regiment or in the British Royal Navy or were apprenticed to "prudent and humane masters or mistresses" in the colony by the Customs Office.[10]

As early as 1811, when the liberated Africans were first settled in the colony, members of the white population expressed fears about the impact their presence could have on the stability of Bahamian society. In a petition presented to the president of the council, William Vesey Munnings, in August 1811, a group of inhabitants voiced misgivings about the recent introduction of recaptives into the island of New Providence and the possibility of further arrivals. These developments, as the petitioners pointed out, provided "a just ground of serious apprehension for the lives and properties of the Inhabitants." They were especially concerned that the influx of Africans would increase Nassau's free nonwhite population, many of whom were unemployed and thus, they believed, likely to resort to criminal activities. The petitioners also noted that the free people of color already formed at least three-fourths of the "Parish Poor" in New Providence.[11]

In protesting against the policy of introducing recaptives into the colony, the petitioners also resorted to constitutional arguments. Although they did not question the right of the Imperial Parliament to legislate for the colony, the petitioners took the view that the details of the operation of any imperial law should be modified to reflect local interests. They asserted that the right of West Indian colonies to regulate their internal affairs, with royal approval, had been long admitted and was "indisputable" and that the introduction of recaptives despite local opposition would represent a violation of that constitutional right.

Pleading the urgency of the situation, the petitioners requested Munnings to reconvene the House of Assembly to consider the matter and take further action. He expected that the members of the Assembly (fifteen of whom had signed the petition) would impose a tax on the holders of African apprentices that would discourage other inhabitants from accepting them. Since such an action would run counter to imperial legislation, Munnings assumed that the Assembly would include the tax in the annual revenue bill. This, as he noted in a dispatch to the Earl of Liverpool, would force him to give his assent to the bill with its objectionable clause in order to prevent the loss of a considerable portion of the colony's revenue.[12]

Contrary to Munnings's expectations, the Assembly did not introduce a tax on holders of apprentices but joined the Legislative Council in addressing a petition to the king in council in November to press for restrictions on the further entry of recaptives into Nassau. The petitioners pointed out that three slave vessels had recently been captured and 451 Africans emancipated by the vice admiralty court in Nassau. Although 91 Africans were recruited for the military and naval services, the remaining 360 had been distributed, under indentures ranging from seven to fourteen years, to the inhabitants of Nassau. They claimed that if the Africans were prepared to hire themselves out as agricultural laborers, after their indentures expired there would be little reason to regret the introduction of the recaptives. However, they argued, in the West Indies free people "of all descriptions" were unwilling to work as field laborers at the prevailing wage rates and concentrated in the towns where few found regular employment and many turned to begging and crime "to eke out a precarious subsistence for themselves and their Families." The petitioners were convinced that the liberated Africans, like other free nonwhites, would "readily fall into all these habits and notions which already render their Brethren unfit for the pursuits of Husbandry and averse to them." They also warned that the presence of the Africans would lead to increased demands for poor relief, which was already proving a financial burden to the community. Given these circumstances, the petitioners maintained that the unrestricted introduction of recaptives, without the development of "new and unexpected sources of Industry," held the prospect of "terror and dismay" for the colony. Finally, they claimed that since the Africans were not British subjects and therefore had no right to residence in any British territory, any imperial legislation that attempted to confer that right in the West Indies, contrary to the wishes and interests of the colonies, was a contravention of their constitutional privileges.[13]

Both petitions were explicit about the social problems that the continued influx of the recaptives into the colony was expected to create. More immediate concerns, however, were unexpressed in those petitions. First, the petitioners must have been aware that the further introduction of recaptives would upset the delicate balance between free nonwhites and whites in the town of Nassau and its environs. In New Providence, before the arrival of the first liberated Africans, the free nonwhites were already challenging the numerical predominance of the whites. In a census of the population taken in that island in December 1810, whites numbered 1,720, and free blacks and free coloreds combined totaled 1,074. As the officials who conducted the census admitted, however, the figures for the nonwhites underrepresented their numbers.[14]

The second of these concerns was economic, for slave owners objected to a scheme that threatened to depress the value of their slaves by allowing the recaptives to compete on the urban labor market. This consideration remained important in shaping the attitude of white colonists toward the introduction of liberated Africans throughout the slavery era. Writing in 1836, Dr. John Richardson referred to the early 1830s as "a period when the prejudices of the Colonists were exceedingly opposed to the introduction of Africans as free labourers who might come into competition with their slaves."[15] These anxieties are best explained by an examination of the nature of the liberated Africans' participation in the urban labor market of the early nineteenth century.

The terms of employment for the African apprentices varied and were similar to those of the slaves. First, there were those who were hired out by their holders to other persons. The wages of these apprentices were paid directly to their holders, who then provided the apprentices with "the usual Clothing and Provisions prescribed by Law for Slaves, with the addition in some instances of two shillings currency per week." Second, there were apprentices who were allowed to find employment for themselves (on the self-hire system by 1816) but were obligated to pay a specified sum to their holders monthly. These apprentices provided their own food and clothing. Finally, there were those apprentices employed directly by their holders. They received "clothes and provisions in common with the Slaves of the same Holder similarly occupied as the Africans."[16]

The impact of the liberated Africans on the labor market and on slave prices was discernible within a year of their arrival. Slave owners complained that the introduction of the recaptives had depressed slave prices and thus forced them to sell more of their slaves to defray their debts to British creditors. The viewpoint of the colony's slave owners was reflected in an editorial of the *Bahama Gazette* in May 1812:

> The impolicy of the introduction of African negroes into our colonies, under indentures for service, has already been proved by practical experience. The great depreciation of the value of our slaves is amongst the least of the baneful effects of the crafty and intriguing interference of the African Institution. Planters who, a year ago, might have had it in their power, by the disposal and sale of one third of their negroe property, to pay their debts to creditors at home, are virtually reduced to beggary; since from the little present value of that species of property, their all would not now suffice.[17]

The effect of the liberated Africans on the market for slaves was also remarked on in 1815. Appearing as a witness before a select committee of the House of Assembly on a proposal for a general registry of slaves in December of that year, John Stephen, the rector of Christ Church, suggested that the introduction of free Africans had further depressed the value of slaves in a colony with a labor surplus: "As far as I have been able to learn from conversation, I have clearly understood that the value of Slaves in this colony has decreased during the last seven years; which may be owing to various causes, and chiefly to a superabundance of Slaves, to the exhausted state of the soil, and to the Introduction of several Cargoes of Africans seized at Sea, and condemned as lawful Prize, which have been let out to the Inhabitants upon Indenture."[18]

In the years after 1811, some white colonists came to regard the liberated Africans as subversive of the system of slavery. This was a fear largely explained by the perceived impact, on a normally quiescent slave population, of ex-slaves freed by the provisions of an imperial law rather than by the normal process of manumission. In his evidence before the select committee of 1815, Theodore George Alexander, one of the editors of the *Royal Gazette,* expressed the opinion (undoubtedly more widely held) that the presence of the recaptives together with the publicized activities of the abolitionists led slaves to believe that their own emancipation was imminent, "the liberation and dispersion of a large number of Africans who have been brought here as Prize, and apprenticed out, serving to instill into the minds of the Slaves a spirit of insubordination, by creating the expectancy that their emancipation is at hand, and still more strongly impressed upon them by the known interference of a powerful influence in the mother country."[19]

The events of January 1816 must have confirmed earlier apprehensions of the threat to security posed by the liberated Africans. In that month, the black troops of the Second West Indian Regiment, to which many recaptives had been recruited and which was garrisoned in Nassau, threatened mutiny.[20] The white minority was alarmed by "the flagrant impolicy and dangers of keeping so large a Body of Blacks in arms in so small a Colony."[21] There was, however, an even greater feeling of insecurity created by the knowledge of the close links between the black troops and the wider black community, especially those Africans under indenture. In a dispatch to Earl Bathurst, Governor Charles Cameron warned of the dangers that could result from "the long residence of this Regiment in the Colony, their consequent habits of intimacy with the black population, particularly with the Indented Africans whose peculiar situation renders them very disorderly."[22]

The white community's anxieties about the liberated Africans were expressed in a memorial in July 1816 addressed to Governor Cameron. In this memorial they opposed the introduction of 300 slaves seized from a Spanish ship bound for Cuba, which was wrecked at Green Turtle Key. In what was obviously a reference to the threatened mutiny and the Barbadian slave rebellion in April, the signatories argued that the increase of the free African population "would seriously contribute to the present insecurity of the peace and even existence of this Colony already but too much endangered by similar and other alarming causes." Their main complaint, however, was that they exercised no firm control over liberated Africans, who, in their words, existed in a "state of total exemption from restraint and coercion." It is not surprising that the memorialists (reflecting the views of their caste) should have found the recaptives "the most worthless and troublesome class of black people in the Town of Nassau and its vicinity." Their difficulty in dealing with the liberated Africans was partly due to the fact that, unlike the slaves or freedpersons, these individuals had no clearly defined position in the slave society and were therefore something of an anomaly: "Insulated from the rest of their colour by the novel and peculiar incidents of their actual situation and prospects, on terms of inequality with the Slave on one side, and the free-man on the other, they assimilate and associate principally with each other only." Finally, the memorialists pointed out that the introduction of the recaptives would prove "seriously burdensome" in a colony where both the slaves and the free laborers were already underemployed.[23]

The memorial was the first effort in an organized campaign to prevent the distribution in the colony of the Africans under indenture. On 9 July "a great and numerously attended Meeting of the inhabitants," held at the courthouse in Nassau, adopted a resolution that if the Africans were introduced into the colony, no one should accept them as apprentices.[24] It is clear from the complete text of the resolution that those attending the meeting regarded the continued introduction of liberated Africans into the colony as further evidence of the British government's tendency to interfere in local matters. The dispute between the colony's legislature and the executive over the proposed registration of slaves must have strengthened that idea.[25]

Despite the efforts of a section of the white population, the recaptives were introduced and distributed to the colonists in September of that year. In fact, 220 individuals applied for the labor services of 597 apprentices, although there were only 218 available.[26] Whatever fears some whites might have harbored about the free Africans, there were others who were anxious to benefit from labor services without the capital outlay that purchasing a slave involved or paying regular wages to a free laborer. As the signatories of the July memorial had predicted, "some individuals may conceive that the services of a few more negros [*sic*] *gratis* for a time might contribute to their private convenience."[27] In an attempt to mollify the critics of the decision to bring the recaptives to Nassau, and to allay their fears, the Collector of Customs distributed only one-fifth of the apprentices in New Providence and allocated the rest to the outlying islands.[28]

Between 1816 and July 1831, when only 197 liberated Africans entered the colony, white fears subsided and were replaced by a resentment of the efforts by members of the colonial administration to improve the social and economic conditions of the recaptives. Most liberated Africans remained under indenture during those years, but some were allowed to work on their own after 1825, when their indentures expired. In that year the collector of customs, Charles Poitier, purchased with public funds 400 acres of land in New Providence for resale to those Africans whose apprenticeships had ended.[29] He had decided on this course of action because he realized that as apprentices, they had worked primarily as agricultural laborers.[30] This measure was received with hostility by slave owners, who (as Poitier noted in a letter to Earl Bathurst) regarded the emergence of an African peasantry as undermining the structure of slave society:

> Your Lordship will be however no doubt aware, that a powerful interest in the Colonies is hostile to the advancement of these people in the scale of political rights; and consequently the jealousy with which my conduct is begun to be viewed; and in truth as a considerable slave owner myself their ideas are brought home to my own feelings. . . . Neither my Lord, can it be expected that any man who considers it wise and fair . . . to defend his right to the property he has vested, under the sanction of law, in slaves . . . should view with complacency, His Majesty's well clad free Africans coming into our market, bending under the horse loads of provisions, the produce of their voluntary labour, industry and keen desire of acquiring property.[31]

During the administration of Sir James Carmichael Smyth, the improvement of conditions in the settlement of Africans, which was established by Poitier and was known as Head Quarters, became the object of official interest and white resentment. Carmichael Smyth was especially interested in establishing a school for the children of the liberated Africans of that community and had unsuccessfully appealed to the Assembly in 1830 for financial assistance. Members of the Assembly had taken the view that such a project was the responsibility of the metropolitan rather than the colonial government. Although the British government acknowledged its financial obligation, there was a delay in the release of the funds by the Treasury. Carmichael Smyth had, as a result, advanced £1,000 from his own funds for the construction of the school. This concern for the liberated Africans was, as Carmichael Smyth knew, widely resented in the white community: "The interest I took in the affairs of these free Africans could not but be known and talked of in a small community like this, and produced a sour sulky feeling amongst a number of the ignorant & prejudiced white Inhabitants."[32] Given Carmichael Smyth's reputation as a militant abolitionist, his interest in the welfare of the Africans would also have been regarded as another attempt to remove all distinctions between the races—"the leveling effect," as the *Bahama Argus* observed, "being a favourite one of his."[33]

Writing in 1825, Poitier had also remarked on the creole slaves' resentment of the attention shown by the colonial administrators to the liberated Africans despite official attempts to ameliorate their condition: "The unmerited fortunate lot of these Africans, is an irritating substantial cause of Dissatisfaction to the good intelligent creole slaves, who with claims so very superior on public munificence, see not one ray of hope to brighten the dark horizon of their fate: for however modified, to a good intelligent man, slavery is a bitter lot."[34]

In the West Indian Regiment too there was friction between the African-born soldiers and the creoles, whose greater familiarity with European ways, as a comment by Lewis Kerr in 1823 suggested, gave them an advantage in securing promotion: "There generally prevails in our black regiments, a strong feeling of jealousy of the Africans against the Creoles; the latter more intelligent, and consequently possessing many advantages in point of pretension to favor and promotion."[35]

There is, however, no evidence of a sustained antagonism between the liberated Africans and the creoles, whether slave or free. The early tendency of the recaptives to keep to themselves (remarked on by the memorialists of 1816) was eventually succeeded by an easy relationship with the slaves. This can be partly attributed to the fact that (as our later discussion will show) they worked alongside each other, performing similar jobs in the urban setting, on the plantations of the Out Islands, and at sea. Even more important in establishing a pattern of amity was the widespread practice among the liberated Africans of choosing their sexual partners from the creole slaves. In 1827, for example, Governor Lewis Grant noted that many liberated Africans were "connubially connected" with slaves and had families by them.[36] This trend was mainly a reflection of the preference in the transatlantic slave trade for adult males and children.[37] Because of the imbalance between the sexes, male Africans established liaisons primarily with slave women. Such interactions must have minimized the cultural differences between liberated Africans of diverse ethnic backgrounds and a slave population that was by 1834 only 9.4 per cent African-born.[38]

The number of recaptives landed in the Bahamas peaked in the 1830s. Between July 1831 and December 1838 approximately 4,000 Africans entered the colony. This influx resulted in a renewal of the earlier anxieties of the white colonists about the economic competition for their slaves and the dangers of the free black presence. The arrival of the recaptives in large numbers also heightened the white community's awareness of the cultural differences between the creole slave population and the newcomers. These differences became more marked because, in the 1830s, incoming recaptives were increasingly settled in villages in New Providence rather than dispersed throughout the outlying islands.[39] In August 1831 the editor of the *Bahama Argus* commented after a visit to a new settlement of Africans at South

West Bay: "On Tuesday last, we were witness to a Levee held by the Collector of Customs, at which seven of these uncouth savages were the *dramatis personae,* all of whom were armed with machets, and most picturesquely attired in blankets. As these new candidates for *court favour* could not speak one word of English, it was truly gratifying to us to witness the profound knowledge of the Collector, in the Mandingo, Ebo and Koromantyn slangs."[40]

In September of that year, the editor once again called attention to the Africans' unfamiliarity with European ways: "It is really offensive to the eyes of a civilized community, to witness the wanderings of these barbarians to the Custom House and elsewhere, almost in a state of nudity."[41]

The "strangeness" of the liberated Africans was especially apparent in a colony where the mainly creole black population had, by the 1830s, assimilated important elements of European culture. Language was a significant indicator of the extent to which creole blacks were culturally assimilated. In most British West Indian colonies blacks spoke a Creole that combined features of European and African languages. In the Bahamas, however, blacks spoke a vernacular that was closer to the English language, as contemporary observers noted.[42] In an editorial of 22 August 1835 on the "Prospects of the Colonies," the writer commented: "Thus may we justly contrast the Bahamas with the other colonies. Our labourers [are] intelligent—speaking the English language, and not a miserable patois."[43] In that same year Governor William Colebrooke suggested in a letter to James Stephen of the Colonial Office that the creole blacks' assimilation of English culture extended beyond language to include even facial expression: "The language spoken here by whites & blacks, is the English language and with a great many superior to some of the common dialects in England. Another peculiarity with us is that many of the Black people except for the colour of their skins are as much Englishmen, as if they had been born & brought up in that country and the English expression of their Countenances is so marked that one really forgets the African feature in looking at them, so much is there the expression of the 'human face divine.'"[44] This evidence confirms Alison Watt Shilling's observation that there was probably "a smaller percentage of pidgin speakers in the Bahamas than elsewhere in the Caribbean until the beginning of the nineteenth century, when there was an influx of Africans from the captured slave ships."[45]

The unfamiliarity of the recently arrived Africans with European culture was one of the reasons for the denial of full civil rights to them up to 1836. In 1833 an act was passed to remove the civil disabilities of the colony's free nonwhites with the exception of "natives of Africa, or of the Islands contiguous thereto." Although Africans were permitted to give evidence in the law courts, by the provisions of that legislation they could do so only after six years' residence and after producing a certificate from a clergyman or a justice of the peace that they were qualified to testify.[46] In the following year, civil rights were extended to the African-born except for those who had resided in the colony for less than seven years.[47] In 1836 liberated Africans with less than seven years' residence were unable to join the militia, vote at elections for members of the Assembly or for vestrymen, and serve on grand or petty juries.[48]

The cultural argument was most clearly expressed in the discussions related to the refusal of the Assembly in 1834 to admit Africans to the militia. This measure was directed at the newly arrived Africans; up to that point, those of "old importations" had been allowed to serve.[49] Although Africans of long residence had, as James Walker, collector of customs, observed, "not behaved improperly when trusted with Arms, and were now complete British Colonists in language and customs," the ban was extended to all recaptives.[50] This is explained by the panic that followed the introduction of large numbers of Africans in the early 1830s when members of the Assembly attributed to the recent and culturally unassimilated recaptives a potential for violence. In a resolution to Governor Colebrooke in December 1835, the members of the House stated their reasons for excluding the Africans from the militia:

> Located as the Africans in this Island are, in communities or settlements, almost entirely distinct from the other inhabitants, and at a distance from any power which can act with promptness as a controlling force over them; and liable as we are to the arrival and settlement in the colony of an increased number, direct from the coast of Africa, and in a state the furthest degree removed from civilization the House cannot but view the enactment which prohibits the enrolment of such persons in the Militia of the colony, as a sound and wholesome provision, and one which cannot be abrogated without in some measure endangering the tranquillity of the colony.[51]

In the following year, however, the Assembly relented and allowed liberated Africans of seven years' residence to serve in the militia.[52]

The members of the House of Assembly might have regarded the liberated Africans as potentially dangerous, but Governor Colebrooke, and eventually the Colonial Office, saw them as a group that would remain loyal to the British Crown in the face of United States expansionism. During the 1830s, successive governors of the Bahamas had expressed concern about American expansionist tendencies. In 1830, for example, Sir James

Carmichael Smyth observed, "Our near neighbourhood to America, and the anxiety already shewn by the American Government to extend their possessions in these seas, by their establishment at West Key, must not be lost sight of."[53] In 1836 Colebrooke also warned Colonial Office officials not to alienate the economic and political elite of a "Community Connected as this is in so many ways with the neighbouring countries." He noted that though the colony had been settled mainly by Loyalists from the southern states, their ties with the United States had been sustained by the "influence of habit and Education and the effects of Constant commercial intercourse." These ties had, he suggested, been strengthened by the abolition of slavery "acting on the prejudices of the Old Colonists and their descendants."[54]

In this context of uncertainty about the loyalties of white Bahamians, in the event of American aggression against the Bahamas, Colebrooke recognized the possibility of creating "a class of devoted subjects" among the liberated Africans with the help of religious instruction:

> If brought here after Capture they ought to be put down in favorable situations attended with care, and provided for till they can provide for themselves. Then indeed would our interference be a blessing to them, and call forth their gratitude. They are peculiarly susceptible of kindness and in a short time become reconciled & eventually a most useful and valuable people. In a few years with the help of the Moravians and other Missionaries, & the Expenditure of a few thousand pounds, we could raise a rampart of them in this quarter, which would enable us to bid a bold defence to our American Neighbours—and we should reap a peaceful harvest for their labours.[55]

The evidence indicates that the Colonial Office endorsed Colebrooke's view of the importance of the liberated Africans in the Bahamas as a bulwark against American encroachment. In fact, Lord Glenelg, the secretary of state for the colonies, regarded them as being of central importance in the event of a maritime war against the United States. As James Stephen explained in a letter to Lord Fitzroy Somerset in March 1838,

> the Western Shores of the Bahama Channel being now entirely incorporated into the United States of America, might afford shelter to Ships of war and Privateers, which would be altogether unchecked in their operations against the British homeward Bound West India Trade, unless the Eastern Shores of the same Channel should be peopled by a race of persons attached to the British Crown and accustomed to a Maratime [*sic*] Life. Such a population, as it appears to Lord Glenelg, might be collected by due

> attention to the Africans who have recently been introduced from Portuguese & Spanish Slave Ships.[56]

As noted earlier, liberated Africans were either enlisted in the military and naval services or apprenticed to local residents by the collector of customs at Nassau, who was, for most of the years under examination in this chapter, directly responsible for their physical welfare on first landing and their eventual distribution. The main idea behind the system of apprenticeship, by which recaptives initially served an indenture of seven to fourteen years, was that they should learn a skill or a trade so that they could earn a living in the wider society once their term of servitude ended.[57] There was also an ideological justification for an apprenticeship. Abolitionists hoped that during those years the liberated Africans would be Christianized and "civilized," a process by which they would be introduced not only to the Christian religion but also to European social and cultural values. Based on an assumption of European cultural superiority, this idea was an aspect of what Howard Temperley has described as "anti-slavery as a form of cultural imperialism."[58] In an opinion prepared for the Earl of Liverpool in July 1811, James Stephens provides an insight into the reasons for the adoption of a system of apprenticeship in the Bahamas for "condemned" Africans but not for captured creole slaves:

> Africans or new negroes, as they are called, neither being intelligent enough to protect their own freedom, nor able immediately to work for their own subsistence . . . it was necessary in respect of them, to give, for their own sakes, the power of enlisting or apprenticing. But the same necessity did not exist in respect of Creole Negroes, i.e. negroes born in the West Indies. These therefore were to be restored to their freedom without any such temporary dangerous modification of it. Between the two descriptions middle terms might have been found, such as seasoned negroes, or negroes who have been long enough in the W. Indies to have learned some European tongue & some method of gaining a subsistence. But great difficulties would have arisen in drawing the lines between the sufficient & insufficient degrees of *Creolization,* if I may use the term (it would be an insult to these poor creatures to call it *civilization*) which might create fitness & unfitness for immediate freedom in that country; & as every doubt or pretence of doubt would be sure of a construction adverse to them in the Colonial Courts, it was thought best to take the broadest lines of distinction only giving to all Slaves not natives of Africa, the full and immediate benefit of the Act, subjecting native Africans to the powers of enlistment & apprenticeship.[59]

The objectives of the apprenticeship were reflected in the conditions, specified in the indenture, that the employers of the apprentices were required to meet. A contract dating from 1833 stipulated that persons to whom apprentices were assigned should instruct them "in some Art, trade, mystery or occupation." Employers were also obliged to provide apprentices with "sufficient, decent and comfortable food and clothing, medical assistance, medicines and other necessities" during the period of apprenticeship. They were further required to ensure that the apprentices received instruction in the Christian faith and were eventually baptized. Employers were, moreover, expected to encourage the adults to attend church and encourage apprentices under twenty-one to attend Sunday school. This insistence on the employees' responsibility for Christianizing the liberated Africans suggests parallels with the *encomienda* system of colonial Latin America. The indenture, signed by the governor and the collector of customs, was in keeping with the contemporary official view that the recaptive (whether adult or juvenile) was not competent to protect his or her own interests.[60]

Despite these declared objectives, the system of apprenticeship became one by which employers extracted cheap labor from the liberated Africans, providing them few opportunities to acquire further skills.[61] Like *emancipados* in Cuba and Brazil, recaptives in the Bahamas were usually treated no better than slaves.[62] The direction in which the apprenticeship had developed was already clear to Governor Lewis Grant in 1825. He noted that "but few of them have been brought up to Trades, a few of them also to the Sea, many a great many are working on the plantations & working indiscriminately with the Slaves and receiving similar treatment. Many are absolutely sent out on hire to work on the roads or to planters and Salt rakers and to be employed in labour which few proprietors would be willing to hire out their own Slaves (except the worst description) to perform."[63]

Grant's preliminary observations were later corroborated by the findings of a committee (on which he served) that investigated the "state and condition" of the liberated Africans. Their report in 1828 noted that African apprentices, like slaves, were usually employed in fishing, wrecking, cutting wood, raking salt, and agricultural and domestic tasks in New Providence and the Out Islands. In addition, female apprentices, like female slaves, were often sent out with trays of merchandise to hawk about Nassau.[64] Many holders of apprentices were no more than middlemen who sold the labor services of the recaptives to other employers on hire. Although the terms of employment for the apprentices on the hiring system varied, the outcome of these arrangements was usually the same. In an inversion of the conventional situation, it was the apprentice who paid regular "wages" to his original employer, as the report noted: "It is a matter of no consideration with the Holder where or how the Apprentice is employed whether he is raking Salt in the Ponds, felling Timber in an uninhabited Wilderness, or working on the Public roads, the paramount object is the Wages."[65] For many employers, apprenticing liberated Africans was a lucrative undertaking, especially in those cases in which individual apprentices served more than fourteen years under indenture.[66]

On the plantations in the Out Islands, the apprentices were exploited more thoroughly than the slaves of their holders. This is understandable; employers were interested in preserving their capital—the slaves—but had no such interest in the welfare of apprentices, whose labor services they owned for a specified term. On that point the 1828 report commented that "the feeling of sympathy which the Master or Proprietor may naturally be disposed to entertain for the Slave from his being under his special and exclusive protection does not seem generally to have been extended to the Apprentice. To get the labor and make the most of it during the time of the Apprenticeship, has been the paramount consideration with the Holder."[67] Apprentices were also remunerated like slaves and thus given rations rather than cash, a practice that prefigured the truck system of the postemancipation years.[68] Since the indenture failed to establish any minimum requirements for the apprentices' allowances, they were usually given those prescribed by law for the slaves. The official report noted, however, that on many plantations the supplies of food (limited to corn) and clothing were "scant and precarious."[69]

The responsibility of the employers for Christianizing, and by implication "civilizing," the liberated Africans was largely ignored. As the official report observed, "The moral and intellectual improvement of the Africans employed in field or other labour does not appear to have been thought of by the Holders."[70] Religious instruction for the apprentices was hindered by the fact that the activities of the established church were concentrated in New Providence. Liberated Africans tended to join "various Sectarian Conventicles," for the nonconformists had extended their proselytizing efforts to the Out Islands.[71] By 1828, however, the influence of Christianity was still only superficial. Commenting on whether individual apprentices had been instructed in religion, the 1828 report most often noted, "Can say his prayers."[72] Even when the efforts to Christianize were more assiduous, they did not always produce the desired result. In December 1816, J. Sullivan, the collector of customs for Crooked Island and Acklins, observed with chagrin in a report on five African apprentices, "These Africans are in good health, and well fed & Clothed, but make no progress either in Religion or

Morals, Although they have Meetings where Prayers and Psalms are said and Sung, from whence they generally go either to Debauch their neighbours' Wife or Husband or Steal from them."[73]

As early as 1825, Governor Grant recognized that the system of apprenticeship, with its long term of indenture, mainly benefited the holders of the apprentices. Noting the high level of demand for the services of the recaptives, even without a period of indenture, Grant instructed the collector of customs to bind the apprentices only for one year at a time. He took the view that these short-term indentures would allow officials to monitor more closely the treatment of the apprentices.[74] Although there is no evidence that Grant's arrangement for reducing the indenture persisted beyond his tenure in office, successive governors came to question whether the system of apprenticeship had achieved its original objectives. In September 1834, for example, Governor Blayney Balfour, in a dispatch to the secretary of state for the colonies, Thomas Spring-Rice, remarked: "The system of Apprenticeship has had I conceive a fair trial and, where the negroes are not used by the Master as Domestic Servants, I am convinced that it is not beneficial to the African—he neither learns English, nor any useful occupation and is too often subject to harsh and cruel treatment."[75] In the following year Governor Colebrooke also expressed the opinion that a long-term indenture was often of no benefit to the Africans. Referring to the distribution of 245 recaptives in August 1834 on seven-year indentures, Colebrooke observed that "such engagements must constitute a kind of modified slavery, without advantage to the Africans in too many cases."[76]

The reappraisal of the apprenticeship system, with its long-term indenture, was accompanied by experiments with alternative methods of preparing the liberated Africans for earning a livelihood. In 1836, for example, male adults from the Portuguese slavers *Vigilante* and *Criolo* were employed in public works in New Providence under the supervision of overseers. Writing in July of that year, Colebrooke observed, "The object has been to exact, until habituated to exertion, a moderate share of labour in useful works in return for subsistence, and thus to enable them to acquire the means of earning full wages; which they are generally doing."[77] By November he was convinced that a period of six months was long enough for adult Africans to acquire the experience necessary for earning a living. In a dispatch to Lord Glenelg, Colebrooke stated that there was no need for a prolonged indenture for the recaptives: "There can be no ground for withholding from them for any time, the full advantages of their industry on the plea of preparing them to provide for themselves. Indeed with the aid of their more experienced countrymen and encouraged by their example they readily acquire a knowledge of the value of their labour, and work most satisfactorily when their wages are paid to them weekly."[78]

Colebrooke's views on the apprenticeship for adult recaptives were undoubtedly influenced by the conclusions of the Board of Superintendence of Liberated Africans, or African Board (to which responsibility for the liberated Africans had been transferred) after an investigation in 1835. This body had reported that a system of indenture was advantageous to African juveniles "in accustoming them by degrees to the habit of civilized life, and reclaiming them from nearly a savage state." The members suggested, however, that the period of indenture should be shortened from seven years to five in cases in which the apprentice was taught a trade and to three years when he was not. The African Board also recommended that the same system of apprenticeship should not be used in the case of adult Africans, who were presumably less impressionable than children. It pointed out that a brief apprenticeship, no more than six months, would help the Africans to learn the English language.[79]

The changed views on the system of indenture were reflected in the instructions issued to the African Board by Colebrooke in August 1836. Adult Africans (defined as those older than fifteen) were allowed to enter into voluntary agreements with their employers, which had to be confirmed by two members of the board. These agreements, lasting no longer than twelve months, were consciously patterned on those ex-slaves were being encouraged to make with their former masters. The board was instructed to include in the agreements provisions for adequate food, clothing, lodging, medical aid in sickness, and wages of no less than one dollar per month for the first year and increases of a dollar per month in each of the next two years. The principle behind these specific provisions for wages, as Colebrooke noted, was "that the African is entitled to the full value of his labour from the employers for whatever period the engagement may be formed." It was stipulated that those engagements made by the board on behalf of minors should include provision for religious instruction and attendance at church.[80]

In 1838 Governor Francis Cockburn attempted to reverse the changes in the system of indenture that Colebrooke had introduced with Colonial Office approval. When 1,043 Africans, captured from Portuguese slavers, were landed in the colony in the first five months of that year, Cockburn, after consulting with his council, decided to place the recaptives under indenture. He justified this course of action to Lord Glenelg by claiming that "the expectations, entertained by my Predecessors, of the Africans being able to obtain a Living by their own exertions, had not been realized." In these circumstances, Cockburn pointed out, it was felt that apprenticing the Africans would be "the only reasonable mode of fulfilling the benevolent views of the British Government towards the liberated Africans." He also noted that the need to protect the Africans from being "enticed" to Demerara by labor recruiters whose proposals "they could in no way understand or enforce" had influenced this decision.

This decision, ostensibly based on humanitarian considerations, was in fact a lightly disguised attempt to retain for the employer class a labor force over which it could exercise a greater degree of control than it could exert over free-wage laborers. The reintroduction of a long-term indenture for the liberated Africans must have assumed urgency since the apprenticeship system for the ex-slaves was in the last months of its existence. The concern for control was reflected in the articles of agreement by which adult Africans were indentured for four years and in which a penal provision was introduced. Any form of misbehavior or violation of the articles of agreement by the indentured African was made punishable by the nearest magistrate by imprisonment with hard labor for a term not exceeding ten days or by confinement in the stocks.[81]

Cockburn's arrangements were short-lived because the Colonial Office had already decided to dispense with a system of apprenticeship for adult Africans. In a circular dispatch of 15 May 1838 to governors of the West Indian colonies, Lord Glenelg stated that experiments in some colonies with allowing Africans to work for their living had "tended to establish the conclusion that the restriction of an Apprenticeship is unnecessary and may be safely dispensed with." The only exception to that ruling was African children without mothers or relatives to provide for them, who would continue to be apprenticed for terms not exceeding five years. In concluding his instructions, Glenelg noted that "a complete and fair experiment" should be made to settle the Africans without recourse to an apprenticeship.[82] Cockburn was subsequently ordered to cancel the indentures of all adult Africans.[83]

In 1839 the House of Assembly attempted, with Cockburn's connivance, to circumvent the Colonial Office's ban on a system of indenture. It used the technique of including an extraneous clause, which gave the governor the power of "disposal and control" of the recaptives, in a bill extending to them the privileges of British subjects. Supporting the need for this provision, Cockburn noted in a dispatch to the secretary of state for the colonies, Lord John Russell, in December of that year: "Since the Indentures of Adult Africans were ordered to be cancelled the want of such a Power has been clearly proved. The Africans beleive [*sic*] me my Lord are not on their first arrival sufficiently enlightened to make agreements for themselves." Such a measure, he pointed out, was also justified because there was the danger of Africans being enticed away to the slave countries in the vicinity. It was that possibility, in Cockburn's opinion, that made "the limited control contained in the present Bill of paramount importance to the due Protection of the Africans."[84]

Despite the display of concern for the Africans, the bill was disallowed. Colonial Office officials saw granting the governor such wide powers of "disposal and control" over the recaptives as undue interference with their freedom of labor. In a dispatch to Cockburn in March 1840, Russell stated the Colonial Office position on such an arrangement: "As often as any Africans may be imported into the Bahama Islands you will take the necessary means for hiring them out to service for six or at most 12 months after their arrival, but beyond this you should not interfere with freedom of their labor."[85]

In 1840 Cockburn was once again urging the need for reintroducing an indenture for the recaptives. On that occasion the object of his concern was the salt industry (then the main prop of the colony's economy), which was experiencing difficulty in attracting and retaining a labor force.[86] Cockburn saw the liberated Africans as a possible solution to the labor problem, but he was aware that the working conditions in the salt ponds were no more acceptable to them than they were to the creole freedmen. Although the Africans worked in the salt industry, they were reluctant to sign any binding agreements with their employers. Their usual response to any suggestion that they should enter into such a contract was "No Sign Paper." Writing to Russell in April of that year, Cockburn suggested that only a reinstatement of some form of apprenticeship could avert the problems he anticipated from the Africans' reluctance to sign agreements:

> This determination leads to the risk that when the salt-raking Season is over many of them may be discharged by their employers in which case they may for a time be exposed [to] that degree of want which I much fear would lead them to acts of Violence & Plunder. Nor am I aware of how the difficulty which I apprehend in this respect can be guarded against except by investing the Governor with a Power of making agreements and enforcing a compliance therewith both on the part of Employer and African. This I am aware would be in part a return to the apprentice System, but as I have before stated the Africans are in no way qualified to act for themselves at least Two or Three Years after their arrival.[87]

At the Colonial Office, officials remained opposed to interference with the Africans' freedom of labor and were reluctant to sanction any scheme that might be construed as a new system of slavery. In his response to Cockburn's dispatch, Russell reiterated the Colonial Office's position on the question of a coercive system of labor: "The disinclination which you observed on the part of the Liberated Africans to enter into written Contracts of Labor must not be encountered in the manner proposed. If authority were given to you to make such Contracts for them, the result would be to excite alarm & discontent & to create the necessity for a compulsory system of labor enforced by penalties."[88]

After 1841 the question of indenturing recaptives in the Bahamas was not again a major issue until 1860, when 360 of them were landed in the colony following the wreck of a slaver on Abaco. Governor Charles Bayley assumed the responsibility for distributing them in the colony as apprentices, for two years in the case of adults and four years for juveniles. Prospective employers objected to that proposal on the grounds that "they were liable to be deprived of their services just as the Africans were beginning to become useful." As a result, Bayley eventually extended the indenture period to six years for children below the age of fourteen and five years for persons over fourteen. Neither group would receive wages during the period of indenture. Those older than fourteen, however, were to be paid "the current wages usually paid to servants, or mechanics of similar proficiency, or capacity," after five years' service. The employers' main responsibility to the Africans under these arrangements was to provide them with food, clothing, and, in the case of juveniles, religious instruction. Employers were also expected to give adult Africans "every opportunity and facility for receiving instructions" in a trade.[89]

Although Bayley chose to represent these arrangements as being in "the interests of the Colony and of the negroes themselves," they were clearly intended to benefit the colony's white employer class, which dominated the local legislature. At that point, employers had neither the working capital to offer steady-wage employment nor the ability to command occasional labor from a lower class that could survive without the sale of its labor power.[90] The African recaptives were eventually indentured to salt proprietors, to owners of fruit plantations, and as domestic servants in the Out Islands. In Nassau, many of the recaptives were bound to joiners, carpenters, boatbuilders, and blacksmiths.[91]

In October 1860, Colonial Office officials endorsed Bayley's reintroduction of a system of long-term indenture for the Africans. By that date, the Colonial Office, under pressure from the planters in the major sugar colonies, had accepted the necessity for long-term labor contracts for both Indian immigrants and liberated Africans.[92] Some officials expressed misgivings about aspects of the system of indenture that had been introduced. Sir Frederic Rogers, for example, observed on 16 October that the position of the liberated Africans in the Bahamas would be "very much worse" than in other West Indian colonies. He pointed out that on their arrival in the other colonies, the liberated Africans could be indentured for three years or until they were eighteen and that "during that time they receive for the first year provisions—after that time—wages at the current rate—and always lodging."[93] Despite Rogers's comments, there was no attempt to interfere with those features of the Bahamian system of indenture that he criticized. The major requests for modifications to Bayley's arrangements were that the provisions for the indenture should conform to the guidelines set by Sir John Pakington in October 1852 and that legislation reflecting the changes should be introduced. In a letter to Bayley outlining the secretary of state's views, Chichester S. Fortescue, then undersecretary of state, limited himself to expressions of disapproval about a system of indenture that made no provisions for the payment of money wages: "The Secretary of State believes that the attempt in a free Country to retain unpaid services of labourers after they have become aware of their usefulness, and while they see persons of the same class receiving a high rate of wages around them, will prove as fruitless (if not mischievous) in the Bahamas as it has proved in other places where it has been tried."[94]

In April 1861, legislation "to provide for the care of Africans brought to or otherwise arriving in the Colony from vessels engaged in the African Slave Trade" formalized the system of indenture. By its provisions, Africans under the age of ten could be indentured for a maximum of eight years, those between ten and thirteen for six years, those between thirteen and sixteen for five years, and those older than sixteen for no more than four years. Although the act provided for the cancellation of the indenture if the employer violated the agreement, it was weighted in his favor. First, Africans of all age groups were paid no money wages until after the end of the indenture. Second, unauthorized absence from work, unsatisfactory performance of the duties assigned, or "misconduct" toward the employer could be punished, on conviction before a justice of the peace, by imprisonment, with or without hard labor, for a maximum of twenty days. An antienticement clause also made it a crime, punishable by a fine, to hire or harbor Africans who were still under indenture.[95]

In 1862 and 1863, details of the 1861 legislation were amended, but the basic framework for indenturing liberated Africans remained unchanged.[96] After 1860, however, no more recaptives were introduced into the colony. Although there is no detailed information on the operation of this system of indenture, its existence must have reinforced the practice of wage payment in truck (in goods rather than cash) that already operated in the colony.[97]

In the years after 1811, the influx of liberated Africans into the Bahamas roused the fears and apprehension of the white community and led to demands for their exclusion from the colony. For the whites, the introduction of large numbers of recaptives, especially into the town of Nassau, not only posed a threat to their lives and property but also created competition for their slaves in the urban economy. Despite these initial fears about the liberated Africans, there were always individuals who were willing to employ them under the apprenticeship system. In theory, this system (with its emphasis on religious instruction and the acquisition of a skill) would prepare the liberated Africans for their integration into the Bahamian society and economy after an indenture of between seven and fourteen years. In practice, it functioned primarily as a system of labor exploitation in which the recaptives experienced, in Governor Colebrooke's words, "a kind of modified slavery." The system of long-term contracts was altered in the mid-1830s, and in 1838 all indentures for adults were canceled. After rejecting proposals for a long-term indenture in the early postemancipation years, the Colonial Office gave its approval for the reintroduction of such a system for the liberated Africans in 1860. In freedom, the system of indenture used in connection with the liberated Africans continued to operate as a form of unfree labor.

Chapter Five

THE ESTABLISHMENT OF A DEPENDENT TENANTRY

Although many rural slaves enjoyed extensive autonomy, verging on freedom, in the years after 1800, there were others who negotiated the terms of their postemancipation dependency. On the Out Island plantations, new labor arrangements that would become pervasive after full emancipation, such as labor tenancy and sharecropping, had evolved by 1836. By the mid-1880s the share system was a significant feature of the rural economy in the Bahamas. One contemporary observer remarked in 1886 that it "prevails to a very large extent throughout the Bahamas especially at the pine-apple growing islands."[1]

Labor tenancy and sharecropping originated and developed in the context of the diverse labor regimes that were adopted in the transition from slavery to free labor. These two forms of labor management created a class of "dependent cultivators" whose tenure on the land was rooted in informal contracts.[2] As noted in chapter three, a system of labor tenancy had existed on some plantations by 1828. Although the evidence pertains to the liberated Africans, it is reasonable to assume that in this as in other matters, the treatment of the recaptives was closely patterned on that of the slave population. By this system, African apprentices and slaves divided the six-day working week between the fields of their holders or owners and their provision grounds, from which they were expected to maintain themselves and their families. The grant of this concession was probably prompted by the realization that maintenance costs on slave plantations, without a major export staple, exceeded the income that the slaves or indentured Africans generated.

During the period of apprenticeship, the voluntary agreements by which employers and predial, or land-working, apprentices signed contracts stating the terms of their employment formalized arrangements that had already been worked out prior to emancipation. In 1835, for example, provisions were made for predial apprentices to maintain themselves under certain conditions. Instead of working a five-day week for their masters, who would then supply them with rations and clothing, the apprentices were allowed to cultivate a plot of land for their "own support and maintenance" for two and one-half days a week. These "voluntary engagements" were signed for a one-year period.[3]

Sharecropping arrangements, unlike labor tenancy, first emerged during the apprenticeship years.[4] Before the widespread adoption of sharecropping, there were individuals who recognized that agricultural production would survive on many of the colony's plantations only if a form of tenancy were introduced since few proprietors could afford to employ wage labor. In his report on a visit to Eleuthera in May 1835, Special Justice Thomas R. Winder observed, "How much benefit the proprietors of large tracts of Land in the neighbourhood [east of Rock Sound settlement] might themselves derive from settling their Estates, in small allotments to these people; thus forming a numerous and happy peasantry."[5] In June of that year, the editor of the *Bahama Argus* suggested that small-scale production based on family labor would become increasingly important in the colony's economy: "Cotton and indeed other productions, must henceforth be raised by different means than heretofore. There are some rich crops, which may perhaps repay the expenses of hired labour on plantations, where little outlay is required, or great prices may be obtained; but these instances are rare. . . . The small cultivators, attending to their own grounds, and employing their families in weeding, hoeing, etc. are every where succeeding, and we must look to them in the Bahamas." By that stage, as the editorial noted, sharecropping had already been introduced on some of the colony's plantations. The editor asserted that such a course of action, more widely adopted, would keep land in production and provide a steady income for the proprietors: "If they would generally settle their apprentices in this manner, as some are now doing, granting them leases on a rent payable in cotton, or other produce, not exceeding one-third of the crop, allowing a third for the farmer's expenses and improvements, and another third for his subsistence, they would derive an improving income."[6]

The trend toward sharecropping arrangements on some of the colony's plantations during the apprenticeship years is illustrated by the case of Robert Millar, a proprietor on Eleuthera, which was the leading producer of food crops for the local market and pineapples for the export trade. In 1836 Millar manumitted 56 of his apprentices at Millar's Settlement and negotiated voluntary agreements with some heads of families to remain on his estate as tenants.[7] The official report of those developments suggests that a sharecrop arrangement was involved in which Millar exploited a "family-labour form of production": "Voluntary agreements were . . . entered into between Mr Millar and the heads of families, to remain on the estate and to work the same upon terms very liberal and beneficial to the people, and calculated to promote their industry, portions of land being allotted to each family, and every facility afforded them of fulfilling the contracts entered into, and comfortably maintaining themselves and children."[8] The report gave no information on the size of the holdings allocated, the crops that were grown, or the division of the crop yields between landlord and tenants on Millar's plantation. There is evidence, however, that Millar concentrated on cotton production on his estate up to 1835.[9] It is likely that Millar's tenants worked on terms described by Thomas Winder in 1836: "There are not many [tenants] settled on the lands of their former employers, when they do so, they work on shares, one third of the produce being for the land owner and the remainder for the labourer."[10]

The evolution of sharecropping relations during the apprenticeship reflected the economic interests of both landlords and tenants. The apprentices gained access to land by remaining on the estates, and proprietors retained the labor services of ex-slaves for plantations that they feared would otherwise have gone uncultivated. The early success of Millar's sharecropping experiment in binding his former slaves to his estate is evident from an 1837 report by Thomas Winder: "These labourers having a distinct interest in the produce of their industry and in the protection of the property entrusted to them appear to be sensible of the advantages their own good conduct has obtained for them, and having tasted the sweets of their labour, *and not likely, in my opinion to be soon detached from the Estate* [emphasis added]."[11]

In the transition from slavery to freedom, labor tenancy and sharecropping were only two of several methods by which labor was organized. In the Bahamas, emancipation did not result in the general adoption of wage labor. In fact, with the exception of pineapple cultivation and salt production, which were centered on a few islands, employers were unable to offer steady wage employment in the Out Islands. This situation is best explained by the fact that landed proprietors in most islands, without a profitable export staple to replace cotton, lacked the operating capital to finance a wage system. Although an export trade in pineapples had developed with the United States by 1832, pineapple production was confined to areas where the soil was considered suitable. As Governor Carmichael Smyth noted in that year, "The real truth is that these islands with the exception of salt do not offer any real encouragement for the employment of capital. Pine-apples to a very large extent have lately been cultivated; but they only answer in particular situations, and in a particular soil."[12] By 1834 very few of the colony's exports were produced "by the land, or the labour of the Inhabitants," and the mainstays of the colonial economy were the salt industry and wrecking. Cotton was by that stage "little more than a nominal article of Export."[13]

The limited opportunities for wage employment were often the subject of official comment. C. R. Nesbitt, administrator of the colony in 1842, observed in a dispatch to Lord Stanley that most of the colony's land was owned by private proprietors who cultivated only a small portion of it and offered "no continuous employment on it for money wages."[14] In 1846 H. F. Cartwright, a stipendiary magistrate in the Out Islands, remarked on "the proprietors of land not having means or knowledge of an available staple article to employ labour."[15] As late as 1866, Governor Rawson wrote about "the Out Islands where the greater part of the population live upon the produce of their fields, with no opportunity of earning wages as labourers."[16]

In the postemancipation years, labor was organized and paid in several ways. First, there was wage labor, which was most widely used in New Providence and those islands that produced salt and pineapples for export. In Eleuthera, San Salvador, Abaco, and Long Island, some proprietors found pineapple production sufficiently profitable by 1847 to offer wage employment.[17] Second, laborers were paid in a combination of money wages and kind. This was the scheme under which recently arrived liberated Africans were employed immediately after full emancipation. After 1838 liberated Africans were encouraged to sign agreements for one-year terms with their employers.[18] In December 1838 C. R. Nesbitt, then colonial secretary, forwarded to Thomas R. Winder the "approved scale of provisions and allowances applicable to the case of Africans recently arrived who are not qualified to make their own bargains":

Weekly.	Eight quarts of Corn or an equivalent
Daily.	Six ounces of fish or four ounces of meat, one gill of molasses, or two ounces of sugar, and two ounces of tobacco, or weekly at the above rate.
Clothing.	Two suits of Oznaburgs yearly or more if necessary, one suit of woollen yearly; one blanket yearly, one straw hat, one cotton handkerchief, one knife; and necessary cooking utensils.
Wages.	One quarter dollar weekly.[19]

Essentially this arrangement was one that met the subsistence needs of the liberated Africans in exchange for their labor. As noted in chapter 4, the system of paying recently arrived recaptives partly in kind persisted into the 1860s.

Payment of labor in money wages and kind was also a feature of contracts signed between proprietors and ex-slaves to work on their estates. In his directions to Thomas Winder in 1838 on the form that these one-year contracts should take, Nesbitt pointed out, "In cases in which the remuneration or any part of it is to be made not in money, but in kind, the contract must specify with all practical precision the nature and amount and quality of the articles to be supplied to the servant, and the time when and place or places at which articles are to be delivered."[20] One surviving example of such an agreement is that between James Farquharson, proprietor of Prospect Hill, Watling's Island, and Jacob, "free Negro labourer," which was signed on 22 April 1839. Jacob was contracted to perform the duties of a herdsman and was paid $12 a year at the rate of $1 dollar a month. He was also given three suits of clothing a year, "a negro house to live in," and the "usual medicine" in addition to "as much land" as he could find time to cultivate.[21] This mode of payment (in cash and kind) clearly reflected the shortage of capital among proprietors who produced for the limited local market.

Finally, labor was organized and remunerated along the lines of the "labour-service system" described by V. I. Lenin with reference to Russian agriculture in the late nineteenth century. As he observed, "labour service in return for land is very widespread in the shape either of half-cropping or directly of work for land rented, for grounds used, etc."[22] Despite the differences in the detailed arrangements for the share and labor tenancy systems, they were two aspects of the labor service system. In both instances labor was paid in kind: in produce in the case of sharecropping, and in land in the case of labor tenancy. Both systems guaranteed landowners a dependent and resident labor force by making land available to tenants.

Seagoing activities like wrecking and sponging were, like agricultural enterprises in the postemancipation years, organized along the lines of a labor service system rather than on a wage basis. Laborers in these economic activities were paid on a system of shares that had been used during slavery.[23] Like sharecropping, the system of shares used in wrecking and sponging served to restrict capital outlay for wages.

In the postemancipation years absentee proprietors recruited a labor force for their estates mainly by the share and labor tenancy systems. Writing in 1884, Governor Henry Blake noted, "Whenever estates are cultivated they are in almost every case cultivated on the metairie system. Indeed it is the only possible system here except the owner is living on the spot and daily superintending the labour."[24] For landed proprietors resident in Nassau, the main attraction of sharecropping lay in the fact that it provided a labor force without the need for paying cash wages or supervision costs. Landowners hoped that land cultivated by tenants would retain its value. It was also anticipated that the former slaves would work more productively as tenants on the share arrangement since they had a "direct interest in the produce of their industry and in the protection of the property entrusted to them."[25] Proprietors, moreover, expected that the share system would provide them with an income without risking scarce capital. As the editor of the *Bahama Argus* remarked in an editorial on sharecropping in 1835, "What a revenue, without risk, might the judicious landholder thus derive!" The discussion in chapter 1 on the recruitment of overseers for slave plantations demonstrated that some landowners had used planting on shares as a strategy for spreading risk. It is clear that proprietors also expected to benefit from the labor of the family unit on their estates. As the editorial in the *Bahama Argus* pointed out in a discussion about the possibility of producing pineapples on the share system, "the work should be performed by him [the tenant], with his family, at little cost."[26]

Proprietors had little difficulty in attracting ex-slaves to engage in sharecropping, for it provided land in a context where few freedpersons were able to purchase land. There was in the Bahamas (as elsewhere in the British Caribbean) an enthusiasm for land ownership among the former slaves. In 1840 Governor Francis Cockburn had remarked on "the prevailing inclination amongst the lower Classes to possess Lands at all risks and hazards."[27] Official policy on the devolution of Crown lands, however, served to thwart the ex-slaves' ambitions to own land. As early as 1836 Lord Glenelg, the secretary of state for the colonies, had ordered in a circular dispatch to the Governors of the West Indian colonies that Crown lands should no longer be sold for less than £1 per acre. According to Philip Curtin, "This document accepted the views of both [Edward Gibbon] Wakefield and the West Indians that too much land was dangerous for the production of staples."[28]

The main idea that informed both metropolitan and colonial policy on Crown lands was to create a rural proletariat by limiting land ownership. These ideas were expressed in the case of the Bahamas by John J. Burnside, the surveyor general, in a letter to Governor Cockburn in July 1838 in which he suggested changes in the regulations governing the sale of Crown lands. He recommended that individuals applying for Crown lands should purchase an allotment valued at a minimum of $75. He pointed out that "by fixing the minimum extent to purchase at $75 it will bring into the market only those persons whose industrious habits have enabled them to lay up the requisite sum and which may be fairly considered as giving them a right to claim the privileges of being freeholders, and it may stimulate others to work as hired labourers until they have acquired the requisite sum to enable them to the like privileges."[29]

Regulations on the sale of Crown lands in the immediate postemancipation years severely restricted the ownership of land by the ex-slaves. This was clear to Nesbitt, who remarked in 1842 that former slaves and liberated Africans "continue desirous of possessing land but their limited pecuniary means do not admit of their purchasing the same under the present regulations."[30] The attempt at an enclosure movement was not wholly successful. In the Out Islands, freedpersons, away from official scrutiny and control, had unimpeded access to extensive Crown lands. Frustrated by high prices in their efforts to purchase freehold land, they resorted to squatting. Some former slaves who worked initially on the share system eventually moved off the privately owned property and squatted on adjoining Crown lands.[31] Many chose, however, to participate in the labor tenancy and share system.

Despite the obstacles to landownership, there were ex-slaves who purchased land. In Eleuthera, for example, liberated apprentices bought Crown land at the settlement of Pitman's Cove in 1835 for an average price of £5 sterling to engage in the profitable business of producing pineapples for export. It was then estimated that an acre of land planted in pineapples could yield an income of £100 to £150 sterling after expenses.[32] Most of the land suitable for pineapple cultivation in Eleuthera, however, was the property of private proprietors who often owned tracts of several hundred acres.[33] As a result, ex-slaves who were unable to purchase land were often prepared to work on shares. Evidence for this development is provided by an advertisement for the sale of a pineapple plantation at Pitman's Cove that appeared in the *Observer* in August 1838: "The plantation consists of two distinct Tracts, joining each other, and the whole, with the exception of a small Turtle Pond, of the very best Pine Apple land. . . . Several persons have applied to the Subscriber offering to work on shares."[34]

The arrangement by which tenants cultivated the land assigned to them on the share system was relatively uncomplicated. Landlords supplied the land and received in turn from their tenants, who provided the labor, a share of the crop yield. In the early years after emancipation the division of the crop varied with soil conditions. An official report for the year 1847, prepared by H. F. Cartwright, described the "conditions of tenancy on the estates" throughout the Bahamas in this way: "On some Estates if New Land one half, if old one third of the produce; and on others from two to three days labor are given for the privilege of cultivating the land."[35] There is evidence that those tenants who cultivated crops such as Indian corn, Guinea corn, and ground provisions often divided only the corn crops with the landlord and kept the rest of the crops for their own subsistence. As Governor Henry Blake explained in 1887, "the cultivators consider that the corn crops only ought to be considered as shareable with the owner, all ground provisions being the property of the cultivator."[36]

The 1847 report (as is clear from the passage cited above) mentioned the existence of the labor tenancy system on some of the colony's estates. It was, in effect, a continuation of the earlier practice by which apprentices divided their time between laboring on their employers' land and on land assigned to them that they worked on their own account. The system of labor tenancy, as it operated on Watling's Island and Long Island, was described by Cartwright in the same report: "The terms of most of the agreements are, that the labourers shall give the two first days in each week in labour to the Proprietor of the land, and receive in return as much land as he can cultivate—in which case he receives wages for work done on other days." It is difficult to establish the extent to which the system of labor tenancy was adopted after emancipation or whether the practice continued throughout the nineteenth century. Unlike the share system, this form of labor service is not mentioned after 1847 in the sources consulted.

Tenants who worked on the share system (as well as on the system of labor tenancy) had a measure of security of tenure on the land they cultivated. By 1847 it had already been established by custom that tenants could not be ejected without reasonable notice and an opportunity to reap the crops they had planted. Writing in 1847, Cartwright observed, "By custom it has become a rule to give six months notice to the tenant to quit possession, and where the tenant pays rent in kind or gives two days labor per week in lieu, he is entitled to remain until he has reaped all the growing crops planted by permission of the Landlord."[37]

In the early years of the operation of the share system there was little to complicate the basic share contract described here. The landlord provided the land but contributed little else to the production process. Few landlords attempted to exercise supervisory functions or control decisions on production methods. In fact, as we have argued, one of the main initial advantages of the share system for the absentee proprietor was that he incurred no supervision costs. This situation changed in the case of pineapple production in the latter part of the nineteenth century.

Most sharecropping agreements throughout the nineteenth century seem to have been verbal and informal. As early as 1847 the main features of these tenancy agreements were firmly established by custom. There is evidence, however, that on the estates owned by the heirs of Charles Farquharson on Watling's Island, written contracts, signed in the presence of a justice of the peace, were used in 1865. Contrary to the general practice, there was also on these estates an attempt to supervise the tenants who worked on the share system.

The share system based on written contracts was not introduced on these estates in Watling's Island until 1865. In the immediate postemancipation period there had been a general reluctance among the ex-slaves on that island to work on shares. A description of economic conditions in the Bahamas between 1837 and 1840 noted of Watling's Island, "Almost abandoned by the Landed Proprietors being unable to cultivate their lands by hired labour and the working class not being willing to work on shares; the old plantations are converted into grazing farms—sends a small supply to the Nassau market."[38] Until the early 1860s estates on the island concentrated on raising stock for the Nassau market, but they came increasingly into competition with foreign suppliers. As Governor Rawson noted in his report on the Blue Book for that year, "Cattle for slaughtering are imported from Cuba and Florida."[39] It was perhaps in the light of these developments that the emphasis on the Farquharson estates shifted to agricultural production on the share system.

The move to establish the share system on a formal basis on the Farquharson estates in 1865 was precipitated by the proprietors' desire to make them profitable operations. This resolve was reflected in their decision to appoint an attorney and agent, Nassau merchant William Marshall, to manage the estates on their behalf. Marshall in turn selected Alexander Forsyth of Rum Cay as his local attorney.[40] On a visit to the Prospect Hill estate in 1865, Forsyth discovered that a large proportion of the proprietors' share of the crops had not been paid for some time. Previous managers had arranged with some tenants (without the owners' authorization) for the proprietors' share to be waived in exchange for making repairs on the estate. As Forsyth reported in September 1865, "On my arrival I visited the above Estate [Prospect Hill] and found matters in a Bad state, as nearly all the Proprietors Rights or Shares as Rent, had been ceded, for an *undefined period,* for imaginary work which had never been properly performed, and in my opinion never would have been or was intended to be performed by the Tenants & others, the Contracting parties!" He also found that tenants abused the custom by which they were allowed to cultivate "free or picking fields" without payment of a share to the proprietors and that this abuse "prevented some persons having a larger and better picking field, than the field from which they give thirds besides this is open to another objection the people choose the best land for their picking fields, and plant all the small articles in them, by which the proprietors are defrauded of their just rights."[41] In August 1865 Forsyth delivered an ultimatum to the Prospect Hill tenants. They had the option of remaining on the estate, after signing a contract, or leaving once their crops were reaped: "All who wish to remain, on the Estate giving one third of what they raise are welcome to do so[,] all who do not like this agreement are equally welcome to leave, after they take in the crops that are now planted, as you are all free men now."[42] Forsyth's last statement suggests that many former slaves had continued to reside and work on the estate as tenants after emancipation.

In the written contracts that have survived from 1865, the rights and obligations of the tenants on the Farquharson estates were explicitly stated. In the contract that was signed by the tenants who worked on William J. Hall's and John Harrison's tracts of land, for example, the owners made it clear that one-third of all the products of the land should be delivered to their resident manager. The crops specified in this contract were corn, sugar cane, plantains, yams, cassava, potatoes, beans, peas, pumpkins, melons, and groundnuts. This agreement also mentioned the tenants' responsibility for keeping the land in good condition and emphasized the manager's supervisory functions: "The persons or tenants aforesaid . . . promise to be honest faithful and careful of the interests of the owners of said land by not destroying the Standing woods by fire or abandoning the fields to weed before the same is worn out, and generally to obey all lawful orders of the aforesaid Jacob Deveaux Senior[,] Manager as regards the portions of the said tracts to be farmed and cultivated."[43] These provisions were clearly intended to discourage the use of the slash and burn agricultural techniques commonly employed by Bahamian cultivators of that period.[44] Any person who failed to comply with the terms of the contract had to pay £2 sterling to the other party. This agreement could be renewed after a period of one year "by mutual consent of both parties."[45]

The detailed nature of the contracts signed by tenants on the Farquharson estates in 1865 is also demonstrated by the fact that even the number of pigs that could be kept on the estates was specified. An addendum to one of these agreements reads, "Every Tenant, working on Farquharson lands are [*sic*] hereby allowed the privilege of keeping free of Rent, or charge one Breeding Sow and the Barrow increase from the same, any person wishing to keep a larger number of Hogs must deliver one pig from each Litter for the owners of the land in lieu of Rent."[46]

Separate agreements were signed by these persons who performed the duties of manager on the estates. The manager's main function was to monitor the performance of the tenants. The contract signed by Jacob Deveaux, Senior, for example, mentioned that he had been employed "for the purpose of directing and controlling the tenants." For the performance of his duties Deveaux was allowed to keep one-fourth of the crops, which he collected from the tenants, and given "the use of cultivation free of all Shares or Rent Three Acres or twelve tasks" of the land he managed.[47]

During the latter part of the nineteenth century landlords who rented "pineapple lands" on the share system also began to take a more direct interest in the production process. By the mid-1880s they extended credit to the share tenants and supplied them with pineapple slips, manure, and fertilizer. The cost of these inputs was the first deduction from the proceeds of the sale of the crops, which were marketed by the landlords. With this increased financial involvement landlords came to exercise a greater measure of supervision over the agricultural activities of their tenants. Thus Henry Blake observed in 1886 of pineapple production on the share system in the Bahamas, "Here the initial expense of purchase of slips, and planting, have necessitated the use of capital and with it, of supervision."[48] The landlords' provision of these inputs was reflected in the share of the crop yields they received. In the late nineteenth century it was usual for landlords who rented pineapple land on the share system to receive one-half rather than one-third of the net proceeds.[49]

These developments followed on a heightened interest in pineapple production after 1865 when the economic boom based on blockade-running during the American Civil War came to an end.[50] Governor Rawson admitted in 1866 that blockade-running had not "increased the commercial relations of the Colony with any other Country." He suggested that it had, however, focused the attention of the colony's merchant class on the commercial possibilities of local resources: "It has turned the attention of the Mercantile Community to the means of developing existing resources, and of opening up new employments for the population of the Out Islands, and fresh sources of profitable industry and commerce for all portions of the Colony."[51] The "existing resources" to which Rawson referred were pineapples and sponges.

The interest in the development of the pineapple industry by the merchant class after 1865 coincided with a sharply increased demand for tropical commodities by the industrialized countries of the North Atlantic. W. Arthur Lewis has noted that the rapid rise in tropical exports after 1870 reflected in part "the growth of demand resulting from the increase in the national incomes of the leading industrial states."[52] In the Bahamas the expansion of the markets for certain foodstuffs led to increased production.

In the case of pineapples, the stimulus to production came from a demand for both canned and fresh fruit. As the administrator of the colony noted in 1881, "The cultivation of pineapples has had an impulse given to it by the enormous demand for canned preserved pineapples, operations of which are on an extensive scale in New Providence."[53] It was with the hope of profiting from this demand that landlords advanced loans, pineapple slips, manure, and fertilizer to increase productivity and output.

The demand for pineapples was also reflected in the increased purchases of land by Bahamian merchants to extend its production. This trend was already discernible in 1869. Governor Sir James Walker pointed out in his report on the Blue Book for that year that "notwithstanding the discouraging return of the present year and the general precarious character of the pine cultivation, large tracts of land have been lately purchased with the view of extending it."[54] One result of this trend was the concentration of pineapple lands in the hands of a few individuals. Thus Charles Mooney of the Baltimore Geographical Society remarked in 1905, after a visit to the Bahamas, "Although there are pineapple soils on all the islands, and particularly the larger ones, yet the industry is centred on Eleuthera and Cat Islands. On these the value of the lands has increased greatly, and they have now come into the possession of a comparatively few wealthy men. The fields are owned either individually or in partnership."[55] In the "palmy days of pineapples," J. W. Culmer controlled Eleuthera; W. E. Ambrister and C. T. Sands, Cat Island; Michael A. Knowles, Long Island; and J. S. Johnson, Abaco.[56] By 1893 the J. S. Johnson Company was incorporated in the state of New Jersey with capital of $400,000. This company had purchased, among other things, J. S. Johnson's interests in canning factories and in sisal and pineapple plantations amounting to 20,000 acres.[57]

Despite the growth and prosperity of the pineapple industry in the late nineteenth century, the share system remained the dominant form of labor organization. Although pineapple production was sufficiently profitable to make a system of wage labor feasible, the share system continued to have important advantages for merchant-landlords who were intent on maximizing profits. First, it was a means of minimizing costs by restricting the outlay of working capital. Second, the landlord benefited from the additional labor of his tenant's family, which, in fact, constituted "a cheap labour reserve."[58]

The rapid extension of the pineapple industry in response to the export stimulus created an increased demand for a stable labor force that would provide steady supplies of this commodity. Initially merchants experienced difficulty in attracting such a labor force, for most persons on the Out Islands supported a relatively independent existence by engaging in subsistence farming and seagoing activities. As chapter 6 demonstrates, merchants recruited and retained this labor force by the operation of a credit system whose effect was to bind laborers to regular employment by the creation of a debt relationship.[59]

Most cultivators who produced pineapples on the share system in this period relied on their merchant-landlords for credit in the eighteen months that elapsed between the planting and the reaping of a crop of pineapples. The evidence indicates that these tenants came increasingly to depend on advances of cash and provisions from their landlords because they concentrated on the production of pineapples to the exclusion of subsistence crops. These developments and their consequences were noted by the resident justice of the island of San Salvador in his report for 1885: "Although the export [of pineapples] is large, there is no visible benefit among the majority of the small proprietors and the labouring classes who, here, as on some of the Out Islands neglect other and necessary agricultural pursuits. The consequence is that ground produce is very scarce, and should any unforeseen circumstances arise to retard the growth of pineapple crops in the field, the usual method of bartering of the fruit of the coming season will have to be entirely adopted, this in some cases has been already done."[60]

Pineapples were not the only export commodity produced on the share system. By the first decade of the twentieth century, sisal, which had initially been produced by wage labor on plantations in islands like Andros, was cultivated on San Salvador by share tenants. Writing in his annual report on San Salvador for 1900, Resident Justice W. K. Duncombe described the arrangements for the cultivation of sisal: "A large portion of this land [on the southern end of the island] is leased by the Bahamas (Inagua) Sisal Co. Ltd. and they permit a large number of persons to cultivate it as tenants and the overseer of the Company collects as rental from each tenant one-third of the total production. This system is adopted throughout the island by the land-owners."[61] The adoption of the share system for sisal production is explained by the investors' need to restrict capital outlay, for the Bahamian industry was already experiencing low prices as a result of the poor quality of its product and competition from efficient producers like Mexico.

In the twentieth century, two factors converged to undermine the importance of the share system. The first of these was the growth of opportunities for lucrative wage employment in the southern United States and in New Providence. In the period 1905–24, the development of southern Florida attracted Bahamian laborers in large numbers. The economic prosperity in

New Providence in the 1920s based on bootlegging, tourism, and the land and construction booms also resulted in the depopulation of the Out Islands. The second factor was the decline of the colony's pineapple industry in the early decades of the twentieth century and with it a decrease in the merchant-landlords' demand for labor.[62] Exports of pineapple in 1892 were valued at £56,000; in 1927 they were worth only £7.[63] Although the share system has survived to the present day, it has ceased to be an important form of land tenure in the Bahamas.

Both the labor tenancy and share systems developed before full emancipation as part of the general trend toward the redefinition of productive relationships in the years after the decline of cotton as an export staple. In the immediate postemancipation years, these labor systems were adopted by absentee proprietors, most of whom had no capital to operate a wage system and regarded a dependent tenantry as a more profitable arrangement for extracting surplus than direct production. The share system was retained throughout the nineteenth century mainly because this precapitalist form of production and employment involved lower costs than wage labor. Unlike *mètayage* in the British Windward Islands, the share system in the Bahamas did not result in the elevation of the ex-slaves and their descendants on the social and economic scale, nor did it provide a stimulus to the development of an independent freehold peasantry.[64] In fact, it was the share system that kept the estates of the absentee landlords intact and financially viable by lowering labor costs. In the Bahamas, under the share system, tenants remained basically "permanent hired hands" whose main resource was their labor power.[65]

Chapter Six

THE CREDIT AND TRUCK SYSTEMS

The Control of Credit and Labor

The labor systems that emerged by the immediate postemancipation years did not remain static but evolved in response to economic change. The most important economic factor in this development was the increased external demand for commodities like salt, pineapple, and sponges by the late 1860s.[1] To respond effectively to the export stimulus, merchant-investors in the production and harvesting of those commodities needed a stable labor force. As we shall see, the mobilization of this labor force often resulted in the introduction of an element of coercion into the existing labor systems. There were control mechanisms that enabled a white mercantile minority to recruit and retain laborers and thus consolidate its position as a ruling elite in the postemancipation period. Rather than a monopoly of land, the important elements in this elite's economic and social control were a monopoly of the credit available to the majority of the population and the operation of a system of payment in truck.[2] The credit and truck systems frequently left the lower classes in debt and, as a governor of the colony in the late nineteenth century remarked, in a position of "practical slavery."[3]

By the time of emancipation in 1834, the merchant class in the Bahamas, based in Nassau, had risen to a position of economic and political dominance. Most of the merchants at the time were either Loyalists or descendants of Loyalists who had settled in the colony after 1783. The prosperity of this urban mercantile group was based largely on its role as middleman in the colony's import-export trade. This role was extended after 1787, when Nassau was made a free port and opened to trade, in certain enumerated commodities, with the Spanish and French colonies.[4]

It should be noted that the merchants in the Bahamas were, unlike those of most other British West Indian colonies of this period, an "agrocommercial bourgeoisie."[5] As Loyalists, they had been eligible for land grants in the Out Islands, on which they had established cotton plantations under the supervision of resident overseers.[6] With the decline of cotton production at the beginning of the nineteenth century and the emigration of impoverished cotton planters, the merchants (many of whom were landowners) were unchallenged as the leading economic group. In the political sphere, too, the merchants were ascendant, and by 1834 they dominated the colony's House of Assembly.[7] It was the beginning of a political control that lasted into the twentieth century.

The techniques of control that the merchant class employed in the post-emancipation years were clearly based on their experience in dealing with the free population during the slavery era. There is evidence, for example, that in the years before emancipation the merchants used their position as the major creditors to dominate the poor white population politically. Governor James Carmichael Smyth hinted at this state of affairs in a January 1832 dispatch in which he commented on petitions from some colonists asking for his removal from office. He suggested that the merchants were already in a position to pressure sections of the poor white population to support their viewpoint: "The poor fishermen at Abaco, who have forwarded their petition, I have never seen. Few of them can read; or write beyond signing their names. They live by catching turtle & looking after wrecks and vessels in distress. They draw their flour and other necessary supplies from Nassau & are entirely under the influence and guidance of those shopkeepers and vendue masters in this town, with whom they deal, and by whom they are furnished with the few comforts they possess."[8]

The link between the role of the merchants as creditors and their political ascendancy was more strongly made by Governor William Colebrooke in a dispatch to the secretary of state for the colonies, Lord Glenelg, in February 1836. Referring to the general election of 1834, Colebrooke brought to Glenelg's attention developments that set the pattern for nineteenth-century Bahamian politics:

> I have adverted to the last Elections having taken place before the Abolition of Slavery, and the condition of the Inhabitants of the Out Islands not enabling them at that time to become candidates, the Elections had been in a great degree nominal. The Merchants resident at Nassau for the most part sought and acquired the seats and some who were unknown to the Constituencies were thus nominated in Extensive and thinly populated districts where but few Electors could attend. In closer communities a commercial interest had grown up by the dependence of the poorer classes on the Merchants for their necessary supplies, and the debts they had thus generally contracted.[9]

Payment in truck also had a precedent, during the period of slavery, in the treatment of the free African apprentices. Like the slaves, the liberated Africans were (as noted earlier) often given rations rather than cash for their labor, a practice that prefigured the truck system for the postemancipation period. The financial advantages to the employer of payment in kind were clear from a case cited by Governor Lewis Grant in 1827:

> Two of them [had been employed] in Field work and the third in raking salt in the ponds of Turks Islands, in the beginning of their apprenticeships. They were afterwards and up to the present day, employed in cutting Ship Timber and quarrying stones on behalf and for the profit of said Lightbournes family—These are the hardest species of employment in which Negroes are employed here. The Holder Lightbourne would be earning two Dollars and a half for each pr. week and the African would be receiving from him each 8 Quarts of corn pr. week and two suits of Osnaburgs pr. ann; which together would not cost the Holder one days earnings of the Africans—a quarter Dollar pr. week which was given also, I believe to the African might make the weekly cost to the Owner about one days earnings.[10]

It is not unreasonable to suggest that the truck system of the postemancipation years was nothing more than the wider application of a practice used in connection with the free Africans during slavery.

The key to the economic and political dominance of the merchant class in the postemancipation years was the widespread need for credit among the colony's laboring classes, which was largely attributable to the nature of the Bahamian economy in that period. In the early postemancipation years the opportunities for regular wage employment outside the island of New Providence were, as noted earlier, limited to pineapple production and salt raking—both of which were concentrated on a few islands of the archipelago. With the notable exception of the sisal industry, the payment of labor in major economic activities, like wrecking and sponging, was organized on a profit-sharing basis rather than a wage basis.

Without regular wages, most members of the Bahamian lower classes came to depend on credit.[11] Whether they were involved in agriculture (as tenants or freeholders) or in wrecking or sponging, poor black and white Bahamians had to provide for themselves and their families until their crops were marketed or the proceeds of the wrecking and sponging voyages were divided. A comment by Rodolfo Stavenhagen on the Agni of the Ivory Coast in the twentieth century is applicable to the situation of the agricultural producer in the Bahamas of the nineteenth century: "The majority of cultivators live on their projected future income, that is, long before the harvest or sale of produce, the agriculturist contracts debts which must be repaid out of the proceeds of the harvest."[12] In the absence of financial institutions to serve their needs, the Bahamian lower classes sought credit from the merchants who were directly involved in these major economic activities.

The main function of the credit system in this period was to provide advances of commodities rather than cash to the individual. Although cash advances were not unknown, these were largely confined to the sponging industry, where they were made with some frequency only after the late 1880s. An examination of the credit system in the three main economic activities of the nineteenth and early twentieth centuries will show that the terms under which credit was advanced were similar and that the result of this system was often to involve the laboring classes in a cycle of debt.

The evidence indicates that the laborers' indebtedness was an outcome that the merchants anticipated. For the merchant, the practice of providing commodities on credit was an effective mechanism for recruiting and through the ensuing indebtedness, maintaining a labor force for the economic ventures in which he had invested. This use of the credit system was suggested to the official and employer classes largely by their perception of the work habits of the Bahamian of the Out Islands, which supplied most of the colony's labor force. It was generally believed that the Out Islander had no incentive to work beyond the point of subsistence because he had few needs to satisfy. It was a viewpoint articulated as early as 1847 by H. F. Cartwright, a stipendiary magistrate, who suggested that, by contrast, the laborers on the larger islands were prepared to work steadily, for wages, so that they could imitate the consumption patterns of their social superiors.[13]

The perception that the Bahamian lower classes of the Out Islands were indolent was based on the fact that they were incompletely proletarianized. In the Bahamas, as elsewhere in the British West Indies and later in Africa, the black population was regarded as "working" only when it was engaged in wage labor.[14] As late as 1857 Governor Charles Bayley observed that there was as yet no wage-earning proletariat in the colony:

> The condition of this island [New Providence] and some other out islands is peculiar—strictly speaking and adverting to the ideas raised by such a designation in Great Britain, they can hardly be said to contain any labouring population at all. I mean, that they do not contain as any country on the continent of Europe does, a body of inhabitants whose daily subsistence entirely depends upon their daily wages, and who have no other means of support but that which is derived from the regular savings of agricultural or domestic services.

Most Bahamians had neither the need nor the inclination to work for wages on a regular basis. In the immediate postemancipation years, with few opportunities for wage labor, they had survived mainly by subsistence farming and seagoing activities. Bayley described the mode of existence of the majority of the Bahamian population:

> We have a population of small free holders, owning patches of ground, the produce of which eked out by the proceeds of wrecking or sponging or fishing amply suffice to furnish all that a genial climate allows the people to deem necessaries of life. A few acres or less than a few acres of ground which produce Indian corn, oranges, limes or Bananas afford to the majority of our population a subsistence almost equal to their wants & which is more than equal when it receives the accession of occasional salvage—casual wages—the proceeds arising from the sale of shells and sponges.[15]

Bayley believed that this situation was the result of a liberal land policy and took measures to restrict the availability of land to the lower classes.[16] It may be argued, however, that in the Bahamian context the lower classes had avoided proletarianization mainly because they were able to make a living from the sea.

In the latter part of the nineteenth century the credit system served to bring subsistence producers into the market economy as laborers. The change became necessary because of the increased demand for labor on a regular basis following the expansion of the pineapple industry and the development of the sponge trade.[17] This use of the credit system was described by Governor Henry Blake in a dispatch of August 1884 in which he attempted to explain the origins of the credit and truck systems in the colony. For the Out Islander an advance of merchandise from the merchant-investor was the initial inducement to provide labor for pineapple production or sponging: "The owner—generally a shopkeeper—requires labour for his ship or on his land. The sponger or 'farmer' is indolent, and not disposed to work beyond his immediate necessities. To secure labour some inducement must be held out, that will at the same time bind the labourer to his work, and that inducement is the opening of an account by advancing food and clothing, to be repaid out of the proceeds of the share in the voyage or crop."[18] Once indebted, the laborer was less likely to opt for subsistence production instead of steady labor for his employer.

The credit and truck systems flourished in certain areas of economic activity. The earliest mention in the records of a system of payment in truck after emancipation is an 1840 reference in connection with the salt industry. Early in that year Governor Francis Cockburn had visited several of the

Out Islands where salt production was the main economic activity. In a subsequent dispatch to Lord John Russell, Cockburn described the conditions of employment of the liberated Africans who were in great demand as laborers in the salt ponds: "In some instances they work on Shares, in others they receive from their employers, Eight Quarts of Indian Corn—2 lbs of Salt Fish or Meat, 2 Hs of Molasses or Sugar Weekly—Two Dollars a Month as Wages and three suits of clothes annually with Medical attendance when sick."[19] This description of the remuneration of the liberated Africans in the period after emancipation provides the clearest evidence for the continuation into freedom of practices that had been developed during the period of slavery. In fact, the formula for the payment of Africans in 1840 was little different from the method of payment in kind and cash described by Governor Lewis Grant in 1827.[20]

Payment in truck was not, however, used only in the context of wage labor. In the Turks Islands, which were until 1848 administered as part of the Bahamas, the large-scale salt producers bought the shares that had been distributed to poorer members of the community and paid for them in truck. As Governor Cockburn reported in 1843, "it is in no way to be doubted that the greater part if not the whole of the shares given to the poor and lower classes are again obtained from them by such persons as Mr. Stubb [a major producer] by paying for them in articles of the lowest quality which are charged at the highest prices."[21] Further evidence of a wider use of the truck system was provided in 1847 by the stipendiary magistrate for the area that included the Turks Islands and Inagua: "The truck system is much in vogue here & nothing but a Savings Bank can remedy the many evils attendant upon it. Every leaseholder is a shopkeeper and every labourer pays weekly 100 per Cent. on the prime cost in the US of America for the necessaries of life."[22]

The most detailed account of the operation of the truck system in Inagua was given by Louis N. Duty in two letters to the *Nassau Guardian* in April and May of 1889.[23] Duty had served as a government official some years earlier and had observed the practice (reminiscent of the "tommy shops" of early industrial England) of paying laborers their wages in substandard goods in stores owned by their employers:

> During the period of my official life there the Truck System was in full sway and I have a lively remembrance of the *modus operandi* having been personally present on numerous occasions on pay day in the office of the greatest Salt Rakers and Merchants of Inagua, and the only kind of payment I ever saw made to the large number of labourers—male and female

> employed in that establishment was by paper orders stamped with the employer's name, and which orders could only be exchanged at his stores for the necessaries of life, spirituous liquors and tobacco. I have heard stalwart men on more than one occasion plead in the most earnest and abject terms for only one shilling in cash from the week's labour, and in some instances the plea was granted, not as a right but as a great favour, and this I aver was the universal mode of payment current amongst the Salt Rakers and Merchants at Inagua in a greater or lesser degree uninterruptedly during my stay in that port with the single exception I have mentioned.[24]

In that context the truck and credit systems were twin aspects of the merchants' exploitation and control of labor. Of central importance to the operation of both systems were the stores owned by the merchant-employers at which the employees were forced to make their purchases. Duty's letter of 4 May provides illustration:

> At the time to which I referred in my [earlier] letter, this system was in full sway at Inagua [and] the stores of the employers of labour with the single exception I before alluded to, were general magazines from which their *employés* were expected to get all they needed, even clothes for themselves and families. . . . Articles of the lowest quality were marked at the highest prices and the employer was accommodating enough to give goods in advance to the *employé* which was deducted from the amount of his wages: *by this means the employer was always able to demand the services of the employé who always remained hopelessly in debt, and thus the system as practised at Inagua, was but a modified form of slavery* [emphasis added].[25]

The laborers' dependence on credit in the salt-producing islands can be partly explained by the nature of salt production and the uncertainties of the weather. Salt was produced by solar evaporation, but this process was often interrupted by heavy rains. The interruption in salt production often left the salt rakers unemployed and forced them to seek credit from the resident merchants. This was the situation in Inagua in 1881, when salt production was abandoned because of unseasonal rains. Laborers needed credit to support themselves while they were unemployed and had reluctantly taken advances from their employers. The correspondent for the *Nassau Guardian* in Inagua reported: "We are sorry to say that in some instances sons of toil have had to take *truck* at a terrible disadvantage . . . they are charged . . . some 25 to 50 per cent more for their necessaries than any ordinary customer with cash calling for a pound of pork."[26]

The salt rakers' reliance on credit and the indebtedness that often followed gave the proprietors, as Duty pointed out, a control of labor. Controlling the labor force was important throughout this period because the merchant-employers had difficulty attracting and retaining laborers for the salt ponds. The reluctance of laborers to engage in salt raking was due mainly to the arduous working conditions. In 1835, Governor Balfour had accurately predicted that after emancipation employers in the salt-producing islands would be able to attract laborers only by offering high wages.[27] Comments by Governor John Gregory in 1852 indicated that the unattractive working conditions in the salt industry were unchanged and that high wages, relative to those paid in other forms of employment, were still necessary to attract laborers.[28] It can be argued that in this context the truck system served to offset the high wages that employers were compelled to offer, while the credit system and concomitant indebtedness reintroduced an element of compulsion that was regarded as necessary to retain the labor force.

By the early 1880s the truck system had become firmly established as the mode of payment used in the salt-producing islands of the Bahamas. The effect of this development was to place most of the salt rakers outside the cash economy. Payment in truck was accepted by the inhabitants of those islands mainly because there were few alternative opportunities for employment. So firmly entrenched was the truck system in Long Cay, Fortune Island, for example, that when stevedores hired by the Atlas Company in 1880 were paid wages in cash, fears were expressed about how this money would be spent.[29]

The entrenchment of the truck system in the salt industry by the 1880s is partly explained by declining prices and the shrinking market for Bahamian salt that resulted from increased American production of mined salt and the imposition of a protective tariff in the United States.[30] In these circumstances it became difficult for salt proprietors to obtain credit. Shortage of cash forced the proprietors to rely even more on the truck system to reduce costs. In 1888 L. D. Powles described one example of the truck system in Ragged Island: "In this particular island, when a vessel comes in, the principal salt-owners take their net, go hauling [for fish] and divide the take among the men who carry the salt on board. In this way they shipped 38,000 bushels of salt at a profit in less than five months."[31] In this variant of the barter system the salt proprietors exchanged one commodity (fish) for another (labor power).

Reliance on credit and payment in truck were also the experience of the tenants and peasant proprietors who produced pineapples for export in the late nineteenth century. Rural cultivators without cash reserves needed credit to support themselves during the eighteen-month period between planting the pineapple slips and harvesting the fruit.

The usual source of credit was the Nassau merchant who was the absentee landlord of the tracts of land in Eleuthera that the tenant farmed on the share system. For the tenant the credit relationship began when the merchant-landlord provided the pineapple slips and (by the 1880s) manure or fertilizer.[32] During the long wait before the harvest, the merchant advanced provisions and sometimes cash to the tenant at credit prices. These debts were eventually repaid by the tenant's share of the proceeds of the crop, which, by the terms of the agreement, was consigned to the merchant for marketing. The credit arrangements for the peasant proprietor were slightly different. Credit was advanced to the peasant in the form of goods, and his crop was marketed by the merchant.

It should be noted that the merchant acted primarily as a marketing agent for some peasant proprietors. Peasants found this arrangement convenient, for the merchant organized the shipping of the fruit. Peasants who attempted to remain independent of the merchant were often without transportation for this perishable produce. This was the situation described by Governor Sir William F. Haynes Smith in 1896: "Where the land is owned by the cultivator the large dealers who are for the most part owners of land worked on the half system buy and the would be independent man is 'ringed' out. He has no means of transport and at times as if in despair he brings his produce to the waters edge at the shipping places and sits down to watch it rotting there."[33]

At the end of a season, tenants were frequently in debt to the merchants. Without a cash income they were compelled to return to the merchant for further credit in the following season. The effect of the credit system was to perpetuate the tenants' dependence on the merchants. As the colonial annual report on the Bahamas for 1897 noted, "the method [of credit] tends to the elimination of any independence on the part of the labourer."[34] The system also generated a great deal of distrust and suspicion between tenants and landlords. Haynes Smith observed in 1896: "The owner alleges that the cultivator cheats him by secretly selling portions of the crop; the cultivator alleges the owner cheats him in the price he charges for the truck and in the statement of his accounts."[35]

The experience of the peasant proprietors with the Nassau merchants, whether the latter were acting as creditors or as marketing agents, was not appreciably different from that of the tenants. Like the tenants, the peasant proprietors often had little cash income. Although the merchants received cash for the pineapples that they sold on the peasants' behalf, the usual practice was to pay the peasants in kind.[36] Peasant proprietors escaped the truck system only by selling their produce directly to American shippers who came to the pineapple-producing islands in search of fruit.[37] In his report for 1882 on the settlement of Rock Sound, Eleuthera, the assistant resident justice noted, "Two firms in Baltimore sent out vessels and purchased in *cash* on their own account. The Magistrate remarks, that this new feature in the trade, i.e., paying in cash—introduced by the American speculators—was a boon to the poor planters, who have been accustomed to receive 'truck' as payment for the fruit—a system which is pernicious and disadvantageous in the extreme."[38]

In the 1890s some tenants resisted the merchants' exploitation by illicitly selling a portion of the pineapple crop. This practice became so widespread that C. Tyldesley Sands, one of the major owners of pineapple land in Eleuthera, found it necessary to offer a reward of a hundred dollars for information leading to the conviction of tenants who disposed of pineapples in this way.[39] Sands complained in 1898 that the purchasers of those pineapples paid only one shilling per dozen, whereas he was paying the in-kind equivalent of two shillings per dozen for the first crop and one shilling and three pence for the balance.[40] One suspects, however, that what was important to tenants was payment in cash without deductions for credit advanced.

It is clear that it was the merchant class that benefited from its business relationship with the rural cultivators. First, the credit and truck systems stabilized the labor force for pineapple production on land owned by the merchants and guaranteed steady supplies of fruit for export. Second, the merchants profited from assuming the middleman role in supplying merchandise to the rural producers and marketing their produce. For the cultivators, however, there was usually no surplus to save or reinvest.

By the beginning of the twentieth century, payment in truck had been extended to encompass workers employed in the pineapple canning factory at Governor's Harbour, Eleuthera. Wages were paid in the form of tokens that could be exchanged for commodities, initially at local stores and later exclusively at the company store. This form of the truck system was described by "Eye Witness" in a letter to the *Nassau Guardian* in September 1906:

> For the last few years the Factory checks and cheques on the Nassau Bank [were] the only money [that] could be seen in circulation. In fact the Factory Tin Checks were used all the year around until this year when the Proprietors sent around to all the stores a notice stating that they would not redeem them and forbidding any store taking them. This caused quite a disturbance when it was found that the Pineapple Factory had built a large store and had imported a very large stock, and forced the labourers to spend their tin checks as they refused to settle with them until the Factory closed.[41]

The method of payment outlined above was clearly intended to reduce the employees' real wages below their nominal wages.[42]

It was against this "deplorable transaction" that the Truck Act of 1907 was directed. This legislation was introduced by Sir William Grey-Wilson, who was anxious to remove a "genuine grievance" and improve labor relations.[43] The provisions of the act removed the two main sources of worker dissatisfaction: it required that laborers be paid in "the current coin of the Colony," and it prohibited employers from insisting that employees spend their wages at a particular shop.[44]

The credit and truck systems were integral also to the sponging industry, which was the mainstay of the colony's economy in the late nineteenth and early twentieth centuries.[45] Credit was essential for the sponger, who, before he earned any income, had to maintain his family for the six to twelve weeks that he was away and also to contribute to the provisioning of the schooner used on the sponging voyage. The main source of credit was the merchant who in most cases owned and outfitted the schooner and acted as agent for the sale of the sponges. Spongers had no alternative source of credit because the existing banking institution was not geared to serving members of the lower classes, who had neither collateral nor security. The sponger's position was accurately described by W. E. Pritchard, a merchant involved in the sponge trade, in a letter to the *Nassau Guardian* in 1892: "No Banking House, or money-lender would advance a sum of money today, at the ordinary rate of interest, without a joint note as security. Should a sponger apply to the bank of Nassau, or to some of the five per cent.-a-month money-lenders for the loan of a sum of money to 'go on his own book,' I wonder how he would succeed?"[46]

Before 1896 the credit advanced to the sponger who had signed on for a voyage was usually in the form of goods rather than cash.[47] These goods, which included basic foodstuffs and articles of clothing, were usually supplied from a store owned by the outfitter and were more expensive than the same items purchased for cash. Although the merchants chose to explain the high credit prices in terms of the legitimate cost of doing business, it is probable that their monopoly of credit was a more important factor.[48] There is certainly nothing to suggest that their risks were of a magnitude to justify the consistently high level of the credit charges.

The system of advances had clear disadvantages for the spongers. First, merchants often sold them inferior goods at prices ordinarily reserved for goods of the best quality.[49] Second, spongers were often forced to accept goods they did not want and then had to sell them at a loss to obtain cash. There were, however, some spongers who found the advance system useful. Involvement in sponging often led the men of Andros and the Out Islands to neglect agricultural pursuits. The advance supplied food in situations in which the sponger had made no provision for his family's subsistence. As the Reverend F. B. Matthews, then stationed in Andros, remarked with more than a touch of irony, "There is no 'worriation about wittles' so easy and kind are the merchants in advancing unlimited flour."[50]

The sponger was expected to defray his debt to the merchant at the end of the voyage. On the crew's return, the merchant often acted as agent for the sale of the sponges by tender at the Nassau Sponge Exchange. In the years before 1886, the amounts offered by sponge buyers were written on small printed forms and handed to the broker, who indicated the purchaser without stating what price had been paid for the lot of sponges. In a dispatch of April 1887, Governor Blake described the system in use until 1886 for the sale of sponges and division of the proceeds: "After the sale of cargo, the total amount of which was not made known to the men, they were paid off in the merchant's office each man receiving generally but a few shillings, which, he was informed represented the balance due to him after the payment of the vessels outfit, the amount of which he did not know, and of his private debt, of the items of which he knew nothing."[51] Clearly the system provided the merchants with ample opportunity to cheat the spongers.

On the completion of a voyage and distribution of the proceeds, spongers were often still in debt to the merchants. Having no private resources, they were compelled to sign up for another voyage and obtain further advances to feed their families. The effect of continuing indebtedness was to force the spongers to work on a regular basis. If a balance was left to the spongers after deductions, it was paid to them in truck rather than in cash. In these circumstances it was difficult for spongers to accumulate the funds that would allow them to bypass the credit system.[52] The combination of the credit and truck systems resulted in constant indebtedness and chronic poverty for the spongers.

The spongers were certainly aware that they were being exploited by the merchants. One of their main objections to the existing organization of the sponge trade was the secrecy that surrounded the sale of the sponges and the division of the proceeds—matters that were naturally of interest to them. They strongly suspected that the merchants were able to adjust the accounts to benefit their own interests. The spongers' response to the merchants' exploitation (real and suspected) took the form of selling all or a part of the catch, at better prices, to persons who had established depots for purchasing sponge in Andros, the main sponging center, in 1884. The establishment of these depots provided spongers with the opportunity to evade the control the Nassau merchants exercised over sponging operations.

Although the merchants knew about these developments, they had no legal recourse since the captains and crews were part-owners of the sponges. The merchants pressured Blake to introduce legislation making it a criminal offense for a sponger who had been outfitted by a merchant to sell the sponges anywhere except at the Nassau Sponge Exchange. Blake was aware, however, that both sides had cause for complaint. He was opposed to certain aspects of the credit system and to the truck system, and he was determined to introduce legislation to deal with them. Blake knew that he would encounter difficulty in passing any measure opposed by the sponge merchants, who dominated the House of Assembly. He eventually extracted a promise of support for his proposed legislation from the merchants only after threatening to enforce a law that imposed a 2 percent tax on the sale of sponges.[53]

The legislation that was enacted in 1886 to regulate aspects of the sponge fishery made concessions to both spongers and merchants. The system of paying the shares of the crews in truck was abolished, and limits were placed on the value of advances that could be made to the captains and seamen. The act also stipulated that the agent should provide, on request, a copy of the accounts of the sponges sold and a detailed statement showing how the net proceeds had been divided. The most important provision of this legislation, however, was that stipulating that the market for sponges collected by crews outfitted by Nassau merchants be limited to the Nassau Sponge Exchange. Crew members who disposed of sponges in any other way were made liable to prosecution for larceny.[54] The effect of this provision was to reassert the merchants' control over the sponging industry.

Despite the attempt to improve the spongers' condition by legislation, their position remained largely the same after 1886. The advance system was retained, although limits were placed on the amounts that merchants could recover from an individual sponger's share at the end of a voyage. An attempt by the mercantile interests in 1892 to repeal the limit was blocked by officials of the Colonial Office, but the provision was eventually dropped in the 1905 enactment of new legislation regulating the sponge fishery.[55]

With or without legal restrictions, the sponge merchants continued to make large advances of provisions and cash to the spongers, and interest rates remained high.[56] It was usual for contemporary commentators to blame the spongers for insisting on large advances. Such demands, however, undoubtedly suited the interests of merchants anxious to retain the services of spongers in the face of increasing opportunities for other employment in the first two decades of the twentieth century. This practice constituted, in Alan Knight's phrase, "debts-as-perks."[57] The result of these large advances was an indebtedness that spongers came to accept as an inevitable condition of their involvement in the sponging industry.

Three additional factors should be taken into account in explaining the indebtedness of the spongers and their continued reliance on the credit system. First, a sponging voyage was, for the spongers, an uncertain undertaking. Although the proceeds of their labor were divided with the merchants, the risks were not shared. For example, the spongers were in debt to the merchants for trips interrupted by bad weather. Second, even when there was a cash balance left to the sponger, it was likely that he would spend a large part of it on entertainment after the deprivation of a long voyage. As Roscow Shedden, Bishop of Nassau, remarked of the sponger in 1927: "Barrooms are many, liquor flows in abundance, women are easy. After many weeks at sea in a life of enforced abstinence and celibacy, he will be only too likely to have his fling as soon as opportunity offers."[58] Third, the provision of the 1886 act that specified that merchants should furnish spongers with a statement of accounts on request was of little value to the majority of spongers, who were illiterate. It was a common practice for boys to sign on as spongers long before completing an elementary education.[59] As a result, the spongers constituted, in the apt description of an official, "a large illiterate, floating population."[60] The spongers' lack of education, as Pritchard admitted in 1892, gave the merchants many opportunities to cheat them: "One of the difficulties the merchant has to contend with is [the] ignorance of the large number of those who cannot even write their names, or have not sufficient knowledge of figures to discover when they are being cheated, supposing the broker is so inclined."[61]

The persistence of these problems after 1886 ensured that spongers remained indebted to and ultimately dependent on the merchant class. It was a fate that some escaped in the early years of the twentieth century by migrating to the southern United States, where relatively lucrative employment was available.[62] In the years after World War I there was also the competing attraction of bootlegging. As the acting commissioner for Mangrove Cay admitted in his report for 1922, bootlegging and employment in Florida provided these laborers with financial rewards that the sponging industry had never given them.[63]

It is not surprising that the merchants prospered throughout the period under examination, the distribution of sponge-trade proceeds being heavily weighted in their favor. These merchant-financiers profited from all stages of the sponging operations in their capacities as outfitters, owners of schooners, brokers, and often owners even of the drays that conveyed the sponges to the purchasers. The capital that the merchants accumulated from the sponger trade consolidated their position as the major source of credit in the colony and strengthened their influence in and control over the society at large.

The credit and truck systems were more than mechanisms for the recruitment and retention of a labor force and surplus appropriation. The adoption of these systems can also be explained by the capital structure of the industries we have examined. In their discussion of these systems, contemporary observers give us little idea of the extent of internal differentiation within the mercantile sector; but there is evidence that some merchants had little capital themselves or access to credit at moderate interest rates. Writing in 1886, after the failure of the Public Bank of the Bahamas, John Gardiner observed:

> I am only mentioning facts well known to most people in Nassau when I say that when the Bank failed, nearly every merchant in Nassau of any importance, except three or four, were found to be more or less heavily in debt to the Bank or its late Cashier. These merchants paid off or are paying off their debts to the Bank by borrowing money, often it is said, at very heavy interest, from other sources, so that they have, to all intents and purposes, no capital available at the present time for mercantile operations.
>
> Mr. Smith would have us believe that there is an available Banking Capital in the Colony of £70,000. Suppose there is; the greater part of it belongs to some half-dozen people, representing only a very small proportion of the members of Nassau; the others have no capital worth speaking of, in many cases none at all.[64]

It is likely that the situation Gardiner described lasted throughout the period under examination. For merchants of limited means, the economic exploitation of the labor force by the credit and truck systems might have been dictated by their need to cover the high cost of credit.

By the end of the nineteenth century the truck system had proven its effectiveness as a mechanism for maximizing profit at the expense of the laboring population and was for that reason widely adopted by employers in the colony. So widely was the truck system used that L. D. Powles commented in 1888 that "there are very few among the working classes of the Bahamas who know what it is to handle cash at all, except domestic servants and skilled work-people."[65] In 1896 Governor Haynes Smith also noted that "the spirit of the truck system appears to saturate every transaction."[66]

Shipbuilding and pilotage were two minor economic activities in which the truck system was used. Powles had visited Grand Bahama during his travels as a stipendiary magistrate and observed the operation of the truck system as it affected shipbuilding: "Shipbuilding goes on here to a limited extent, but owing to the prevalence of the truck system the unhappy workman derives but little benefit therefrom. Mr. Adderley brought to my notice a case in which men building a schooner for a Nassau merchant were being paid, at a low rate of wages, in flour instead of cash. We 'sampled' the flour, which was invoiced to them at 1L. 16s. a barrel, and found it not fit for human food."[67]

In the Biminis, payment for piloting, which was the main source of employment for the white population, was also made in truck. As the acting resident justice explained in his report for 1897, "Most of the white population depend entirely on ship-boarding or piloting, and as their services are not required except the wind is southerly it can be easily seen that there is plenty of time wasted. Even when employed they are paid in provisions and these provisions are generally sold at a sacrifice to obtain a little cash."[68]

In the southern islands of the archipelago, the truck system was used throughout the latter part of the nineteenth century. With the decline in salt trade by the 1880s, steamship labor became the main source of employment for the male population. Steamship lines like the Atlas Company, which served West Indian and Central American ports, called at these islands to engage laborers for loading and discharging cargo at those ports. Initially, Long Cay on Fortune Island was the base from which stevedores and deck hands were hired, but by 1882 Inagua had become the main center of labor recruitment.[69]

It was hoped that this new source of employment would provide a steady cash income for laborers in islands where the truck system had for so long prevailed. In 1880 a Long Cay correspondent to the *Nassau Guardian* pointed to the novelty of laborers' receiving their wages entirely in cash.[70] Four years later, however, most of the steamship lines had reverted to the practice of payment in truck. The foreign employers had quickly learned the local practices for exploiting labor.[71]

The extensive control that one local employer in Fortune Island exercised over his labor force through the truck system was described by Allan Eric after a visit in 1895:

> Fortune Island is virtually owned by one man whose name is J. A. Farrington. He is known as "King John," because he virtually owns the island and everybody upon it. He has a little West India negro blood in his veins. The negroes upon the island are always in debt to "King John," who keeps a general store, well stocked with all that delights the eye and stomach of the negro. The latter, being indolent and lazy, care not how much they become indebted to "King John," who, pursuing a thoroughly busi-

> ness method, allows them to liquidate by working for him, and he hires them out, such of them as he does not need on the island, to the Atlas steamers when colored men are wanted. So the negroes go on getting into debt to "King John" and working for him, so that they are not only subjects of, but subject to the autocrat of Fortune Island.[72]

The practice of paying steamship laborers in truck continued as late as 1897. In his report for that year, the resident justice of Long Cay mentioned its existence and the dissatisfaction it created among the laboring population: "A great deal of discontent has prevailed owing to the 'truck' system," with the laborers "asserting that the balances due them on the termination of their voyages, are not paid them in cash, and that they are compelled to wait for long periods before obtaining a settlement."[73]

At the beginning of the twentieth century, another version of the truck system was used in Inagua in connection with laborers employed on one-year contracts with American companies in Mexico, Panama, and countries on the South American mainland. These laborers were signed on by a local agent, who received a commission of one dollar for each man recruited. From that commission the agent met local expenses incurred on behalf of the companies. The agent's own main sources of income were the store he kept and the variant of the truck system he operated. The laborers were paid one-half of their wages in cash in the country of their employment, and the other half was paid to them on their return to Inagua.[74]

It was the agent's practice to allow (and actively encourage) the laborers to run up debts, sometimes as much as £40, that were huge by the standards of those times. There were several techniques by which the agent ensured this result. First, laborers were signed on long before the steamship arrived to convey them to their place of employment. During the waiting period they were encouraged to take advances of food and drink. Second, while the laborers were absent in Latin America, their contributions toward maintaining their families were paid in truck at "exorbitant rates" by the local agent. If a laborer's wife resided on an island other than Inagua, an additional charge was made for shipping supplies to her. Finally, the agent deliberately delayed settling the accounts on the laborers' return to Inagua. Laborers waiting to be paid were often forced to rely on the agent for food and other supplies.[75]

Action to end these practices was initiated by Sir William Grey-Wilson, who was strongly opposed to any form of the truck system,[76] and in 1907 legislation protecting emigrant laborers was enacted.[77] Grey-Wilson's comments in 1911 indicate that the act had removed the worst abuses of the system of recruiting laborers: "The position of the contract labourers under the new legislation, is vastly better than it was. Now the labourer cannot squander his pay in advance of earning it, & the temptation to do so is thereby greatly reduced. Now the Employer is not tempted to delay the departure of engaged labourers, because the cost of such detention is no longer chargeable to the labourer. Now those for whom the labourer makes provision in this colony are not paid in truck."[78]

Although blacks formed a majority of this dependent labor force, the credit and truck systems were not primarily racial in orientation but were key elements in a "machinery of class slavery" in which merchants dominated both whites and blacks.[79] The credit system and the indebtedness it induced constituted an effective means of mobilizing and maintaining a stable labor force, and payment in truck served to perpetuate the indebtedness. These systems were, however, more than methods for the control of labor. They must also be seen as techniques for increasing profits both by reducing labor costs and by creating a captive consumer market for the merchants' overpriced commodities. For the laboring classes the systems established a cycle of exploitation and impoverishment, but for most members of the mercantile elite they facilitated capital accumulation. In the Bahamian context, the merchants had replaced slaves with a dependent laboring population susceptible to their economic and social control.

Official efforts to legislate against the worst abuses of the credit and truck systems were prompted mainly by the realization that worker dissatisfaction might disrupt the output of major export products. It is difficult to escape the conclusion that the reform measures were intended to be acceptable to the merchant class. These measures were aimed primarily at abolishing the truck system but did not significantly affect the way in which the credit system operated. The credit system by itself, however, had the effect of keeping cash payments for labor to a minimum.

Payment in truck persisted in some of the colony's industries into the twentieth century despite the enactment of legislation to end the practice. Up to 1908 merchants involved in the sponging industry (like the operators of the pineapple-canning factory) made payments in the form of tokens that could be redeemed in goods.[80] There is also evidence that the truck system was practiced in the salt industry in Inagua as late as 1935. Writing in September of that year, Cyril Stevenson referred to the continued existence of such a system:

> To point out the disadvantage that "unorganized labour" is subject to, I might mention the "Truck System" which is carried on continually at Inagua,

> Bahamas. During my visit there I came across many people who were the victims of this "Truck System." In plain language it is simply this: "You want my Job? Buy from me, regardless of the price." Therefore the little money that labourers do make is wasted away this way, and in view of the fact that this is contrary to our statute laws.[81]

The decline of the credit and truck systems was largely the result of developments in the export sector. As we have argued, it was the expansion of export markets for sponges and pineapples that led to the intensified use of these forms of labor control. By the 1930s, with the decline of the sponge and pineapple industries, these systems were no longer necessary to mobilize and retain a labor force. Their effectiveness had, moreover, been undermined by the widening of opportunities for profitable wage employment in Florida and New Providence.

It is clear that the credit and truck systems were not restricted to Belize, as O. Nigel Bolland and William Green have stated; Green has asserted that "there was no system of advances and no company store in the sugar islands before or after emancipation."[82] The evidence indicates, however, that these systems existed in the sugar colonies of Trinidad, Tobago, British Guiana, and Jamaica in the postemancipation years and served some of the same purposes in those countries that they served in the Bahamas and Belize.

In British Guiana in the 1860s and in Trinidad in the 1870s, the credit and truck systems provided supervisory personnel on the sugar estates with a source of additional income. Their main victims were the indentured Indian immigrants who comprised the largest section of the plantation labor force. It was a common practice in British Guiana for the wages of indentured immigrants to be paid through their drivers, who often retained as much as 25 percent for themselves. Laborers were also required to spend their wages at shops operated by the drivers. This coercive authority of the drivers was largely derived from their power to assign tasks to estate laborers.[83]

In Trinidad the credit and truck systems were sufficiently widespread in the mid-1870s to warrant comment by the editor of the *San Fernando Gazette,* who, in May 1875, deplored "the unfair and unprincipled system of trucking carried on by some Estates."[84] Managers and overseers, or their wives, supplied estate laborers with commodities on credit at inflated prices. Indentured immigrants were obliged to purchase these goods because they were allowed a market day only once a month and often only once in two months. Debts incurred in this way were then deducted from the immigrants' wages.[85] Another practice was for the estate management to delay paying their laborers, sometimes for as long as seven weeks.[86] It is possible that the delayed payment of wages was designed to keep free laborers working steadily on the estates since they were unlikely to move away before being paid. But it was certainly intended to force laborers to resort to credit provided by the supervisory staff.

In Tobago in the late 1880s those sugar proprietors who still employed wage laborers on their estates turned to the credit and truck systems in an attempt to cope with the crisis in the sugar industry. The sharp fall in the price of muscovado sugar on the international market in 1884 had resulted in the collapse of the London firm of Gillespie Brothers, which had provided more than half of Tobago's sugar estates with credit and supplies.[87] In this situation the proprietors, who were almost always merchants of some description, used credit and truck to reduce labor costs. The laborers' objections were noted in an editorial in the *San Fernando Gazette* of 9 February 1889, which urged "the substitution of cash payments for labor generally, instead of the system of advancing merchants' goods to the laborer and then at pay-day to impound his earnings in payment of the same."

Although the examples of the operation of the credit and truck systems in the British West Indies have not been discussed in equal detail, it is possible to make certain generalizations. A common feature of these colonies was that those members of the lower classes who were involved in the market economy usually needed loans for production and consumption. In the absence of financial institutions to cater to their credit needs, they resorted to informal sources of credit—mainly landlords, employers, or entrepreneurs with whom they were associated. The need for advances to cover subsistence made the laborer vulnerable to control and manipulation by the employer class and facilitated the emergence of credit and truck systems. It may be argued that these systems of labor control appeared in those British West Indian colonies where the roles of employer, landlord, or entrepreneur and of supplier of subsistence and production loans were combined in a single individual and where there were few alternative opportunities for employment.

The ability to offer employment and credit undoubtedly gave a measure of coercive authority to the employer (as the cases of Belize and the Bahamas clearly demonstrate), but the existence of a narrow range of employment opportunity was a necessary condition for the successful operation of the credit and truck systems. In Jamaica, for example, there were planters who owned and operated plantation stores in the postemancipation years. A truck system appeared, however, only in the 1860s, when laborers were forced to rely on estate employment because of drought and high food prices.[88] It is also significant that in British Guiana and Trinidad the credit and truck systems were applied to indentured Indian immigrants who were restricted, by the terms of their contracts, to laboring on the estates to which they were assigned.

In a discussion of the systems of domination in the British West Indies after slavery, O. Nigel Bolland has argued that "the entire question of the relation of the control of land and the control of labor is dialectically connected throughout the Caribbean."[89] Our analysis of the situation in the Bahamas has shown, however, that the restriction of access to land was not essential to the creation of a stable labor force. The key to the control that the Bahamian agrocommercial bourgeoisie exercised over labor lay in its monopoly of capital in an economy where forms of nonwage payment were widely used and where, as a result, the laboring classes depended on credit. It was the credit system that drew the subsistence-oriented Out Islander into the market economy, into a cycle of debt, and thereby into steady labor for the merchant-investor. In the pineapple industry, merchants extracted labor not only from tenants on the share system but also from peasant proprietors through the credit and truck systems. It can be argued that the establishment of credit relations between the peasant proprietor and the merchant involved a "concealed sale of labor power."[90] In the Bahamas, the credit and truck systems were important elements of an intensified labor coercion in the slow and oppressive transition from slavery and subsistence farming to a system of wages and markets.

Chapter Seven

RACE, CLASS, AND URBAN POLICING

The extensive control that the white mercantile minority came to exercise over the colony's economy and its labor force in the postemancipation years was reinforced by its ability to shape policy on the systems of social control.[1] This small elite dominated the colonial state, which had a monopoly of both law-making and coercive agencies like the police.[2] As a result, the police force (reflecting the priorities of the propertied classes) functioned primarily as an agency for guaranteeing a stable business environment for the exploitation of the colony's resources by the late nineteenth century. An important aspect of the police force's duties was to suppress internal disorder, which might threaten the lives and property of the dominant class. Thus it helped to preserve the "established hierarchical relationships" of colonial society.[3]

The problems of social control—policing—were not new. Social control had been a basic and inescapable difficulty of slave society itself; how best to regulate and maintain order on the plantations and in the urban setting had been a perennial worry for the slave-owning and colonial orders. In fact, policing activities were central to the maintenance of the slave systems throughout the British Caribbean.[4] As Elsa V. Goveia observed in her discussion of the West Indian slave laws of the eighteenth century, "the experience of the British colonies makes it particularly clear that police regulations lay at the very heart of the slave system and that without them the system itself became difficult to maintain."[5] This problem clearly changed with the coming of black freedom, but in societies where colonial elites attempted to maintain the existing social and economic order, policing remained a major concern.[6] This chapter examines the reorganization of the police force in the Bahamas between 1888 and 1893. The discussions about this reorganization, involving members of the white ruling class and colonial and metropolitan officials, reflect the perspectives of those groups on the role of the police in colonial society and also provide some insight into techniques of control that were more widely employed throughout the British Empire in the nineteenth and twentieth centuries.

The question of reorganizing the police force in the Bahamas was raised by the secretary of state for the colonies, Lord Knutsford, in 1888. He suggested that a strengthened police force would be a suitable replacement for a detachment of the West India Regiment, whose withdrawal from the colony was imminent.[7] The withdrawal of the scattered detachments of the regiment from the Bahamas, British Honduras, Barbados, Trinidad, and British Guiana had been recommended in 1881 by a royal commission appointed in 1879 to study and make recommendations for improving the defense of British commerce and colonies. The commission had suggested that these detachments should instead be concentrated in the colonies of Jamaica and St. Lucia, which were of greater strategic importance.[8]

In his response to Knutsford's suggestion, Sir Ambrose Shea, governor of the colony, expressed the view that the internal security of the colony might be undermined rather than improved by any attempts to strengthen the police force. He warned that in any disturbances in which race was a factor (in his view such disturbances were an ever-present possibility), a more efficient police force recruited locally might take sides with the black population:

> In the proposal to increase the Police organization as a substitute for the Military Force I feel there lies a danger that the public security would be weakened and not confirmed by such a Measure. While I see no reason to complain of the general conduct of the black population, I am without much faith in the temper they would exhibit on any occasion in which their race prejudices were excited, and when I consider that it is this class from which the present Force is drawn and any addition to it must also come, I see a peril in the increased efficiency their training would give them with the great probability that it would be found in the time of trial on the wrong side.[9]

Shea's views on the probability of disturbances were (as he admitted) not new; other colonial governors had expressed similar misgivings earlier in that decade. In fact, these views had formed an important part of the arguments advanced by the governors for retaining the military forces after the Colonial Office had announced that the garrison would be withdrawn.[10] In most cases these concerns were based on a racial stereotype of "the black and coloured peoples" as easily excitable and with little power of self-control.[11] These ideas, as they related to the Bahamian context, were most clearly expressed by Sir Charles Lees in a dispatch to the Earl of Kimberley in December 1882, in which he said: "The population of the Bahamas is docile and law-abiding but your Lordship is aware that it is almost entirely composed of a race easily excited, and when under the influence of passion, capable of but little self control."[12]

Official attitudes toward the withdrawal of the troops in the 1880s, however, were largely shaped by the views of the white mercantile elite, which had controlled the economic and political levers of power in the Bahamas since the period of slavery.[13] In the Bahamas there were none of the divisions in the ruling class that existed in England, where, at this stage, there was a "complex competition for political power and social influence by different class factions."[14] This ruling group had homogeneous interests and was, moreover, bound by family ties and a similarity of social attitudes. The political dominance of this group was aptly described in 1888 by L. D. Powles, who observed that "the House of Assembly is a little less than a family gathering of Nassau whites, nearly all of whom are related to each other by blood or marriage."[15] The local black and colored population had, however, no countervailing influence in official circles.

In 1888 Shea's opposition to the withdrawal of the troops and the strengthening of the police force reflected in part the opinions of this influential white minority. As he observed in a dispatch to Knutsford in November of that year, "the feeling is universal among the white population that if left to a black Police Force with their local sympathies and connections, property and life would be safe only so long as there was no special incitement to a violation of the Law, and that the most dangerous element would then be found in the Police Body itself."[16]

The views of the white elite in 1888, as described by Shea, did not differ significantly from this class's earlier position on the withdrawal of the troops. In 1885 all the members of the House of Assembly had signed a memorial to Governor Henry Blake that asked for a reconsideration of the decision to withdraw the garrison. As they pointed out, "Such a step as this we cannot but regard as one that will be absolutely fatal to the future progress of the Colony; its good government will be placed in jeopardy, and insecurity to life and property will, under these circumstances universally prevail."[17]

Although the members of the House did not identify the source of their disquiet in that memorial, they regarded the threat of internal disorder as coming primarily from the "black and coloured peoples" whom they perceived as hostile to the white minority. These fears of the white population were reflected in a comment made by Blake in a dispatch of August 1885: "While I cannot speak too highly of the general conduct of the population, the fact remains that there is a strong feeling on the part of the black and coloured peoples against the white population of Nassau. I have heard this from too many sources to have any doubt on the subject."[18]

An incident of 1886 in which a black policeman had been shot by an insane white man had further convinced the white population of the likelihood of social disorder stemming from racial antagonism.[19] On that occasion the hostility of the black population toward the white Bahamians was apparent. As L. D. Powles reported, "A member of the New York Yacht Club, who knows the Bahamas thoroughly once said to me, 'I was here the day Sands was arrested and I never shall forget it as long as I live! No one who saw that crowd could doubt there was an undercurrent of race hatred with which the White Conchs will have to reckon sooner or later.'"[20] United by their fear of the black majority, the whites were opposed to the augmentation of a police force recruited from the local population.

Although Shea did not share the exaggerated racial fears of the white Bahamians, he was concerned that the colony's fragile prosperity, based on the production of sisal, should not be jeopardized by social upheaval. During his tenure as governor he had promoted sisal as the solution to the colony's social and economic problems and had done much to attract British capital investment to the colony.[21] Shea recognized, however, that the continued influx of capital would depend on the maintenance of a stable business environment.[22] It was for all these reasons that he concluded that the withdrawal of the troops would be a dangerous experiment, especially since the colony was not linked to the outside world by telegraph. He suggested that the security needs of the colony might be met by stationing a gunboat there and urged Knutsford to take "the improved economic prospects" of the colony into account in making a decision on the matter.[23]

The Colonial Office's response to Shea's plea for the retention of the troops in the Bahamas was generally unsympathetic. Colonial Office officials took the view that the maintenance of internal order was the responsibility of the colonial rather than the imperial government. It was also felt that imperial defence considerations took precedence over the domestic concerns of the individual colonies. Edward Wingfield observed, for example, in a minute of 19 December 1888, "It seems to be generally agreed that there is a strong antipathy of the black population to the small handful of whites in the Bahamas which does not exist in anything like the same degree in any other Colony—but they cannot expect the Imperial Govt. to maintain troops there merely to preserve internal order."[24] Similar sentiments were expressed by Major George S. Clarke, secretary of the Colonial Defence Committee, who had been asked to comment on this question: "The idea that imperial troops are to [be] employed to police colonies in peace time cannot be entertained for a moment. I think this might be pointed out. But, further, it is on a handful of *black* troops that the community now appears to rely & for the retention of which it pleads. I cannot see why a 'black man' called a soldier is a better safeguard against disorder than his brother a little differently dressed and called a policeman."[25]

In his comments on the black man as soldier and policeman, Clarke demonstrated an ignorance of the reasons for the West India Regiment's effectiveness in defending the social and political order in the Bahamas up to that point. The West India Regiment had been kept loyal and dependable by a deliberate policy of recruiting its members from several ethnic groups from Africa and from different West Indian colonies. This policy had been pursued since the establishment of the West India Regiments in the late eighteenth century. As Roger Norman Buckley has pointed out, "Although the West India Regiments were composed chiefly of recruits from various African nations, as well as a diminishing number of Creoles, no apparent attempt was made to form companies of Africans belonging to a single national or language group, or even of Creole soldiers. On the contrary, the *Description and Succession Books* show that companies were heterogeneously formed of, for instance, Ibos, Hausas and Creoles. The reason for this organization was, no doubt, the time-honored principle of divide and rule."[26] It is not surprising then that the West India Regiments acted to buttress the slave systems throughout the British Caribbean.

The evidence indicates that this strategy of divide and rule persisted well into the nineteenth century. In 1860 Governor Charles Bayley of the Bahamas was asked whether the soldiers of the West India Regiment stationed in the colony could be relied on for the "suppression of sedition, tumult and turbulence." He reassured the Duke of Newcastle, the secretary of state for the colonies, that the regiments could be relied on "for firmness and fidelity" in any disturbances when certain conditions (which the forces in the colony obviously satisfied) were met:

> The negro creoles, so far as I have observed, have strong local attachments. They each profess (& I believe feel) an ardent affection for the island which gave them birth; & invariably consider its attractions superior to those of the others. The Jamaica Creole despises Bahamas, the Antigua Creole Barbadoes [*sic*] & the Barbadian despises all other islands but his own. With prejudices or affections so vehement, it is evident that no Creole soldiers could safely be trusted to act by themselves against a tumultuous or seditious movement of their own countrymen in their own island. *But in any regiment moderately well disciplined and containing natives of all the*

> *islands & of Africa, the local sentiment of a part would be lost & swamped in the military subordination of the whole body* [emphasis added].[27]

After reading Bayley's dispatch, Newcastle was convinced "that if called upon to suppress internal disturbances the difficulty would be not to stimulate but to restrain the eagerness of Black Troops."[28]

In 1866, after the Morant Bay rebellion in Jamaica (which had been brutally suppressed by white imperial troops), a request for comments on the reliability of black troops in the event of a disturbance was made by the secretary of state for the colonies, Edward Cardwell, and evoked a response similar to Bayley's quoted above. After consulting with the members of his executive council, Governor Rawson reiterated Bayley's view that "Black Troops may be relied upon as an efficient Force for repressing Black Populations." In fact, it was generally agreed that the recent events in Jamaica had confirmed that view.[29]

The Colonial Office's position on the withdrawal of the West India Regiment was clearly stated in a dispatch from Knutsford to Shea in January 1889. Knutsford pointed out that it was the duty of the colonial government to make suitable arrangements in anticipation of the withdrawal of the troops, which would remain in the Bahamas only for a limited time. He also suggested (on Clarke's recommendation) that the members of the police force, like the troops, might be recruited from the West Indian colonies "to prevent any feeling of local sympathy between [the] Police and the inhabitants of the Bahamas."[30] As that recommendation indicates, both colonial and metropolitan officials were concerned about recruiting men for the police force from outside the colony, believing outsiders unlikely to become emotionally involved in the event of civil disorder.

Shea did not take action to implement the Colonial Office's recommendations until November 1890, when he was convinced that the withdrawal of the garrison was imminent. By that time he had clear ideas about the composition of a reorganized and strengthened police force. In a dispatch to Knutsford in that month Shea announced his intention to recruit policemen from Barbados. This plan was prompted by the example of British Honduras, where a police force had been recruited from Barbados to replace the West India Regiment and had been found satisfactory. Shea also expressed an interest in securing the services of a contingent of Sikhs who would account for twelve of the seventy to eighty policemen whom the colonial government proposed to enlist.[31]

Shea's proposal to enlist Sikhs for the police force demonstrates the tendency to apply more widely the techniques of control used in one area of the British Empire. His suggestion was clearly based on the reputation of the Sikhs as a loyal fighting force. In the aftermath of the Indian Mutiny, when the Indian Army became essentially an army of occupation, the native element in the reorganized army was recruited mainly from "the martial races" of the Punjab and Nepal, who had demonstrated their loyalty during the campaigns of the mutiny.[32] Sikhs and Gurkhas were subsequently employed in other parts of the British Empire in Africa and Asia.[33] In Africa, for example, the military establishments that accompanied the extension of British rule in the late nineteenth and early twentieth centuries relied on Indian troops. As William F. Gutteridge has observed, "In parts of East Africa, especially Nyasaland, the nucleus of army units was actually formed by Sikh volunteers from the Indian army, who in some cases remained in Africa until 1911."[34] In 1890, however, there were no precedents for combining blacks and Indians in the ranks of the military or police forces.[35]

Shea's proposal to recruit Sikhs was received with little enthusiasm at the Colonial Office. In his response to Shea, Knutsford advised that the employment of Sikhs would be very expensive and expressed the view that even if they could be induced to serve in the small numbers Shea proposed, it was uncertain how they would interact with a West Indian population and with their "comrades" in the police force. Knutsford concurred, however, with Shea's view that it would be best to recruit the police force from outside the Bahamas. He also agreed that Barbados would be the best center for recruitment, but he called Shea's attention to a recent report by Major General Goodenough on the defense of the West Indies, which had pointed to the advantages of recruiting forces from a wide area in the British West Indies. Goodenough had observed, "The more the field is enlarged the better the chance of selection of good men, and of having in the ranks men of various pursuits and more extended experience."[36]

The main purpose of the legislation of July 1891 that provided for the organization of a new constabulary in the Bahamas was to create a police force that would eventually be recruited entirely from abroad. Under this act a constabulary force was established that was quite distinct from the existing force.[37] It was anticipated that the police force would be gradually phased out by the resignation of its members and their enlistment in the new constabulary. But the conditions of service in the new constabulary were made deliberately unattractive so that the members of the police force would be unlikely to enlist in it.[38] For example, the salary of a constable was set at £36 per year instead of £52, which a member of the existing police force received.[39] Although the number of the constables was initially fixed at forty, it was expected that this figure would eventually be increased to seventy-five. The officers of this force consisted of a commandant, one inspector, one subinspector, one sergeant, and two corporals.[40]

The new constabulary was, by design, distinctly military in character. In the first place, the constables (like the troops) were isolated in barracks away from the local population.[41] The Constabulary Act specified that members of the constabulary in Nassau had to reside in barracks. This rule extended even to subofficers and constables, granted permission to marry, who were assigned quarters in the barracks. The desire to prevent constables from forming local ties of friendship or romance, evident in the rules on accommodation, also prompted the regulations relating to marriage. These regulations pointed out that "with the sanction of the Governor upon the recommendation of the Commandant, the Sub-officers, and a proportion of the Constables not exceeding ten per cent., or such lesser number as there may be accommodation for in Barracks may be enrolled upon the strength of the Force as married with leave."[42]

Second, the constabulary was expected to perform primarily military functions. It was envisaged as an organization of last resort whose members would be specially trained to suppress social unrest rather than as a body whose main duty would be to police the local population. These ideas were clearly conveyed in a comment by the colony's attorney general in his report on the Constabulary Act in July 1891: "For some time at least there must be the two forces, one doing civil duty entirely, the other isolated and kept in Barracks, performing when necessary and advisable civil duty as a Police, but especially trained and disciplined, and kept in hand for any emergency."[43] The role of the constabulary in the Bahamas, at this stage, may be usefully compared with that of the army in colonial Africa, which, as Gutteridge has written, "because of its isolation, concentration and exclusiveness is the reserve line in maintenance of internal security."[44]

Several factors may be adduced to explain the quasi-military character of the constabulary. First, policy makers at the colonial level expected that the new security force would perform functions similar to those performed by the troops it replaced. As Shea had observed in January 1891, "the new Constabulary force recruited from abroad and living in Barracks should be equal to all the requirements for the preservation of internal order."[45] Second, the military character of the constabulary reflected the experience of the colonial secretary, Captain H. M. Jackson, who was mainly responsible for the reorganization of the police force. He had pursued a military career in the Royal Artillery before he entered the colonial service. Between 1880 and 1884 Jackson had served as inspector general of police in Sierra Leone, where he had reorganized the police force. He had also been sent on special service to the Gold Coast in 1881 in connection with the threatened Ashanti invasion.[46] In this early period of colonial rule in Africa, as Gutteridge has observed, "the distinction between police and army was hard to draw."[47] In Sierra Leone, for example, the police force was often used to "pacify" the inland peoples as the British extended their control into the interior from the coast. Finally, the character of the constabulary was determined by the police forces on which it had been modeled, because in both British Honduras and Sierra Leone the police force was at this stage a paramilitary body.[48]

Although attempts were made to extend the field for recruiting, as General Goodenough had recommended, the members of the new constabulary were eventually recruited exclusively from Barbados. The inspector general of constabulary in Jamaica, on being consulted, had expressed the opinion that suitable recruits from that colony were unlikely to be attracted by the low salaries being offered in the Bahamas. Jackson also took the view that since the troops were due to be withdrawn from the Bahamas by November 1891 at the latest, the matter of recruitment should not be delayed by enlisting and training members of the constabulary in several different places. He recognized, moreover, that recruits coming from the same colony would form a more cohesive force. He observed that "it would be . . . of unquestionable advantage that the new force, before entering on their duties here, be accustomed to work together, and be bound together by the tie of a common country."[49]

Jackson was almost certainly influenced in his choice of Barbados as the main constabulary recruitment center by his own experiences with Barbadians in West Africa. In fact, Jackson's observations about the Barbadians suggest that he regarded them as the West Indian counterparts of the "martial races" of India:

> I have had some experience of Barbadians, having had detachments of West India Regts. under my command in bush fighting in West Africa, and having also had a nucleus of them in the Sierra Leone Police, a force which I entirely recognized. During the tribal disturbances in Freetown in the end of 1883, when the police had to turn out with sidearms nearly every night for some weeks I specially selected these men for difficult and dangerous work, and I never found them wanting in discipline, though they were of course exciteable as the coloured race usually are. The Police Force of Barbados is of proved efficiency and there are many natives of Barbados in the Trinidad Police which is an excellent Force.[50]

In the Bahamas of the late nineteenth century, the white elite was not embarrassed to admit the direct link between property interests and the formation of the new constabulary. Thus a select committee of the House of Assembly, reporting in 1893 on the progress of the colony during the previous five years, noted, "A well-appointed Force was recruited at Barbados, and is now quartered in the Barracks at Nassau; a guarantee both to the local public and to investors abroad, that their interests will be safeguarded by an efficient administration of the law."[51]

In the years after 1891 the response of the local population to the Barbadian constabulary was hostile. This initial hostility may be explained by the fact that the Barbadians were strangers. As early as September 1892 Jackson noted that "the marked hostility evinced by the natives of Nassau to strangers has rendered the command of the dual force of native police and of constabulary enlisted abroad, one of exceptional difficulty."[52] The strained relations culminated in disturbances, involving the constables and members of the local population, that broke out in the black suburb of Grant's Town on 15 April 1893. In a memorandum on the causes of the disturbances Jackson suggested other sources of the hostility toward the constabulary. It was a common complaint that the constables were aggressive and "unnecessarily rough" in their treatment of prisoners. Jackson also pointed out that the members of the old police force resented the newcomers: "The second cause of hostility appears to be the not unnatural dislike to the new Force, felt by the members of the old Police Force, who know that they are to be gradually replaced by the Constabulary and thus feel themselves looked on as an inferior Force. They regard the Constabulary as interlopers, who are taking the bread out of their mouths depriving them and their friends of a convenient means of earning a livelihood and in any case of friction with the people they might be expected to side with the latter."

Official awareness of the widespread resentment of the constabulary by black Bahamians influenced the way the police force was reorganized after the disturbances. The main suggestions for changes in the force came from Jackson, who was anxious to remove the sources of hostility to the Barbadians. He recommended that the old police force be allowed to survive and be given clearly defined duties relating primarily to the policing of the suburbs, where they would deal directly with their fellow Bahamians. The main responsibility of the constabulary, however, should remain the protection of the property interests of the white minority. Jackson's conception of this division of "control work" between the police force and the constabulary was articulated in the memorandum to which we have already referred: "Any collision between the police & people is more likely to occur in the suburbs, & by placing those in charge of a permanent and improved Force of police recruited wholly locally, risk of such collisions would be minimized, while for the protection of that part of the town where property of large value would be endangered by a riot, or for the suppression of any organized disturbance in the suburbs, the better drilled & disciplined Force would always be together and at hand for use as a combined body under its own officers."

In this plan for reorganization, the military aspects of the constabulary were once again emphasized. Jackson proposed, for example, that the constabulary be split into three divisions. It was anticipated that one division would be on street duty, one off duty, and the third on reserve. It is difficult to escape the conclusion, after reading Jackson's proposal, that the constabulary was kept in a state of preparedness to handle any domestic crisis that might arise: "One Division would be on Street duty at a time, & the Division off duty should join the general daily drill, and after that be allowed to rest and go on pass, &c., while the Division next for duty should be in barracks as a reserve, and should not be allowed on pass but should supply all necessary barrack fatigues & be available for special messengers, fire duties, &c. The two Divisions not on street duty combined would form a sufficiently large body to gain the full benefit of drills & exercises in becoming well accustomed to work together."[53]

Such a state of preparedness was, in Jackson's view, warranted by the likelihood of popular disturbances. While he was willing to concede that most members of the "colored class" were law-abiding, he believed that the danger of disorder came from a permanent "lawless class": "The large majority of the coloured class is, and will continue to be, on the side of law and order, but there will always exist a certain lawless class, to be influenced by unscrupulous persons for their own ends, & therefore there must always remain risk of popular disturbances, a factor to be borne in mind in settling the organization of the police Force."[54]

Given the considerations that informed official policy on the reorganization of the police force, it is not surprising that the propertied classes came to repose confidence in the constabulary. As the committee of the executive council that had investigated the Grant's Town disturbances observed of the constabulary, "these men, under efficient officers, are capable of being converted into a well disciplined Force; quite sufficient, in conjunction with the Police and with an occasional visit of a Gunboat, to protect the various interests committed to its charge."[55]

The way the police force was reorganized has more than local significance; it demonstrates techniques of control that were used by the colonial authorities at the periphery of the British Empire. The recruitment of Barbadians to serve as constables in the Bahamas was in the imperial tradition of selecting agents of control from among the colonized. A key element in this control was that men recruited in one area were often deployed to keep the natives of another area in check.[56] Throughout the nineteenth century, for example, the West India Regiments were used extensively in West Africa to subdue the indigenous peoples.[57] In India the preservation of British control after the Mutiny depended on the support of "the martial races" of the Punjab and Nepal. Native African troops or *askaris* were also used by European governments in their efforts to conquer and control the African continent in the late nineteenth and early twentieth centuries.[58] In all these contexts the colonial state deftly manipulated religious, caste, ethnic, and community differences in a successful attempt to exert control on behalf of a dominant economic class that was often nonresident.

Chapter Eight

MERCHANT HEGEMONY AND THE MAKING OF IMMIGRATION POLICY

The mercantile oligarchy's control over the lawmaking process in the colony's House of Assembly allowed its members to consolidate their position as a ruling class. Laws and government policies often reflected their class interests and concerns. This chapter examines one example of the merchants' involvement in policy making: the enactment of restrictive immigration legislation in 1928 and other laws in the early 1930s that were designed to limit economic competition from "trading minorities."[1] In this instance, laws were clearly used to defend the existing social and economic order.

The earliest demand for restrictions on immigration to the Bahamas was made in 1925 by R. J. Bowe, a businessman and member of the House of Assembly for Exuma. At a meeting of the House on 30 April of that year Bowe proposed the appointment of a select committee that would consider, among other things, the advisability of allowing only first-class passengers of incoming ships who were not natives of the colony to enter the colony. Such a committee would also consider the question of the "total exclusion of Chinese, Syrians, Turks, Arabs, Gypsies, Hindoos and Egyptians."[2]

Bowe's proposals for measures to restrict immigration were prompted, as he later explained, by the examples of the colonies of Jamaica and Bermuda. In Bermuda, laws restricting immigration had been passed by 1925. It was, however, the Jamaican experience with the Chinese and the Lebanese that provided Bowe with evidence supporting his demand that these minorities be excluded from the Bahamas. He was convinced that Jamaicans were forced to emigrate primarily because of the economic activities of those trading minorities. As he observed in a letter to the *Nassau Guardian* in December 1926, "Is there any wonder that you have Jamaicans coming to this country in such large numbers? They are being pushed out of their own country by Celestials from the Far East and 'Jewestials' from the Near East. I have seen Jamaicans in nearly every place I have visited even on the Isthmus of Tehuantepec, driven to seek a living in an alien country by foreigners, permitted to enter by a Crown Colony Government much against the wishes and protests of the native Jamaican."[3]

It was the economic success of the Chinese and Lebanese in Jamaica that alerted Bowe to the challenge that the "middleman minorities," already resident in the Bahamas, could pose to native businessmen.[4] In his 1925 speech proposing the appointment of the select committee to consider the immigration issue, Bowe pointed to the possible dangers from the Chinese and the inroads that the Greeks and Lebanese had already made in commerce. As a House of Assembly report states, Bowe "thought that before they knew it there would be a colony of Chinese here who would capture the entire grocery and dry goods trade of the Colony. The sponge industry was entirely in the hands of Greeks and there were a number of Syrians here some of whom used to live in stables when they first arrived and could now buy the whole property." Bowe's proposals were received with little enthusiasm by his fellow legislators and by the articulate members of the wider society. Assemblyman L. W. Young seconded Bowe's motion for the appointment of a select committee on immigration but was mainly concerned to keep out "certain people such as gypsies who came here and practised their arts among the people." Whereas Bowe regarded the presence of these minorities as a threat to native businessmen, R. T. Symonette, a wealthy businessman, was inclined to view this economic competition as the natural consequence of the free enterprise system: Symonette thought "if people came here and took business away from the local people they ought to be given credit for doing it. He would like to see some more live business men come here."[5]

A select committee was appointed in April to consider the immigration issue, and a bill was eventually drafted that would prohibit the landing in the colony of any immigrant who was a "Chinaman, Syrian, Turk, Arab or Gipsy or of any other immigrant who has been sentenced for a felony or misdemeanour without the consent of the Governor."[6] When Bowe moved for a second reading of this bill, however, a motion was adopted that postponed its discussion for six months.[7]

Although Bowe's proposals on immigration restrictions were not adopted, he defined the parameters of the debate on the immigration issue. Later in the decade there would be demands for the restriction of immigration from the West Indian colonies, especially Jamaica, but the question of the middleman minorities remained central to the debate. It is to the history of these immigrant groups in the Bahamas and the patterns of their participation in the economic life of the colony that we must now turn.

Certain features of the political and economic structure of the Bahamas have a direct bearing on our discussion of the economic activities of these immigrant groups. Those immigrants who arrived in the colony in the late nineteenth and early twentieth centuries found a society controlled by the white merchant class, which exercised extensive political and economic power. By the late nineteenth century, the formal political structures had long been dominated by that group. White control of the House of Assembly was maintained by the use of the open ballot and bribery of the electorate rather than by a restrictive franchise.[8] In 1917 Sir William Allardyce, then governor of the colony, was prepared to admit that "the colony is really run by a few merchants in Bay Street who are Members of the House of Assembly and control a majority of votes there." He further noted the difficulties involved in offering advice to members of the legislature in a self-governing colony: "I do what I can to guide them, I periodically render advice officially and otherwise, I endeavour to influence them to the best of my ability when I get the opportunity to do so, but as a *SELF-GOVERNING COLONY* they are hypersensitive of advice and the debates? . . . in the House clearly indicate this."[9] The decisions of the Executive Council also reflected the will of the ruling local clique. Although the Letters Patent of the Governor indicated that the function of the Executive Council was solely advisory, a local law provided that the "Governor-in-Council means the Governor acting by and with the advice of the Executive Council."[10] The implication of this legislation was pointed out by Sir Alan Burns, who had served as colonial secretary of the Bahamas in the 1920s: "As there is generally an unofficial majority in the Bahamas Executive Council, and as most of these officials are members of the House of Assembly, the legislature also, to some extent, controls the executive."[11]

The economic dominance of this small ruling group was, as was previously argued, based on ownership of land (though not a monopoly over it), its function as the major source of credit for the majority of the population, its role as middleman in the import-export trade, and its control of retailing. Members of the merchant class also prospered in the early twentieth century from involvement in bootlegging activities during the Prohibition years, the development of tourism, and the real estate and construction boom that was an extension of land speculation in Florida.[12] Immigrant groups like the Chinese, Greek, and Lebanese, which ventured into commercial and other business activities, thus found themselves in direct competition with the local merchants.

The Greeks

The first group of Greeks entered the Bahamas in December 1887 to engage in the sponge trade. Although the evidence suggests that this group of twenty-four men had external financial backing, there is no precise information to link their venture to a particular firm.[13] It is likely, however, that the sponsor was the Vouvalis Company, packers and exporters of sponges, which had established a business in London in 1882. This company is known to have been one of the first major firms to establish a sponge business and warehouse in the Bahamas. Originally a Greek-based company, Vouvalis expanded its operations in the late nineteenth and early twentieth centuries to include Africa, Cuba, the Bahamas, and Florida, which were major sponging centers.[14]

The arrival of this group of Greeks was immediately perceived by Bahamian sponge merchants as a threat to local control of the sponge fisheries. In a letter to the *Nassau Guardian* in December 1887, "J.B." (the initials of Joseph Brown, a leading sponge merchant) observed, "Twenty four aliens have arrived, experts in the gathering, clipping and packing of sponge, and if I am rightly informed, determined to handle it themselves in all stages from the gathering to the packing, thus excluding native labour. If the experiment should be successful, it is quite probable that we should soon have hundreds of men in our midst, whose ways are not our ways, who would form a distinct section of the population, and who would only continue to remain here until such time as the sponge beds become exhausted or the business ceases to be profitable."[15]

The letter from "J.B." went on to suggest that a law should be enacted to protect the sponge fisheries against the "encroachment of aliens." A plea for protective measures was also made in a letter written in a spurious "dialect" by "Efrum Clark," a sponger, in the same issue of the *Nassau Guardian:* "i ain got de time to rite you a long letter bekors ise gwine on a vyge, but i hear say dat sum grekes is kum to go a spungin an i tink dat it is a hard kase to low furinirs to kum here an spile our biznis an our livin an i hope dat de majoritis will look into dis ting an arks de house of semli to look into dis ting an put a stop to dese grekses an purwent dere getting spung." One suspects that this letter was also written by "J.B." to dramatize the threat that the entry of Greeks in the sponging industry represented to the native spongers.[16]

A further demand for protective legislation against the economic competition of the Greeks was made in a petition signed by 14 of the 29 members of the House of Assembly and 141 other citizens and presented to the governor of the colony, Sir Ambrose Shea, in March 1888. The arguments presented in this petition in support of the suggested legislation emphasized not only the need to protect local resources from foreign intrusion but also the dangers of attracting foreigners who would not easily be integrated into Bahamian society:

> We are quite sensible of the advantages that may be derived from persons of foreign birth settling among us if their object is to make this their permanent home to amalgamate with our people, and willing to become citizens, thus bearing their share of those burdens which it is necessary to impose for the preservation of law and order. Such a class of emigrants we should welcome as a desirable addition to our population. But it is evident that the Greeks who have or may come here can never be made amenable to such conditions, as difference of race and language both forbid—so they can have but one object, and one only, and that is to gather that product of nature which has hitherto been the backbone of our prosperity, and upon which the very existence of a large portion of this community exists.[17]

This early attempt by Greek interests to gain a footing in the Bahamian sponging industry by introducing Greek spongers was unsuccessful. As a report of April 1889 by the American consul in Nassau, Thomas J. McLain, Jr., noted, "The experiment of introducing fishermen from the Mediterranean towards the close of 1887, which caused great indignation and much local excitement at the time, proved an utter failure. After a few months' trial the Greek spongers were withdrawn it having been shown that they could not compete with the natives, and those who had embarked in the undertaking suffered a considerable loss in both time and money."[18]

It is most likely that the unsuccessful experiment with Greek spongers in the late 1880s determined the later role of the Greeks in the Bahamas sponge trade. With their expertise in the selection of sponges, their knowledge of the market, and their international marketing connections, later Greek immigrants concentrated on buying, packing, and exporting sponges. Initially many of these immigrants came to the Bahamas as buying agents for the Vouvalis Company. Among them were Theophanese Tiliacos, Pericles Maillis, Nicholas and Theophilous Mangos, and George Miaoulis.[19] Some of these immigrants eventually established their own sponge businesses after they had accumulated some savings. One of the earliest independent buyers of sponges was George Damianos, who established his business as early as 1890.[20] The date of the establishment of his business suggests that he was among the original group of Greek immigrants who arrived in the Bahamas in 1887. Other early Greek buyers of sponges included the Christofilises, Christopher Esfakis, and Pericles Maillis.[21] By 1924 the Greek community had established its control over the buying and exporting end of the sponge trade. An editorial in the *Nassau Tribune* in August of that year noted that the Greeks "practically control the sponge business of the island" and estimated that they spent approximately £20,000 annually in wages.[22] Despite their growing economic importance, the Greeks were not accepted socially by the white Bahamian elite.[23]

Although most Greeks tended to engage in the sponge trade, by the 1920s they had begun to venture into other areas of business. Theophilous Mangos, for example, established the Model Bakery in 1924. By 1927 there were four branches of this bakery, and Mangos had opened the Parisian Store, which, with its stock of ladies' wear imported from Paris and its perfumes, catered to the lucrative tourist trade.[24] Some Greek immigrants operated stores that sold fresh fruits and vegetables imported from the United States. The first of these was the California Fruit Store, which was owned by M. G. Bantouvanis.[25] By 1930 there were two other fruit stores owned by Greeks, the Olympia Fruit Store and the Acropolis.[26]

Another area of Greek enterprise was the restaurant business, which was primarily dependent on the winter tourist trade. In 1926 D. N. Photiades, who had previously operated the Central Lunch Stand, operated a fruit and vegetable delicatessen and light lunch business called The Grand Central.[27] Other restaurants owned by Greeks included the Bahamas Restaurant, which was operated by Steve Plakaris & Company, and the Prince George Restaurant, whose proprietor was Jim Glico.[28]

By 1925 the Greek community was firmly established in the Bahamas. Although the sponge trade had acted as the original attraction for Greek immigrants, the sharp increase in the size of the community after World War I was due largely to the arrival of individuals who joined friends and family members who had migrated earlier.[29] This increase is clearly discernible from the censuses of population for the Bahamas. Greeks were not listed separately in these censuses, but it is reasonable to assume that the category "those born in other parts of Europe" referred mainly to them. In the census for 1911 there were only 30 persons in that category.[30] This increased only to 47 by 1921.[31] By 1931, however, the number had risen to 131, or .2 percent of the entire population.[32] In 1930 there were still only 11 Greek families in the colony.[33]

The Lebanese

The first Lebanese came to the Bahamas in the 1890s. They were part of a significant exodus of Christian minorities escaping from Turkish misrule in Syria, which then belonged to the Ottoman Empire. It has been estimated that between 1870 and 1900 approximately a million people emigrated from that territory.[34] By the 1880s and 1890s there was "a formidable movement" of Lebanese into the Americas.[35]

The Amourys and the Bakers were among the first Lebanese to arrive in the Bahamas. It is known that Joseph Kalil Amoury came to the Bahamas in 1891 and established a business in 1895.[36] A store owned by the Baker family was established as early as 1894. In the Bahamas, as in other parts of the world where they settled, the Lebanese started out as itinerant peddlers before they engaged in "retail trade of a more fixed variety."[37] Newspaper references to the early business activities of the Lebanese immigrants in the Bahamas confirm this. The *Nassau Guardian* in May 1897 carried this item on the street-vending activities of the Lebanese:

> Dialogue Heard on Bay St. between Mr. Wellred, a Distinguished Traveller, and Mr. Bornhere a Citizen.
>
> Mr. W.—And who is that bandit-looking gentleman disposing of small wares, while I am informed that shopkeepers are not allowed to place even a box on the sidewalk?
>
> Mr. B.—a Greek, Syrian or some other nation like that.[38]

In May 1902, a writer who signed himself "Shopkeeper" complained in a letter to the *Nassau Guardian* about the peddling activities of the Lebanese:

> Now, this morning I went in the Public Market and drew No. 7 [a policeman] attention to one of these Assyrians in the Fish Market going from stall to stall selling Singlets and Shirts, and I explained to him how I was ordered to take in anything exposed in the Public streets and told him to report it. When he answered they are Pedlers [*sic*]. They are different from you—there again outside on the eastern side of the Fish Market was a man with two barrels—Rice, Sugar and Grits in fact a regular Grocery store with scales and weights—and on the western side was a man with a wheelbarrow with Matches, Tinware, ect. [*sic*]."[39]

The evidence indicates that these peddling activities by Lebanese immigrants continued into the 1920s. One informant remembered that in 1906 Lebanese peddlers with satchels on their backs hawked dry goods from house to house in Nassau and traveled to the Out Islands, where they supplied the people with pins, buttons, and cheap textiles.[40] Another informant recalled that in the 1920s some Lebanese, equipped with yardsticks, sold cloth outside the Market Range.[41] These early peddling activities were important to the later success of the Lebanese in business. It was by this method that they were able to steadily accumulate capital that they later reinvested in more ambitious enterprises. As peddlers they had small overhead expenses, and (as the quotations from the *Nassau Guardian* indicate) their selling activities were not circumscribed by the regulations affecting the shopkeepers. Important too for the later business activities of the Lebanese was the fact that as peddlers they catered to the lower end of the market and became associated in consumers' minds with inexpensive goods and value for money.

By the 1920s most of the Lebanese families, with one notable exception, had opted for the role of middleman between producers and consumers in the dry goods trade.[42] Two Lebanese-owned stores, those of J. K. Amoury and K. S. Moses, already dominated the market for inexpensive dry goods. These business concerns had certain advantages over their native competitors. Both merchants relied on low profit margins and quick turnover of goods, and both recognized the importance of advertising.[43] They also made regular sales because their owners had an insight into the psychology of the consumer that did not come as readily to the proprietors of the older established businesses. The merchandising techniques practiced by the Lebanese businessmen may be contrasted with those of the Bahamian merchants. A 1924 article in the *Nassau Tribune* pointed to the business practices of most native merchants: "Many of our merchants buy wrong. Too many profits have to be made by other handlers before it reaches them and, in some cases, too much profit is expected by the local merchant who does not realise that quick turnover and small profits is better than large profits and no business. . . . Merchants hold their goods too long. They should have periodical sales. They should find means of attracting the attention of the purchaser, of making him come to the store. This can only be accomplished by periodical sales, courtesy and advertising."[44]

Although J. K. Amoury's merchandising techniques were similar to those of K. S. Moses, Amoury's business had certain unique features. As early as 1923, Amoury was involved in the wholesale trade as well as in retailing.[45] In 1924 the Amoury Trading Company, importers, exporters, and commission merchants, had offices in New York, Nassau, and Bahia, Brazil.[46] This was a family business that supplied merchandise to the family retail outlets in Nassau and to other Nassau merchants. This is clear from a news item in the *Nassau Tribune* early in 1924: "Mr. T. J. Amoury of the Amoury Trading Co. of New York and Nassau returned in the *S.S. Miami* after having spent the Xmas season in Nassau with his family. This Company does a very large export business to all parts of the world and is a valuable asset to the Nassau merchant. The trade has grown considerably since Mr. C. T. Fajer has established an office in Nassau and conducted a campaign in person. Right methods and the goods to deliver always spell success. Mr. Fajer has both."[47]

Supplied by a family firm based in New York, J. K. Amoury had certain advantages over its competitors in the dry goods trade in Nassau. The Amoury Trading Company bought in large quantities and thus received significant discounts. The direct purchase of the products in New York eliminated the middlemen, who made the goods of competitors more costly. It is also most likely that the Amourys, having a clear idea of the products their clientele demanded, sought out those manufacturers who could supply them at the lowest prices. The regular contact with New York, a major retailing and manufacturing center, also kept the Amourys aware of the latest fashions. An advertisement for J. K. Amoury in July 1925 informed the ladies of Nassau that "Mrs. Amoury has returned from New York. This means the newest things in Colours, Styles, Patterns, etc."[48]

Another important aspect of the business activities of the Amoury Trading Company was its role as commission merchant. This was an area that had previously been the exclusive preserve of the native Bahamian merchants. The company's presence in New York must have given the Amourys the opportunity to spot market trends and secure the distribution rights for products with a large sales potential. In 1923 the company was already the representative in the Bahamas for the National Cash Register Company, Monroe Calculating and Adding Machines, the Remington Typewriter Company, Story and Clark Piano Company, and Federal "Radio."[49] Some of the products these companies produced, like the radio, were only then coming into popular use in the United States.[50]

By 1925 the Lebanese were a tiny but conspicuously successful trading minority.[51] Their economic success can be explained by a combination of competitive prices, imaginative merchandising, and business acumen. One of their strengths was that family members were usually involved in their business enterprises. The observation made about J. K. Amoury on his death in 1926 provides some clues about the Lebanese approach to business: "Aided by a help-mate of singular devotedness and ability, he built up an extensive mercantile business both here and in New York, and reared a family of 10 children, to all of whom he gave a thoroughly religious and business training."[52]

The Jews

As our discussion of the activities of the Lebanese community has demonstrated, business in Nassau became more competitive in the early 1920s. The number of Jewish businessmen in the Bahamas at that stage was insignificant, but the operations of the Home Furniture Company, which was partly owned and managed in Nassau by a Jewish family, the Garfunkels, are worth examining because they provide a further example of aggressive merchandising techniques. The Home Furniture Company was opened in Nassau in February 1923 by M. Garfunkel, who had recognized the colony's need for a store dealing exclusively in furniture. The store, a branch of a Miami-based company, was able to offer low prices to the consumer because its merchandise was purchased and shipped to Nassau in bulk. In February 1923 the *Nassau Tribune* reported an interview with Garfunkel in which he explained the reasons for his competitive edge:

> Mr. Garfunkel . . . told our reporter that his business can remain in Nassau, even if it did not show a profit, as purchases are made for two stores. Buying in large quantities as it does, the company gets 5, 10 and even 12 per cent discount, with an additional 2 per cent occasionally. Then there is a saving in freight by having goods shipped in carload lots which the smaller man cannot have, especially on dressers, buffets, chairs and rockers, beds and springs, which are bought direct from manufacturers, thus eliminating the middle man and collaring the jobbers' discounts.[53]

The techniques employed by Garfunkel to attract customers to his store ranged from regular sales and newspaper advertising to the use of promotional gimmicks and premiums. In a context where the idea of a sales promotion was unheard of and pricing strategy was inflexible, the use of these techniques could easily be perceived by native merchants as "unfair competition." Garfunkel's techniques were, however, successful with the Bahamian consumer. As the *Nassau Tribune* commented after his death in 1924, "His methods of business were strange to Nassau; his persistent and aggressive advertising; his talk and stories; his general manner and liberality made him successful in business and popular with his customers."[54] Garfunkel's son, who succeeded him as manager of the Nassau store, continued to use his father's marketing strategy.

The Chinese

The Chinese settled in the Bahamas as early as 1879. A news item in the *Nassau Guardian* in December of that year noted, "It is astonishing how the Chinese settlers are thriving in our midst. We have now about a dozen Celestials who are patterns of industry, ingenuity and perseverance." Earlier in that month one of these immigrants, Pan Young, had opened a restaurant on East Bay Street and a "Panorama of Shell-work."[55] The Chinese to whom R. J. Bowe referred in 1925, however, were not these early settlers, whose subsequent fate it is difficult to determine, but others who came to the colony in the early 1920s.

Among the early immigrants of the later period was Luis Chea, who arrived in Nassau in 1923. He came to the Bahamas from Guantanamo, Cuba. It is reasonable to assume that Chea had left there because Cuba was at that stage experiencing an economic depression and that he was attracted to the Bahamas because it was enjoying an unprecedented boom that was due to bootlegging. Chea obviously came to the colony with capital, for he was soon able to establish himself in business. In May 1923 he opened the New Chinese Restaurant, which served American and Chinese meals.[56] In December of that year he opened a Chinese laundry at the corner of Marlborough and West Streets, close to the New Colonial Hotel.[57] Chea was able to engage in these businesses despite the fact that he did not speak English. In July 1924, when he was tried on a charge of selling beer in his restaurant without a license, the court proceedings had to be translated into Spanish for him.[58]

Chea's business activities established the pattern for later Chinese immigrants. At first they concentrated on opening restaurants and laundries, businesses in which they had prior experience.[59] As new arrivals they were able to recognize the need for these services among a transient population of tourists and people involved in bootlegging activities. Unlike the Chinese in Jamaica of the same period, who catered almost exclusively to the needs of the peasantry and the wage-earners in the towns by opening groceries, the Chinese in the Bahamas initially served a floating population of visitors to the colony.[60] By 1925 the Chinese in Nassau operated three restaurants, which were all located on Bay Street, the main commercial street. The Far East Restaurant was operated by Samuel Wong.[61] In 1924 ownership of the New Chinese Restaurant changed from Chea to Samuel Wong and Henry Wing Wong.[62] Chea, who had briefly operated the Wayside Inn Cafe in 1924, owned and managed the New Canton Restaurant by 1925.[63]

Most of the Chinese immigrants who came to the Bahamas in this period worked in some capacity in the businesses owned by the Cheas and the Wongs. There were, however, a few who sought employment in the wider society. In July 1925 the *Nassau Tribune* carried an advertisement for the services of Lim Wah and Pancho Wong, Chinese contractors, carpenters, painters, and furniture and wood polishers with "many years" of experience in Austria. In September 1926 Cham Wong advertised for a position with a private family as a cook or a footman. In both cases the advertisers gave the New Chinese Restaurant as their point of contact.[64]

The Chinese, like other middleman authorities, relied on the labor of relatives and other members of their ethnic groups. This was a practice that undoubtedly kept labor costs down and allowed them to offer competitive prices. As Edna Bonacich has observed, "The middleman firm is labor-intensive but able to cut labor costs drastically through ethnically-based paternalism and thrift."[65]

The entry of these immigrants into the colony in the early 1920s did not go unremarked. The main concern that the editor of the *Nassau Guardian* expressed in December 1923 was that Bahamian society would be transformed with the continued influx of immigrants: "We have always advocated progress and development for Nassau and it seems that gradually things are beginning to move. The latest addition to the amenities of the town is a hot dog motor van which arrived this week to retail hamburger steaks and such like delicacies, and is owned, of all people by a Jew! The town seems to be becoming more and more cosmopolitan and shortly we may expect to see a Chinese quarter and a Ghetto, perhaps with foreign language papers, if we have not already some of these."[66]

The principal arguments later advanced against the further entry of these immigrants were, however, not cultural but economic. These immigrant groups occupied an intermediate position in Bahamian society and were involved, as middlemen, in the distribution rather than the production of goods. In 1925 Bowe made it clear that it was to these middleman minorities that he objected: "The class of immigrants that I proposed to exclude are not producers but extractors of wealth. We would welcome tomorrow any enterprising people who would go in for farming, or any other industry, but will this element go in for hard work[?] No, I am afraid not, altho' I have seen Chinamen in Mexico cultivating fruit and vegetables in large quantities. If they would do so here we would not object to their presence."[67] By 1928 Bowe's views would receive wider support.

The question of restricting the entry of immigrants who were likely to provide competition for Bahamian merchants was reintroduced in the House of Assembly by A. K. Solomon in August 1928. At a meeting of the House on 13 August, Solomon moved for the appointment of a select committee "to consider what action (if any) should be taken to limit and control the business activities of non-residents of the Colony." He pointed out that action along the lines Bowe had earlier proposed was now necessary and was, in fact, a matter of some urgency. Although Solomon expressed concern about the "undesirable" business methods of the foreigners, it is clear from his speech that their only "crime" had been to compete successfully against the entrenched native merchant class. As he observed, "It was very hard for a man in business, who had gone through the thick of battle and tried all his life to do the right thing, to see the business he had built up and of which he was justly proud drift away, because some foreigner of doubtful character and business methods came in and undersold him."[68]

Solomon's proposal found wide support among members of the House who were directly affected by the economic competition from the ethnic minorities and those who found the rapid economic success of the newcomers intolerable. In seconding Solomon's motion, Bowe once again argued that the immigrants as middlemen extracted rather than produced wealth. His main targets for criticism on this occasion were the Greeks and the Chinese. Bowe pointed out that the Greeks did not undertake the risky business of outfitting the sponging vessels but were concerned only with exporting the sponges. Thus the Greeks reaped where the local people sowed. He also expressed disapproval of the Chinese in the restaurant business who profited from the sale of food that they were not prepared to produce. As Bowe remarked, he did not like to see the Chinese "waiting on the wharf to buy an Out Island chicken for six-pence to sell in their restaurant for three to four shillings."[69]

Members of the House were agreed that the matter of immigration restrictions should be dealt with immediately. Failure to act, it was generally felt, would result in the entry of what T. A. Toote, a successful black lawyer, called "hundreds of undesirables." Toote took the view that if the matter were deferred until the following year, more immigrants would enter, and it would be difficult to get rid of them. Some of the earlier immigrants, he noted, were already being naturalized. It was for these reasons that the select committee appointed to consider the question met during the House's recess to devise a plan of action.[70]

Why did the House of Assembly reverse its position on the immigration issues between 1925 and 1928? Certainly the statements of its members on 13 August 1928 provided little precise information on the reasons for this new hostility. Solomon, for example, spoke vaguely of "what happened during the past year or so."[71] The main source of this hostility was the economic competition resulting from the proliferation of new businesses owned by the trading minorities (especially the Lebanese and the Chinese) after 1925. In some cases these businesses encroached on areas the Bahamian merchants had hitherto dominated.

The Lebanese merchants, as has been argued, dominated the lower end of the dry goods trade by the early 1920s. However, after 1925 the Amourys opened stores that catered to the tourist trade and thus came into direct competition with the established Bahamian merchants, who were heavily dependent on sales from the winter tourist season. The first of these stores the Amourys operated was M. Sraeel, which, as an advertisement in the *Nassau Tribune* in January 1926 proudly announced, was managed by "Mme Amoury, late of Paris."[72] This store offered merchandise of high quality rather than value for money, which the Amoury establishments had previously emphasized. A February 1926 advertisement for M. Sraeel pointed out that its stock of ladies' wear was "all of exceptional quality, style and good taste."[73] This store followed the Amoury tradition, however, in one important respect: at the end of the season there was a sale.[74] In January of the following year Miss V. S. Amoury opened a shop in the new Hotel Fort Montagu that carried a complete line of high-grade ladies' wear.[75] Later in 1927 she opened yet another shop, which was described as "The Shoppe of Beautiful Things," on Marlborough Street opposite the New Colonial Hotel.[76]

After 1925 the small Chinese community expanded its operations in the food business and entered the dry goods trade for the first time. In 1926 Hong Yick & Company acquired the Sunlight Bakery and established the Chinese Bakery.[77] In February of the following year Lim Wah opened Waufle's Lunch on Bay Street.[78] Perhaps the most important Chinese business venture launched in these years was the Chinese Republic Silk Store, which was opened in 1926 and was owned by Samuel Wong. This store sold Chinese silks, Christmas presents, and toys as well as French toilet goods. In this enterprise the Wongs relied on marketing tactics such as newspaper advertising, sales, and the use of premiums, which the Garfunkel family had pioneered in Nassau. Typical of this more aggressive approach to merchandising was the store's opening offer: "We also wish to inform the public that for every Dollar spent with us in the first three days of opening, *WE GIVE PREMIUMS* which hold good at either of the following: Chinese Republic Silk Store; Lunch Room, Cor. Bay and East Sts and the favourite old place New Chinese Restaurant. Give us a trial—Money back is our guarantee, if not satisfied."[79]

The competition in the dry goods trade was further increased by the opening of two stores on Bay Street during the course of 1926. Both of these stores competed for clientele of the established Bahamian stores and made it clear that they were prepared to offer more competitive prices. One was Cooper & Yanowitz, which opened in October 1926 and advertised itself as "The Store with a Conscience."[80] The other was Ariswo, which opened to business in December of that year. An early advertisement stressed that it would offer merchandise at less expensive prices than existing stores: "Watch for Ariswo 505 Bay Street. Let London's Famous West End Tailors solve your Clothes problem at Half your Present Cost."[81]

In this increasingly competitive business environment, it is not surprising that the native Bahamian merchants, with their more traditional business methods, felt economically threatened. This anxiety was reflected in the rumors that circulated in the business community in 1926 that J. Garfunkel, the manager of the Home Furniture Company, would be entering the dry goods business. The content of the advertisement placed by Garfunkel in the *Nassau Tribune* to dispel these rumors brings out clearly the difference between Garfunkel's approach to business and that of the Bahamian merchants:

> Yes, WE are Not in the Dry Goods Business. It having come to our attention that certain parties are starting a rumour that 'Garfunkel has gone into the dry goods business, and is cutting prices just out of meanness, etc.' we want to say the following:
>
> 1. That this rumour is like most rumours—without any foundation.
> 2. That the people starting this should have verified the facts first.
> 3. That IF Garfunkel was in the dry goods business everybody would know it through the Press, the proper channel.
> 4. That Garfunkel has never cut prices through 'meanness' but through *Good Business.*
> 5. That Garfunkel knows as well as any man or woman in Bay St. that a person cannot exist without a legitimate profit.
> 6. That we are in the Furniture business, AT YOUR SERVICE.[82]

The economic competition between the immigrant minorities and the local merchants did not immediately result in the enactment of restrictive legislation. The evidence suggests, however, that there was a more rigorous enforcement of the existing laws that attempted to regulate immigration into the Bahamas. The Immigration Act of 1920 stated that no immigrant would be allowed to land in the colony "without the special sanction of the Governor in Council."[83] The governor in council was also empowered to prohibit the landing of any immigrant "from any ship or vessel from any place or places outside the Colony." An examination of the minutes of the Executive Council (whose members included some of the leading merchants of the colony) indicates that in the period 1927–33 there was a sustained attempt to keep the further entry of the Chinese into the Bahamas to a minimum. It also shows that the members of the Executive Council delayed the naturalization of Chinese businessmen who had settled in the colony.

At the meeting of the Executive Council on 2 March 1927, landing permits were refused to two nephews of Louis Chea.[84] Permits were also refused in April of that year to Charles Hui Chea and Miguel Chea.[85] A second application for a permit for Miguel Chea was turned down in June.[86]

Landing permits were refused for T. Wong and C. Wong in November 1927 and in April of the following year.[87] In June 1928 the Executive Council did authorize the issue of landing permits to two Chinese men who were to be employed by the Hatchet Bay Company, but conditions were attached that made it impossible for the men to settle in the colony.[88] Applications by the established Chinese businessmen for naturalization were refused by the Executive Council. Louis Chea's applications in 1927 and 1929 were turned down.[89] The applications by Samuel Wong and Charles Chea in 1929 and 1932, respectively, were also rejected.[90]

It is clear that the Chinese were not welcome. The antipathy to the Chinese can be explained by the fact that, although they were the most recent of the immigrant groups, they had become visibly successful in business in a few years. Local merchants also resented most of the business practices of the Chinese. The complaint that immigrants kept their businesses open on Fridays, Sundays, and public holidays, while the shops of local merchants were forced by law to close, referred specifically to the Chinese.[91] Since their business concerns relied on the labor of relatives and ethnic comembers, the Chinese were able to keep them open for longer hours.

It is most likely, however, that the less than welcoming attitude to the Chinese was based not only their conduct in the Bahamas but also on reports from Jamaica that the Chinese were displacing native shopkeepers and that the legislature there had found it necessary to pass legislation restricting alien immigration.[92] As D. Stanley Eitzen has observed, "The wide dispersion of Jews and Chinese helps to reinforce prejudice against them. Because each group is a minority throughout much of the world, '. . . the apprehensions regarding them as a minority are transferable, interchangeable and even cumulative to a degree.'"[93]

The demand for restrictions on immigration, as has been shown, originated in the House of Assembly. On this issue the House was supported by the editor of the *Nassau Guardian,* who remarked in an editorial, "One thing is certain and that is something drastic must be done soon if the local traders are to maintain their position in the Colony."[94] The editor of the *Nassau Tribune,* on the other hand, urged "caution and considered reflection" before any legislation was enacted. In an editorial on the immigration question, he pointed to the economic contribution the immigrant groups had made: "In spite of anything that might be said to the contrary it must be borne in mind . . . that there were no restaurants or cheap boarding houses at which a certain class of visitor to this Colony might be accommodated until recent years, and these have been supplied by foreigners." He also noted that the entry of foreigners into business had been beneficial to

Bahamian consumers: "The foreigners who have been doing business here have, for the most part, attempted to bring prices down to a more reasonable level than we have known them to be for many years."[95] Except for editorial comments and a few letters to the colony's newspapers, there is little evidence to suggest that the immigration issues aroused much interest outside mercantile circles.

The legislation that was enacted in September 1928 sought to restrict immigration to the Bahamas rather than to exclude specifically the trading minorities whose economic activities had prompted this measure. This can be partly explained by the fact that the law was also intended to limit the immigration of West Indian artisans who had been attracted to Nassau by the prospect of obtaining jobs during the construction boom of the 1920s.[96] There was, moreover, a reluctance among members of the House to legislate for the exclusion of competing immigrant groups in too direct a fashion. Ostensibly the emphasis in this law was on restricting the entry of "undesirable aliens"—a wide category that included lunatics, criminals, prostitutes, seditious persons, and anyone "whose presence in the Colony would not be conducive to the public good." The main objective of the framers of this legislation, however, seems to have been to complicate the process of gaining admission to the colony for the prospective immigrant. Passengers who traveled second-class to the colony could land only after they received permission in writing from the immigration officer. This permission could be obtained only after the immigrant produced a medical certificate dated no more than ten days before his or her departure for the Bahamas, a certificate of good character signed by a magistrate, and a deposit of £20. The immigration officer could also ask for "two sufficient sureties," ordinarily resident in the colony, in a bond of £50. Those passengers who traveled first-class to the colony were exempt from these requirements.[97]

Some persons were quick to realize that the Immigrants Act would not meet the requirements of the local business community. Early in September 1928 Asa Pritchard, a merchant and member of the House of Assembly, pointed out in the debate on the bill that it would not prevent "any stranger coming into the Colony to conduct business as heretofore."[98] One correspondent to the *Nassau Guardian,* with the appropriate pseudonym "Bay Street," was even more explicit in his criticisms of the legislation:

> Half measures are often useless. If the tenor of the Immigration bill read, "preventing an immigrant engaging in business here," the mists of obscurity would have been lifted from this most important matter.

> After all, the purpose of the Bill should be to keep Nassau as free as possible from the type of immigrant which of late has added to the number, though not to the quality of business men in the city. . . .
>
> The term "Undesirable" seems to have assumed different meanings to different people; in which case I maintain that the interpretation given by those born here, or at least of long residence is the conviction that the business life of the Colony is sufficiently represented without allowing the encroachment by aliens to any further extent.[99]

By 1930 the members of the House of Assembly were prepared to take direct action against those immigrants who continued to enter the colony and establish themselves in business. The measures taken were intended to limit alien participation in lucrative business activities. Thus a law was enacted that made it illegal for aliens to act as commission merchants unless they had been registered.[100] Another law was passed that licensed motorboats for hire in the Nassau harbor. This legislation debarred any boat that was owned wholly or partly by an alien, or on which an alien was employed, from receiving a license.[101]

These significant restrictions on the business activities of aliens in the colony reflected a heightened concern by merchants facing economic competition from immigrants in an economy that was contracting. As early as 1929 the colonial government had started a policy of retrenchment in its program of public works, and this resulted in widespread unemployment among the laboring population.[102] These developments led in turn to a reduction of commercial activity and, as the *Nassau Tribune* observed, "a certain amount of panic" in the business community.[103] The merchants' problems were compounded by the stock market crash of 1929. The effect of the stock market crash on the 1930 tourist season was clear to the editor of the *Nassau Tribune,* who observed in March of that year, "It is an undeniable fact that something is wrong, so very wrong that few business people are looking forward to the summer with any sense of equanimity; for following on the most disastrous hurricane in the history of the Colony has come a most disappointing season as a result of the stock crash in the United States which will leave the merchants in the city burdened with heavy stocks and but small channels through which to distribute them during the lean months of the year."[104]

Given the deteriorating economic situation in the colony, it is not surprising that the business community agitated for further effective action to exclude foreign competitors. Letters to the editors of both the *Nassau Guardian* and the *Nassau Tribune,* representative of local business opinion, called attention to the "invasion of aliens" who undersold their Bahamian competitors and repatriated their savings.[105] Typical of these letters in tone and content was one to the *Nassau Guardian*, signed "Nassauvian," in November 1930:

> Brielofsky is the latest addition to Nassau's merchants. The newest development is a Clothing Shop in George Street the landlord is an M.H.A. by the way—which has broadcast pamphlets and [is] advertising Five Hundred $50 to $75 Suits at a sacrifice price of $5.00.
>
> These 500 suits mean £500 taken out of the Colony. Our tailors will be deprived of work, our merchants of business, and our Government of the duty on clothing material.
>
> Nassau men who make money spend it in Nassau; it remains to be circulated here. How many homes have foreigners owning stores here ever built? How much money have they ever circulated here? One of them told me recently that all the money he makes went home to his country to support his wife and family. . . .
>
> The existence of our business community is being severely threatened. If "Bermuda for Bermudians," why not "Nassau for Nassauvians"?[106]

The threat from these foreign competitors was so seriously regarded that a deputation of prominent Nassau merchants, including several members of the House of Assembly, called on the governor of the colony, Sir Charles Orr, in November 1930. Among the matters they discussed was "the alien invasion in business." It is interesting to note that one of the two spokesmen of this deputation was R. T. Symonette, who had not been especially alarmed in 1925 by competition from the immigrants.[107] Orr's response to these representations was to prohibit entry into the colony of persons who intended to engage in shopkeeping or storekeeping without a special permit from the governor in council.[108]

With the passage of the Commission Merchants Registration Act and the Boat Registration Act in May 1930 the House of Assembly had adopted the principle of protecting certain areas of business from foreign intrusion. In 1931 there was yet another attempt by members of the House to extend this protection of businesses by enacting a law that would provide for the licensing of shops. Some members saw this as an opportunity for requiring aliens to pay punitive fees for operating their businesses.[109] This viewpoint was clearly expressed by Asa Pritchard, whose comments were reported by the *Nassau Guardian:* "He [Pritchard] would . . . license aliens and put hardships on them so that they would not come here. Every line of business was fully represented here, so why should we part our slice of bread with the outsider?"[110] So strong was the resentment of the immigrant competitors that there were suggestions that foreign merchants who had been established in business in the colony for several years should be expelled.[111] These proposals were opposed by both newspapers in the colony. As the editor of the *Nassau Guardian,* who had supported the restrictions on immigration in 1928, commented, "It would appear that if the restrictions ultimately arrived at are to be as severe as suggested the shops in Bay Street will, by the time these restrictions come into force, be entirely operated by natives. Whether this is altogether desirable is a debatable point, for it must be remembered that the present high efficiency of the business community and the lowered prices of recent years, have been due in no small degree to the stimulus of outside competition."[112]

The legislation of 1933 that provided for the licensing of shops in the colony was not enacted in the form the merchants had originally proposed. License fees for aliens and natives were uniform, but by making the licensing of shops compulsory, the Bahamian merchant class had imposed another form of control over the business activities of their foreign competitors in the colony.[113]

Chapter Nine

LABOR MIGRATION AS PROTEST AND SURVIVAL STRATEGY

In the late nineteenth and early twentieth centuries, large-scale external migration provided lower-class Bahamians with an alternative to "the constraints of the colonial political economy," especially those created by the credit and truck systems.[1] Although the Bahamas supplied labor for the construction of the Panama Canal and other American enterprises in Central America and the Caribbean, the main destination for Bahamian labor was the state of Florida, across the Gulf Stream. This chapter examines the circumstance that prompted the migratory flow to Florida and the consequences of this labor migration for the sending area.[2]

There were two main waves of labor migration to Florida from the Bahamas in the period under examination. The first of these was the migration to Key West, which lasted from the 1870s into the first decade of the twentieth century. This outward movement was succeeded by (and overlapped with) the "Miami Craze," which lasted from 1905 to 1924, when immigration restrictions virtually closed the American labor market to Bahamian labor.

As early as the 1820s and 1830s Bahamian wreckers (primarily from Abaco) had migrated to Key West, where they were largely responsible for that area's emergence as a wrecking center.[3] In 1849 the *Bahama Herald* reported that approximately two-thirds of the white inhabitants of Abaco were leaving or had already left "to take up their abode at Cay West, to become fishermen or wreckers."[4] A factor in the early out-migration of white Abaconians to Key West was racial prejudice. Governor Charles Bayley observed in 1860 that natives of Abaco, who then formed at least two-thirds of the population of Key West, had migrated because they were "disgusted at the civil and religious equality of the negroes."[5]

The establishment of Key West as a center for sponging operations in the 1870s also attracted Bahamian immigrants.[6] J. H. Webb, the superintendent of census in the colony, observed in 1881 that one of the factors that explained the slow rate of population growth in New Providence as compared with that in the rest of the colony between 1871 and 1881 was "immigration—chiefly to Cay West."[7] By the 1880s the expansion of the cigar industry, which had been given new impetus with the influx of Cuban refugees after the Civil War, drew further immigrants to Key West.[8] In 1885 Governor Henry Blake reported periodic migration to Key West by black Bahamians from Nassau: "The black population . . . have begun to migrate periodically to Key West, which the expansion of cigar manufacture for the American market has raised from a village to a comparatively wealthy town. Six schooners are now engaged in this passenger traffic."[9]

Although the economic prosperity of Key West in the late nineteenth century attracted laborers from the Bahamas, the outward movement is largely explained by economic conditions in the sending islands and by the way in which the sponging and pineapple industries were organized. By the mid-1880s the pineapple industry was already showing signs of decline in some areas. One of the problems at this stage was that the land suitable for pineapple cultivation was becoming exhausted. Most cultivators worked the land for a few years without using fertilizers and practicing rotation of crops and then abandoned it for several years to allow it to regain its original fertility.[10] By 1884 the consequences of these agricultural practices were evident, and outward migration to Florida had already begun in the settlement of Rock Sound, Eleuthera. The official report for that year noted that "many are away on the Florida Coast. Quite a number have left altogether for Key West. No inducement for them to remain. The large Pine tracts were worn out."[11] The collapse of the pineapple industry in the early years of the twentieth century led to further migration of the inhabitants of Rock Sound who were not satisfied with mere subsistence.[12] With the failure of cash crop production, the cultivators in Rock Sound turned to wage labor in Key West.

In Abaco and Harbour Island, outward migration was also directly related to the fluctuating fortunes of major export staples. An unsuccessful season in pineapple cultivation was often enough to stimulate emigration. This was the experience of pineapple cultivators in Harbour Island in 1886, when the severity of the winter damaged their crop. Their problem was compounded by the failure of the agents who marketed the crop to pay them. The consequence of these developments, as the official report that year observed, was to reduce "the planters and other laborers to great privation obliging some from sheer necessity to emigrate to Florida."[13] In Key West these emigrants were able to obtain employment for their children at the cigar factories at "increased wages."[14] The difficulties of the pineapple industry also adversely affected related economic activities such as shipbuilding. In 1885, for example, the slowdown in shipbuilding in Harbour Island forced several unemployed ship carpenters to migrate to Key West, where they expected to find steady employment at a higher wages.[15]

In Abaco, the decline of the pineapple industry in the 1890s coincided with the decline of the sisal industry in some other areas. During that decade, British capitalists who had established sisal plantations and provided wage employment in several districts of that island closed operations in the face of low prices and sisal of poor quality.[16] In 1890, for example, the suspension of work on the sisal farm in the Cherokee Sound district left many laborers unemployed and stimulated their migration to Key West in search of employment.[17] In his report for 1893 the resident Anglican priest in Abaco attributed the sharp decline in the number of communicants to "the lack of employment, which has caused many of our men and lads to seek work in Florida, where in lumber yards and on river boats they apparently earn good and regular wages."[18]

Another major area from which labor migrated to Key West was Bimini. In 1890, for example, more than a hundred inhabitants of Bimini, mainly from Alice Town, left for Key West and other areas in Florida in search of work.[19] In Bimini, the decline of wrecking in the late nineteenth century had left the inhabitants with few alternative occupations. Most of the men earned a precarious livelihood from fishing, sponging, and salvage from occasional wrecks.[20] Piloting vessels past the dangerous reefs and shoals that fringed the island also became an important source of employment for the white population, but the services of pilots were required only when the wind was southerly. Furthermore, these pilots were paid in provisions, which they had to sell at a loss to obtain cash.[21]

Labor migration to Florida in the late nineteenth century was also an expression of dissatisfaction by the laboring class of the colony with the way the sponging and pineapple industries were organized. Both industries (as we have established) were organized in such a way that the major part of the profits was appropriated by a white merchant class resident in Nassau, New Providence. In both industries the payment of labor was organized on a profit-sharing rather than a wage basis. In practice, spongers and cultivators were rarely remunerated in cash but paid instead in provisions or "truck."[22] The evidence indicates that there was a direct connection between the operation of the truck system in the sponging and pineapple industries and the exodus to Key West. One of the attractions of Key West for the immigrant laborer seems to have been not merely higher wages but wages paid in cash. As L. D. Powles observed in 1888, "The people of the Bahamas are daily coming more and more in contact with Key West on the Florida coast, and are gradually finding out that there are places in the world where not only a high rate of wages is paid, but the people get paid in cash."[23] Throughout the nineteenth century, the operation of the truck system remained a source of dissatisfaction to the laboring classes of the Out Islands. In 1896 Governor Haynes Smith commented during an official visit to the Out Islands on the discontentment of the inhabitants, which he explained by the fact that "industry and labor in the Colony are enclosed in the bonds of the Truck System which eats into the vitals of all labor in the Colony and destroys all enterprise and energy."[24]

Labor migration to Florida, principally to Key West, in the late nineteenth century was usually permanent. There was little of the oscillating or return migration that was a prominent feature of the movement to Miami and its environs in the early twentieth century. It was also not unusual to move in family groups. As Governor Haynes Smith observed in 1896 of emigration to the United States, "This goes on in a steady stream from each settlement mostly in family parties of two or three at a time. Sometimes a whole collection of families will express disgust with the Colony and leave as at Rock Sound where 40 at once left their substantial houses and went to Florida."[25] This steady outward migration from Abaco, Bimini, Eleuthera, and Harbour Island resulted in a decrease in the population in those areas between 1881 and 1901.[26] In 1896 Haynes Smith estimated the number of Bahamians who had settled in Florida between 20,000 and 30,000, but that figure was probably high.[27] In 1892 the Bahamians in Key West numbered 8,000 out of a population of 25,000.[28]

After 1905, Miami became the most attractive destination for emigrating Bahamians. By 1896 the hotel and railroad magnate Henry Flagler had extended his railway system from Jacksonville to Miami and opened up the latter to development.[29] The accelerated economic activity created a demand for labor that sparsely populated southern Florida could not supply. Laborers were thus provided largely from outside the area.[30] In the first two decades of the twentieth century, unskilled Bahamian laborers migrated to Miami principally for construction and agricultural work. Construction work was available not only in the rapidly growing city of Miami, which early on experienced a land and building boom, but also on the Key West extension of Flagler's railroad between 1905 and 1912.[31] By 1905 the Florida East Coast Railroad had already reached Detroit (Florida City) and resulted in the establishment of large-scale capitalist farms in South Dade that provided winter fruits and vegetables for northern markets.[32] The development of this subtropical region required a large labor force to clear the pinelands, plant groves, and tend vegetable fields. There was also a demand for women to perform domestic service.[33] These laborers were paid higher wages than the Bahamas could offer. It is not surprising then that Miami, as one contemporary observer remarked, should have become "to the Bahamians seeking a livelihood, what Mecca is to the religious Moslem world."[34] Bahamians who were attracted to Miami included not only those who came directly from the islands but also those who came via Key West, where the cigar industry was in decline after 1910.[35]

The higher wages offered in Miami were an important inducement to Bahamians of the laboring classes to migrate in search of employment. In New Providence in 1911 the usual wage rate for unskilled laborers varied between 1/6^{d} and 2/-per day, whereas in Florida the daily wage was from $1.25 to $1.50, or approximately 5/- to 6/- at the existing exchange rate.[36] The Bahamians who earned a regular wage in the colony, however, formed a small minority of the working population in the early years of the twentieth century. Up to this time many Bahamians remained unproletarianized and essentially outside the market economy.[37]

There is no doubt that lucrative wage employment in southern Florida represented an attractive alternative to independent production for many Bahamians in the Out Islands. Some of these independent cultivators were forced into wage labor in Florida because of the effects of droughts or hurricanes. In 1919, for example, many inhabitants of Long Cay, Acklins, and Crooked Island migrated to Florida because prolonged drought had caused food crops to fail. Their situation had been worsened by the fact that the Bight of Acklins was closed to sponging.[38] These were the islands to which Sir William Allardyce, governor of the colony, made reference when he remarked in December 1919 that "both men and women have been obliged to emigrate to Florida in order to obtain, not high wages alone but the means of subsistence and better conditions of living."[39]

In the first two decades of the twentieth century, those Bahamian cultivators who were linked more directly to the world economy by the production of two export staples—pineapple and sisal—experienced shrinking markets and usually unremunerative prices. Many cultivators responded to this deteriorating economic situation by emigrating to Florida. In the pineapple industry there were problems of productivity and marketing. The chief problems in pineapple cultivation by 1908 were exhausted soils and a failure to use suitable fertilizers.[40] But more important in explaining the decline of the pineapple industry was competition from other pineapple producing areas, especially Hawaii and Florida, which dominated the American market with the help of a protective tariff.[41] One result of the problems experienced by the industry was that the smaller cultivators generally abandoned pineapple cultivation. In a petition to the House of Assembly in January 1911, the residents of Tarpum Bay, Eleuthera, pointed out that within the previous five years the "deterioration of stock," the low prices paid for pineapples, and the high tariff had forced most of the smaller cultivators to abandon the industry and devote their time to the cultivation of produce.[42] By 1912 the cultivation of pineapples in the district of Arthur's Town, San Salvador, previously an important center of pineapple production, had "dwindled to [a] mere nothing."[43]

Developments in the sisal industry were equally frustrating for Bahamian cultivators. By the first decade of the twentieth century, sisal had become mainly a peasant crop that provided cash for the cultivator during periods of drought when food crops were affected. However, for most of the period (with the exception of a few years during World War I), the price of Bahamian sisal on the American market remained low. This situation reflected the poor quality of Bahamian sisal and the competition from efficient producers like Mexico.[44] Those years in which low prices for sisal coincided with a failure of food crops usually saw increased labor migration to Florida and elsewhere.[45]

With the decline of the sisal and pineapple industries, laborers displaced from agriculture moved to Florida and other areas where there was a demand for their labor power. In the Out Islands there were few alternative agricultural activities in which these laborers could become involved. A major obstacle to agricultural development in the Out Islands was the lack of roads and regular and reliable transportation links with Nassau and external markets. Although this was a problem to which successive governors had called attention, the House of Assembly, dominated by Nassau residents, had shown little interest in improving the situation.[46] In 1920 a commission of inquiry appointed to report on the general administration of the Out Islands attributed emigration mainly to the fact that there was as yet "no ready and reliable transportation to this [Nassau] or any other market for what is or might be produced."[47]

The main exception to the general pattern of economic decline in this period was the sponge industry. Because of its continued prosperity, labor was usually required for sponging crews. But the spongers' widespread realization that they did not benefit from the prosperity of the sponge trade continued to stimulate migration to Florida.[48] The principal source of this dissatisfaction was the credit and truck systems, which virtually guaranteed that the laborers were always in debt to the merchants. This indebtedness, as "Twist Back" suggested in a 1911 letter to the editor of the *Nassau Tribune,* was the primary cause of the spongers' exodus: "I am sorry to say since I see you last time, all of the sponging boys gone to Florida to look for libin, I did en want them to go Sir but they tell me dem tired workin for notin if they carry all of sponge in de sea for sell they never kin get nough to clear the shop debt and they is gwine to Merica if every body in Bay Street dead."[49]

It was never necessary to recruit Bahamian laborers for work in southern Florida because news of employment opportunities circulated in the colony. Most migrants went to Nassau by the mail boats, which traveled between the islands, and then crossed the Gulf Stream by one of the several vessels engaged in the passenger traffic between Nassau and Miami.[50] At $5 or £1 the fare was within reach of many members of the laboring classes.[51] Until 1917 there were few immigration restrictions to bar the entry of male migrant laborers into Miami. The evidence suggests, however, that immigration officials discriminated against unmarried women of the laboring classes, who were usually suspected of being prostitutes.[52]

Initially it was the young, able-bodied men who migrated to Miami, leaving their families at home. The usual pattern was for these men to spend between six months to a year abroad and then return for a period of rest before migrating again. This movement back and forth was made possible by the proximity of the Bahamas to Florida and the relative ease of communication. The length of time the migrants spent abroad often depended on the type of work in which they were engaged. Agricultural laborers, for example, usually left in October and returned in March, at the end of the harvest. Laborers from Bimini, who were employed primarily as fishermen in Miami, also returned home after the fishing season was over.[53] The oscillating short-term labor migration was reflected in the statistics for migration between the Bahamas and Florida, which were collected only for the period 1911–17 (see table 1).

On their visits home the migrant laborers had an opportunity to display their new prosperity and material possessions. As the commissioner for Fresh Creek, Andros, noted of the returning migrants in 1911, "They bring some extraordinary clothes (and it is now *de rigeur* to change three times on Sunday)."[54] These migrants almost certainly acted as unofficial recruiters of labor in Miami. What government officials deplored as outlandish clothes were undoubtedly perceived by men and women who had not yet migrated as evidence of consumer items that the high wages available in Miami made affordable.

The outward movement of labor to Miami eventually included most of the able-bodied men in the Out Islands communities. In 1916, for example, the commissioner of Long Cay, Fortune Island, noted that at the end of the

Table 1. Statistics of migration between the Bahamas and Florida, 1911–1917

Year	Departures	Arrivals	Net departures	Net arrivals
1911	3,230	1,964	1,266	—
1912	2,628	2,548	80	—
1913	3,422	2,396	1,026	—
1914	3,758	3,059	699	—
1915	1,511	2,702	—	1,191
1916	2,734	1,895	839	—
1917	1,750	2,090	—	340

Source: Annual Colonial Reports for the Bahamas, 1912–1917.

year there were approximately 200 people on the island but only 24 men willing or able to work.[55] In his report for 1920 the commissioner for Watling's Island reported a similar if more extreme situation: "The island is almost denuded of young men. Throughout the whole of the year both men and women have been going to Florida. I regret to report that at the time of writing there is not a single man on the whole island. It seems incredible but it is nevertheless true. If something out of the ordinary doesn't turn up soon, the district will be manless, because the married as well as the single are going."[56]

By 1911 yet another pattern had emerged in the migratory flow to Miami. Increasingly, wives and children joined husbands who had settled there.[57] By 1910 a large population of Bahamians had settled permanently in Miami. The United States census for that year indicated that in a black population of 5,000 there were 3,500 British subjects, most of whom would have been Bahamians.[58] From Miami, Bahamians had distributed themselves in towns such as Coconut Grove, Dania, Fort Lauderdale, West Palm, Beach, and Daytona, which developed along the railway line.[59] In 1915 it was estimated that at least 2,000 Bahamians lived in these communities.[60]

In Miami and the surrounding areas of settlement, Bahamians were employed as domestic servants, farmers, cooks, hotel waiters, bellmen, hackmen, draymen, carpenters, painters, masons, bakers, and laundry workers.[61] On the railroads Bahamians also held jobs as porters and firemen.[62] The majority of the Bahamians who migrated to southern Florida were poor and unskilled, but there were also immigrants from the middle classes, some of whom possessed skills and capital.[63] Some Bahamians with capital established businesses in Colored Town in Miami. These Bahamian businessmen were able to provide their fellow Bahamians in Miami with a wide range of services. The strict enforcement of a policy of residential segregation along racial lines in Miami ensured that "colored" businessmen did not often come into direct competition with their white counterparts for the business of the Bahamian migrants.[64]

The magnitude of labor migration from the colony in the first two decades of the twentieth century, especially to Florida, was reflected in the colony's census figures for 1901–21 (see table 2). During that period, population growth was clearly affected by external migration. The intercensal rate of growth for the period 1891–1901 was 11.5 percent, but between 1901 and 1911 it had slowed to 4 percent. In the years 1911–21 the population declined by 5.5 percent.

Although the censuses alone do not provide emigration figures, it is possible to arrive at rough estimates of the outward movement by using them in conjunction with the data for natural increase (see table 3). It is likely that, for the census period 1901–11, a net loss of 6,180 is too high a figure. Census takers would not have counted, for example, persons from the southern islands of the archipelago who were employed as stevedores on steamship lines or as laborers on one-year contracts with American companies in Central and Latin America. Such persons were usually only temporarily absent. These forms of migratory wage labor ceased after 1914 and therefore did not affect the results of the 1921 census.[65]

After 1920 the migration of Bahamian laborers to the United States was curtailed. Many Bahamians who had worked as seasonal laborers on the farms in southern Florida were prevented from returning to the United States by a law that made passing a literacy test a requirement for entry.[66] This legislation, aimed primarily at the immigrants from southern and eastern Europe, had been enacted originally in 1917 but temporarily suspended later as a wartime measure. After 1920, however, it was strictly enforced.[67] With the passage of the Johnson-Reed Act in 1924 the exclusion of Bahamians from the Florida labor market was virtually complete. Laborers from the Out Islands who had worked in Florida sought jobs increasingly in Nassau, which since the 1920s had been experiencing economic prosperity based on bootlegging, tourism, and the land and construction booms. Although there was a migration of Bahamian laborers to the United States between 1943 and 1966, it was different from the earlier migrations. In the latter period Bahamian laborers went on short-term contracts on a scheme that was supervised by the colonial and American governments.[68]

Table 2. Decennial census returns, 1881–1921

Year	Population	Change	% Change
1881	43,230	+4,359	10.0
1891	47,565	+4,044	8.5
1901	53,735	+6,170	11.5
1911	55,944	+2,201	4.0
1921	53,031	-2,913	-5.5

Source: Report on the Censuses of the Bahama Islands, 1891, 1901, 1911, 1921.

In commercial circles in the Bahamas, fears were frequently expressed that the migration of spongers would endanger the prosperity of the sponging industry, but little effort was made to halt this outward movement.[69] The attitude of the white mercantile elite was reflected in the comments made by the commission of inquiry in 1920 on the question of emigration. Commission members took the view that the loss of population (which meant the loss of a great number of producers) might be harmful in theory, but they observed that emigration had not so far resulted in a financial loss to the colony and that until economic conditions improved at home, emigration must be expected. The commission recommended a policy of noninterference: "We do not therefore think that any effort should be made to stem the outward tide by legislation or that obstacles should be placed in the would-be temporary emigrants' way. But permanent emigration should not be encouraged."[70] This tolerance of emigration by the employer class is perhaps best explained by the fact that the demand for labor in agriculture had decreased. Merchants also benefited from the remittances that migrants sent their families in the Out Islands.

Most colonial governors during this period saw emigration as evidence of the colony's economic decline. Although they deplored the depopulation of the Out Islands, they also recognized the importance of remittances to the economic well-being of the colony. In 1912, for example, William Hart Bennett, the officer administering the government, admitted that there might be a labor problem if large-scale business enterprises were established in the colony, but he commented, "There is however another side of the question that is the undoubted fact that large remittances are sent by most of the emigrants to their wives and families here."[71] Colonial administrators reluctantly accepted the fact that emigration was one solution to the economic problems of a colony that could not support its population. It was for this reason that Sir William Allardyce endorsed the proposal by the Mason and Hanger Contracting Company of New York in July 1917 to recruit Bahamian laborers on contract for war emergency work in Charleston, South

Table 3. Population and loss from emigration in the Bahamas, 1901–1921

	Males	Females	Total
1901 census	25,000	28,735	53,735
Natural increase, 1901–11	—	—	8,389
1911 census	24,975	30,969	55,944
Net loss, 1901–11	—	—	6,180
Natural increase, 1911–21	—	—	8,344
1921 census	23,790	29,241	53,031
Net loss, 1911–21	—	—	11,257

Note: Natural increase is births minus deaths.

Source: Reports on the Census of the Bahama Islands, 1901, 1911, 1921; *Annual Colonial Reports for the Bahamas,* 1911–1920.

Carolina.[72] Between July and October of that year 2,573 laborers left for Charleston.[73]

Labor migration to the United States from the Bahamas in the first two decades of the twentieth century had far-reaching consequences for the sending area. An immediate consequence of the outward movement of men was that wives and children were increasingly relied on to maintain the provision grounds.[74] In certain of the Out Islands this was a continuation of an earlier practice. In Andros, for example, women and children usually tended the provision grounds while the men were away on sponging voyages. In many instances, the land deteriorated during the men's absence in Florida.[75] It was not unusual for some men to remit funds to pay for the care of their subsistence plots while they were away.[76] But the absence of the male members of the household most often resulted in a cycle of neglect that led to an even greater dependence on the wages that migration provided. The process described in the case of the settlements of Rock Sound and Tarpum Bay, Eleuthera, in 1920 was fairly widespread in the Out Islands: "The results of emigration to Florida vary; some are benefitted, while others suffer by leaving their fields and other properties with no one to care for them during their absence, and on their return find their fields in such conditions that to restore them would swallow up the little they bring back and the result is, that back to Florida they go, to earn more money and this is repeated over and over by many."[77]

The withdrawal of men from the rural economy as a result of migration to Florida and to Nassau contributed to the increased dependence on imported food. This trend was discernible in the 1920s when the Bahamas began to import food items like eggs and fresh vegetables, in which it had previously been self-sufficient, and increased its importation of tropical fruits, which it had earlier exported (see table 4). The increased demand for those food items, created mainly by an expanding tourist industry, was not met by local agriculture, as the colonial secretary pointed out in a 1930 memorandum on agriculture in the Bahamas: "One might expect that tourist traffic would create a lively trade in farm and garden produce but in fact it results mainly in a larger importation of food stuffs."[78] Ironically, outward migration, which was in part a protest against mercantile control of the domestic economy, served to enhance the merchants' role as middleman in the import trade.

Remittances from Bahamian migrants in Florida had important effects on the Bahamian economy. Many migrants were able to send money home because they earned more than enough to meet their subsistence needs and therefore had money to save. For Bahamians in Miami, the racial hostility directed at blacks also created a context that was conducive to saving. As the official 1909 report on Governor's Harbour, Eleuthera, explained, "In Miami the black man has to be extremely careful as to how he conducts himself, otherwise his liberty and even his life are endangered, and for this reason alone he abstains from liquor, saves his money and remits to his people at home."[79]

The preferred method of remitting money to the Bahamas was in the form of U.S. currency in registered letters.[80] Postal money orders were not, as was the case with Barbadians in Panama, widely used in the Bahamas in the early twentieth century.[81] Statistics for postal money orders from the United States exist for the period up to the financial year 1912–13 but have clear limitations (see table 5). These figures were presented in aggregate form and did not differentiate between money orders that originated in the state of Florida and those from other migration destinations like New York State. Other evidence, however, suggests that considerable sums of money were remitted to the Bahamas during the years of the Miami boom.

Table 4. Selected food imports into the Bahamas, by value (in pounds sterling), 1921–1929

Food imports	1921	1922	1923	1924	1925	1926	1927	1928	1929
Eggs	—	—	—	3,609	4,145	5,617	5,691	6,275	6,395
Tropical fruits	89	45	255	1,246	780	11,316	8,539	8,978	8,978
Fresh vegetables	—	—	—	844	1,332	1,985	2,933	2,999	4,116
Total	89	45	255	5,699	6,257	18,918	17,163	18,252	19,489

Note: The *Blue Books* give no information on the volume of these imports.

Source: Bahamas *Blue Books*, 1921–1929.

Table 5. Postal money order remittances from the United States to the Bahamas, 1905–1913

Financial year	No.	Total (in £)
1905–6	302	722
1906–7	327	1,121
1907–8	398	1,615
1908–9	509	1,354
1909–10	463	1,339
1910–11	572	1,400
1911–12	541	1,381
1912–13	592	1,556

Source: Annual Colonial Reports for the Bahamas, 1905–1913.

The commissioner for Exuma, for example, estimated that in 1920 migrants' remittances to their families in that island amounted to $15,000 (U.S.).[82] In his report on Clarence Town for 1912, the Commissioner of Long Island noted that as much as $1,000 had arrived by registered mail in one delivery.[83]

The remittances provided financial support for the members of the migrants' families who remained at home. The situation described in the case of the Bight, San Salvador, in 1912 was perhaps typical of many communities in the Out Islands: "The introduction not only of the dollar bill, but the fives, tens and twenties, into the district from Miami has made many a heart glad, it is a common occurrence for registered letters to contain $40 and $50 coming to wives from their husbands and to parents from children."[84]

Remittances seem to have been used primarily to satisfy consumption needs rather than for productive investment. The money was often used to build new houses and "in short time was dispatched to Nassau to procure clothing and articles of food not produced locally."[85] The Out Islands became "remittance societies."[86] In the face of the declining importance of pineapple and sisal production (a situation made worse by the absence of adult males), remittances formed a major source of income. This dependence on remittances made the Out Islands vulnerable to changes in the demand for labor in Florida. Immigration restrictions in the United States therefore resulted in a further decline in the economy of the Out Islands by the late 1920s, as the editor of the *Nassau Tribune* pointed out in October 1929: "It is well known that hundreds of Out Island people went back and forth between Florida and their homes and that thousands of dollars were brought or sent home by these people but the sum that found its way from

Florida must have been much larger than was believed, to result in such a general collapse of the Out Islands when this source of invincible income is withdrawn."[87]

Labor migration had important consequences for the family. The prolonged absence of married men caused their wives to establish liaisons with other men. The existence of such relationships was repeatedly hinted at in official reports of this period.[88] Some of the married men who went to Florida also formed other associations and abandoned their families.[89] It was not unusual for both parents to migrate to Florida, leaving behind children who, without parental care and guidance, developed into juvenile delinquents.[90]

The long-term effect of labor migration was to perpetuate those features of Bahamian society and economy that the migrants were attempting to escape. It reinforced the underdevelopment of the Out-Island communities by depopulating them. More important, the increased dependence on imported food entrenched the position of the mercantile elite as a dominant minority.[91]

CONCLUSION

Despite its unique history, the Bahamas, like other British Caribbean colonies, was shaped by forces such as European conquest and colonization, the institution of slavery, and colonialism. The existence of clear differences and similarities in the historical experience of the Bahamas and the rest of the British Caribbean makes a comparative analysis possible. As Magnus Mörner, Julia Fawaz De Viñuela, and John D. French have observed, "Comparison . . . presupposes similarities as well as differences; to compare that which is absolutely equal or different would make no sense."[1]

My analysis in this book has been informed by an awareness of the current trends in the historiography of plantation America in particular. I have engaged, with varying degrees of explicitness, in the ongoing debates on the transition from slavery to freedom, the internal slave economy, postemancipation labor systems, "systems of domination after slavery," the question of social control in postslavery colonial societies, and labor migration as survival strategy and resistance.

I have argued that the transition from slavery to freedom in the Bahamas began with the collapse of the cotton plantation economy by 1800 and the emergence of a surplus labor force that slave owners found increasingly difficult to employ profitably. In this situation, slave proprietors were prepared to concede greater autonomy to slaves, whom they often could not afford to maintain. Falling profits from agricultural production thus resulted in a redefinition of the social and economic relationship between slaves and their masters, which gradually shifted from a coercive to a contractual one in "a slow and extended abolition."

Although my findings for the Bahamas have clear parallels with "the internal dissolution of slavery" that Rebecca J. Scott has described for Cuba in the period 1860–86, my arguments are primarily a response to Mary Turner's widely influential microstudy of two estates in eastern Jamaica between 1770 and 1830.[2] Turner has demonstrated that the slaves on those estates successfully established informal contract terms for their labor that anticipated postabolition arrangements for wage laborers. Central to Turner's argument was the existence of a labor shortage in Jamaica, after the abolition of the slave trade, which gave the slaves leverage in their negotiations for improvements in their working conditions. In the Bahamas, by contrast, concessions to slaves in the urban and rural settings (which usually involved the slaves' assumption of responsibility for self-maintenance) were a response to the existence of a surplus labor force.

The expansion of the self-hire system in Nassau and the accelerated development of a protopeasantry on the Out Islands after 1800 were indices of the advanced stage slaves had achieved along the continuum from slavery to free labor. Self-hire was a system under which urban slaves functioned as free-wage laborers while they were still property. Without the constraints on time and labor that export commodity production created, rural slaves in the Bahamas operated more as peasants than as slaves before full emancipation.

The discussion of the emergence of a protopeasantry in the Bahamas also contributes to the literature on that group, which has steadily accumulated since Sidney W. Mintz and Douglas Hall established in their 1960 essay on internal marketing in Jamaica that "both the peasant economy and its marketing patterns originated within the slave plantation."[3] My analysis centers on slaves as participants in the market economy, as consumers (an aspect of protopeasant activities on which Roderick A. McDonald has produced an important parallel study of plantations in Jamaica and Louisiana), and as owners of property—a right that was recognized in strict law in 1826.[4] The evidence from the Bahamas challenges the prevailing orthodoxy in the scholarly literature that Caribbean peasantries emerged only after emancipation.

In the Bahamas, the gradual metamorphosis of slavery into a contractual relationship after 1800 overlapped with the introduction of African recaptives who worked in the colony under a system of indentured labor that often proved harsher than slavery. My examination of the experience of the liberated Africans in the Bahamas establishes the fact that the operation of a system of contracts in connection with African laborers was not a post-emancipation development but had a precedent in the slavery era. In the edited volume *Colonialism and Migration; Indentured Labour Before and After Slavery,* for example, the organization of individual contributions reflects the assumption that African contract labor was introduced only after slavery.[5] It was perhaps this assumption that led Stanley L. Engerman, in an overview essay, to write of the transition from "servants to slaves to servants." This oversight is probably explained by the tendency among scholars of the Caribbean to view the use of contract labor solely in terms of the plantation economy.[6]

The system of indenture, suspended in 1838 and reintroduced in 1860 for incoming recaptives, was only one of several labor systems that coexisted in the postemancipation years. In the Bahamas, emancipation did not result in the general adoption of free-wage labor: precapitalist forms of production and employment survived into the twentieth century. On the Out Island plantations, a landlord-tenant relationship involving labor tenancy and sharecropping had evolved between former slaves and their former owners by full emancipation. Former slave owners who lacked the capital to control production through the money-wage nexus resorted to sharecropping, in which family members provided a "valuable labor reserve."[7]

Unlike the *mètayage* system, which Woodville Marshall has described for the British Windward Islands, sharecropping in the Bahamas did not provide a stimulus for the "creation of a self-conscious 'useful middle class of yeomanry.'"[8] With the growth of the export market for agricultural staples like pineapples, the absentee merchant-proprietors introduced a coercive element into the sharecropping system, through the credit and truck systems, that effectively reduced sharecroppers to a rural proletariat. The agrocommercial bourgeoisie also attracted a stable labor force for harvesting commodities, like sponges, for export by an advance system that provided laborers with food and clothing. Up to that point, many Out Islanders, without opportunities for wage employment, had remained on the periphery of the market economy and engaged in activities that provided them a bare subsistence. In the Bahamas, the employer class in diverse categories of employment exercised control over the labor force by a monopoly of the credit available to most Bahamians and the operation of a system of payment in truck.

The experience of the Bahamian laboring classes after emancipation most closely approaches that of their Belizean counterparts involved in the timber industry, which O. Nigel Bolland has analyzed so cogently. As Bolland has shown, the domination of that labor force was based on a combination of the advance and truck systems and a monopoly of land made possible by the white settler oligarchy's control of the colony's political institutions. In the Bahamas, by contrast, the agrocommercial elite did not succeed in effecting an enclosure movement. Although the merchant-proprietors controlled the land best suited to agricultural production, it was difficult to monopolize land in a context where many of the Out Islands were remote and the machinery of enforcement was centered on New Providence. Moreover, the sea provided an important source of subsistence and alternative employment.

The Bahamian experience on the question of labor control in the post-emancipation years reveals the limitations of Bolland's arguments on systems of domination after slavery in the British West Indies. Bolland has provided an essential corrective to the arguments of those scholars like William A. Green who have contended that the availability of land for former slaves was determined by population density. His arguments are based on two major underlying assumptions: that the production of export staples depended exclusively on wage labor created by denying the former slaves access to land and that the ownership of land guaranteed the existence of an "independent peasantry"[9] capable of resisting the domination of the landed classes. The Bahamian case shows, however, that landed proprietors made land available to members of the lower classes on the share system to secure supplies of pineapples for the export market. It also demonstrates that peasant cultivators involved in the production of a cash crop could become a dependent peasantry through their need for credit over the production cycle and their reliance on merchant-creditors for marketing services.

Examples from other areas of the British Caribbean also offer countervailing evidence to Bolland's line of argument. In both the *mètayage* system in the British Windward Islands and the cane farming system in Trinidad at the end of the nineteenth century, sugar proprietors placed land at the disposal of members of the laboring classes to guarantee supplies of cane for their factories and a source of wage labor for estate operations.[10] In Trinidad also, as my research has established, the cocoa peasantry remained vulnerable to the control of merchant-proprietors on whom they depended for consumption loans to survive between the seasons, even after the cocoa trees had come to maturity.[11] The fact is that Bolland's formulation, based mainly on the immediate postemancipation experiences of the sugar colonies, does not take into account the complex arrangements that landed proprietors in increasingly diversified economies made for export production throughout the British Caribbean by the end of the nineteenth century.

In the Bahamas, the scarcely concealed threat of state violence bolstered the domination of the agrocommercial oligarchy that exercised state power. This book, in common with such other works as David Vincent Trotman's on Trinidad and Brian L. Moore's on Guyana, examines the role of the coercive agencies, including the police and the army, in maintaining the existing social and economic order.[12] In all these colonies, the police had become a paramilitary force by the end of the nineteenth century. As I have noted elsewhere, "Questions of class and of race had a powerful influence over the execution of nineteenth-century policing in the British Caribbean."[13]

Bahamian labor migration in the late nineteenth and early twentieth centuries was prompted by a need to escape the material poverty of Out Island existence and resistance to the credit and truck systems. Bahamian labor, like that of the rest of the British Caribbean, responded to the opportunities for employment generated primarily by the expansion of American capital investment. This movement of population was a continuation of the post-emancipation migration tradition of British Caribbean peoples who formed a "migratory labor reserve" for certain countries in the Caribbean and Central America.[14] Velma Newton, Bonham C. Richardson, and Elizabeth McLean Petras have studied aspects of Caribbean labor migration.[15] This discussion is intended as a contribution to that burgeoning historical literature.

The recapitulation of the main conclusions of this book should not obscure the fact that it is primarily concerned with the operation of successive labor systems in the Bahamas. It is thus a contribution to the modest body of historical writing that attempts to reconstruct the patterns of work of the black majority in slavery and freedom in the British Caribbean. In 1783 the economic life of the colony's main settlement in New Providence rested, as Johann David Schoepf noted, on a base of slave labor.[16] More than a century later, the colony's economy depended on the labor of the descendants of the slave population. Writing in 1886 in response to a criticism of black Bahamians as "lazy and good for nothing," James Carmichael Smith, a colored member of the House of Assembly, expressed views reminiscent of Bertolt Brecht's celebrated 1939 poem, "A Worker's Questions While Reading":

> But who performs almost *all* of the hard work done in the Bahamas? Who are the actual cultivators of the soil, and the fishermen of the Sponge-beds and Turtling grounds? Who are the carpenters and masons, the wheelwrights and blacksmiths, the tailors and shoe-makers? Who construct our houses and our ships, our wharves and our streets? Who quarries the stone and fells the timber? *Who built the city of Nassau?* Who man our merchant-ships by sea and who transport our merchandise by land? Who cooks the dinner and cleans the house? Who takes care of the baby at his birth, and buries the old man at his death? Who rocks the cradle and wheels the perambulator? Who makes the coffin and digs the grave?
>
> Is there any kind of work inherent in any industrial function—extractive, constructive, exchange, professional—which coloured Bahamians, West Indians, have not successfully performed?[17]

NOTES

Introduction

1. Gordon K. Lewis, *Growth of the Modern,* 309.

2. The phrase is from Best, "Outlines of a Model," 283.

Chapter 1: The Bahamian Economy to 1815

1. Sealey, *The Bahamas Today,* 3–4, 5–7.

2. Keegan, *The People Who Discovered Columbus,* 46–47.

3. Ibid., 220–22.

4. Craton and Saunders, *Islanders in the Stream,* 64–69.

5. Ibid., 73–76.

6. Ibid., 79.

7. Quoted in Craton and Saunders, *Islanders in the Stream,* 89.

8. Quoted in Feduccia, ed., *Catesby's Birds of Colonial America,* 165.

9. Oldmixon, *History of the Isle,* 12.

10. Quoted in Riley, *Homeward Bound,* 38.

11. Craton and Saunders, *Islanders in the Stream,* 95–97.

12. Oldmixon, *History of the Isle,* 11.

13. Craton and Saunders, *Islanders in the Stream,* 104–48.

14. Bruce, *Bahamian Interlude,* 47. *The Memoirs of Peter Henry Bruce, Esq.* was originally published in 1782, but those matters relating to his Bahamian stay were excerpted in the publication cited above, with an introduction by Richard Kent, in 1949.

15. Schoepf, *Travels in the Confederation,* 2:265–85.

16. *Bahama Gazette,* 11–15 April 1800.

17. Schoepf, *Travels in the Confederation,* 2:271–72. Pieces of eight were imaginary units of currency used to establish rates of exchange between the several coins of European colonial powers that circulated in the Bahamas in this period. For an expert discussion of the currency situation in the Atlantic world before the American Revolution, see McCusker, *Money and Exchange,* 3–26.

18. Craton and Saunders, *Islanders in the Stream,* 179–89.

19. Chaplin, *An Anxious Pursuit,* 7.

20. Siebert, *Loyalists in East Florida,* 1:148–50.

21. Quoted in Albury, *Story of the Bahamas,* 113.

22. Craton and Saunders, *Islanders in the Stream,* 179–93. Peters, "The American Loyalists," 67–68.

23. McKinnen, *Tour Through the British West Indies,* 176.

24. Saunders, "Slave Life, Slave Society," 333.

25. Gray, *History of Agriculture,* 2:678.

26. See advertisement by the Commissioners of Roads, 2 December 1789, *Bahama Gazette,* 15–19 January 1790, 30 April 1815.

27. *Bahama Gazette,* 23–30 October 1784. See also advertisement by Peter Dean and Company, *Bahama Gazette,* 4–11 December 1784. Cf. Hurt, *Agriculture and Slavery,* 66.

28. *Bahama Gazette,* 11–18 July 1789.

29. *Bahama Gazette,* 12–15 April 1791; Peters, "The American Loyalists and the Plantation Period," 124.

30. *Bahama Gazette,* 16 April 1815.

31. See, for example, Colin A. Hughes, *Race and Politics,* 5.

32. Chaplin, "Creating a Cotton South," 174–83.

33. Chaplin, *An Anxious Pursuit,* 7.

34. Craton and Saunders, *Islanders in the Stream,* 123.

35. Schoepf, *Travels in the Confederation,* 2:273.

36. Gray, *History of Agriculture,* 1:551.

37. Gray argued that in the early years after the introduction of Eli Whitney's cotton gin in the American South, "there were no uniform methods of planting and cultivation." Gray, *History of Agriculture,* 2:689.

38. "On the Culture of Cotton," *Bahama Gazette,* 12–15 January 1790.

39. Saunders, "Slave Life, Slave Society," 337. Philip D. Morgan has noted that there were elements of gang labor in the task system used in rice culture in the lowcountry. Morgan, "Black Society in the Lowcountry," 105.

40. Saunders, *Slavery in the Bahamas,* 94.

41. Peters, "The American Loyalists and the Plantation Period," 54.

42. *Bahama Gazette,* 11–18 July 1789, 18–21 May 1790. Cf. Chaplin, *An Anxious Pursuit,* 290; Betty Wood, *Slavery in Colonial Georgia,* 139.

43. Saunders, "Slave Life, Slave Society," 338.

44. Craton, "Hobbesian or Panglossian?," 354. Cf. Campbell, *An Empire for Slavery,* 126.

45. See supplement to *Bahama Gazette,* 30 April 1815.

46. *Bahama Gazette,* 23–27 February 1798.

47. Craton and Saunders, *Islanders in the Stream,* 208 and 424, note 27. The ratio probably reflected the idea, brought from Georgia, that 30 slaves to 1 overseer was the optimum figure. See Betty Wood, *Slavery in Colonial Georgia,* 138.

48. *Bahama Gazette,* 1–4 April 1800.

49. *Bahama Gazette,* 17–24 January 1789, 21–28 November 1789, 3–5 February 1790, 16–19 March 1790.

50. *Royal Gazette,* February 1806. See advertisement by James Wallace.

51. *Bahama Gazette,* 12–16 November 1790. According to Peters, a taskable hand was a field slave between sixteen and sixty years old, whereas a half-taskable hand was one from twelve to sixteen or over sixty years old. Peters, "The American Loyalists and the Plantation Period," 150–51.

52. *Royal Gazette,* 4–8 September 1795, 16 January 1808; *Bahama Gazette,* 4–8 September 1795.

53. Cf. Goldfield, "Pursuing the American Urban Dream," 65.

54. *Bahama Gazette,* 16–23 April 1785.

55. *Bahama Gazette,* 18–21 October 1796. See also notices by Frederick Fine, *Bahama Gazette,* 15–18 April 1800, and Valeria Patton, *Bahama Gazette,* 23 March 1813.

56. Cf. Sarah S. Hughes, "Slaves for Hire," 271–72; Campbell, *An Empire for Slavery,* 81–82.

57. Wills of Edward Turner, 1769; Elizabeth Edgecombe, 8 March 1807; John Lusher, Turks Island, 5 February 1824. Abstracts from Supreme Court Wills. Bahamas Archives.

58. Morris, "The Measure of Bondage," 233.

59. Wills of Will Smith, Grand Key, Turks Island, May 1820; Samuel Mackey, 4 September 1818; John Lowe, 25 May 1824. Abstracts from Supreme Court Wills. Bahamas Archives.

60. Hired slaves were occasionally employed on the Out Islands to maintain the public roads. See, for example, notice by Commissioners of the Roads for Great and Little Exuma, *Bahama Gazette,* 14–18 January 1791. Cf. Starobin, *Industrial Slavery,* 30–31.

61. *Bahama Gazette,* 26–29 July 1796, 22–26 August 1810. See also notice by Commissioners for the Western District, New Providence, *Royal Gazette,* 16 September 1809.

62. See advertisements in *Bahama Gazette,* 4–7 July 1797, 26–29 August 1800, 29 August–2 September 1800, 7–10 May 1799.

63. *Bahama Gazette,* 27 December 1788–3 January 1789.

64. *Bahama Gazette,* 14–21 July 1797, 28 July–1 August 1797, 28–31 August 1798. Cf. Smith, *Slavery and Plantation Growth,* 76.

65. "Extracts from an Act for imposing and laying certain rates, assessments and taxes for the year 1800." *Bahama Gazette,* 18–21 February 1800. Slave owners were exempted from paying a tax on slaves who were apprentices. Cf. Peter H. Wood, *Black Majority,* 205–6.

66. *Bahama Gazette,* 1–5 February 1793. Cf. Sarah S. Hughes, "Slaves for Hire," 282; Peter H. Wood, *Black Majority,* 206.

67. Cf. Aptheker, "Slave Resistance," 166; Hart, *Black Jamaicans' Struggle,* 5–6.

68. *Bahama Gazette,* 2–6 March 1792, 20–23 October 1795.

69. Cf. Ronald L. Lewis, *Coal, Iron, and Slaves,* 88; Morgan, "Black Life," 222–23.

70. *Bahama Gazette,* 9–16 October 1784, 12–19 September 1789, 14–17 April 1795.

71. Cf. Ronald L. Lewis, *Coal, Iron, and Slaves,* 96; *Bahama Gazette,* 18–21 October 1796.

72. See statement by William Wylly to a select committee of the House of Assembly on a proposal for a general registry of slaves, December 1815. Enclosure in Charles Cameron to Earl Bathurst, 24 January 1816. C.O. 23/63.

73. *Bahama Gazette,* 25 November–2 December 1786.

74. See Proclamation of 17 June 1790, reprinted in *Bahama Gazette,* 15–18 June 1790. See also the Proclamation by Robert Hunter of 30 August 1797, reprinted in *Bahama Gazette,* 1–5 September 1797.

75. For an example of the use of the term "free coloreds" to include both free browns and free blacks, see "The Petition of the Undersigned Inhabitants of New Providence [undated]." Enclosure in William Vesey Munnings to the Earl of Liverpool, 22 August 1811. C.O. 23/58.

76. See report of the speech by Chief Justice William Vesey Munnings, 16 March 1819, in *Bahama Gazette,* 17 March 1819.

77. *Bahama Gazette,* 24–27 December 1793, 4 November 1813.

78. Riley, *Homeward Bound,* 140.

79. Nash and Soderlund, *Freedom by Degrees,* 173–78.

80. For an example of a free colored who served an indenture on a plantation, see notice by Henry Glenton, *Bahama Gazette,* 1–8 August 1789. For examples of indentured white servants, see runaway notice by Hugh Dean, *Bahama Gazette,* 1–8 October 1785.

81. *Bahama Gazette,* 18–25 July 1789, 29 July–1 August 1794, 26–29 January 1796; *Royal Gazette,* 21 February 1806.

82. Saunders, "Slave Life, Slave Society," 333.

83. See editorial, *Bahama Gazette,* 3–5 February 1790.

84. See letter from "A Planter," 27 March 1794, in *Bahama Gazette,* 1–4 April 1794.

85. Reprinted in *Bahama Gazette,* 24–27 May 1791.

86. See letter from Thomas Brown et al., 22 December 1790, in *Bahama Gazette,* 4 January 1791. Eve had introduced a prototype of the cotton gin as early as 1796, but it had not gone into general production because its operation was regarded as too complicated.

87. See letter from "A Planter," 16 June 1795, in *Bahama Gazette,* 16–19 June 1795.

88. See extract of a letter from "A Cotton Planter at Long Island," 28 May 1792, in *Bahama Gazette,* 1–5 June 1792.

89. "Cursory Thoughts on the Present State of Cotton Planting in These Islands," by "Urbanus," 8 April 1789, in *Bahama Gazette,* 4–11 April 1789.

90. See editorial, *Bahama Gazette,* 1–4 March 1791.

91. Saunders, "Slave Life, Slave Society," 333; see table 1 in this source.

92. Editorials on "Cotton Planting," *Bahama Gazette,* 11–15; 15–18 April 1800.

93. Editorial, *Bahama Gazette,* 17–24 October 1789. Cf. John Hebron Moore, *Emergence of the Cotton Kingdom,* 89.

94. Editorial on "Cotton Planting," *Bahama Gazette,* 15–18 April 1800.

95. Editorial on "Cotton Planting," *Bahama Gazette,* 18–22 April 1800.

96. Letter from "A Gentleman at Exuma," *Bahama Gazette,* 1–4 March 1791.

97. Editorials, *Bahama Gazette,* 11–14 December 1792, 21–25 November 1794.

98. Letter to "The Planters of the Bahama Islands" by William Wylly, 7 February 1806, in *Royal Gazette,* 11 March 1806.

99. Letter from "A Cotton Planter," *Bahama Gazette,* 16–19 April 1799; Peters, "The American Loyalists and the Plantation Period," 150–51.

100. Saunders, "Slave Life, Slave Society," 333.

101. Cited in Craton and Saunders, *Islanders in the Stream,* 192.

102. Letter from "A Cotton Planter," *Bahama Gazette,* 16–19 April 1799.

103. For an example of a planter who was forced to sell his land and slaves under general court executions, see the notices concerning Mr. Glenton in *Royal Gazette,* 1 July 1809.

104. See editorial on "Cotton Planting," *Bahama Gazette,* 15–18 April 1800.

105. Riley, *Homeward Bound,* 190.

106. McKinnen, *Tour Through the British West Indies,* 154, 160.

107. See supplement to the *Bahama Gazette,* 30 April 1815.

108. For the full text of "An Act for encouraging the cultivation of Corn within these Islands," see *Bahama Gazette,* 16 January 1812.

109. *Bahama Gazette,* 19 December 1813.

110. See notice by John Coakley, 16 December 1813, in *Bahama Gazette,* 19 December 1813.

111. Peters, "The American Loyalists and the Plantation Period," 159–61.

112. *Royal Gazette,* 28 January 1806.

113. Letter to "The Planters of the Bahama Islands," 7 February 1806, in *Royal Gazette,* 11 March 1816.

114. McKinnen, *Tour Through the British West Indies,* 136, 159.

115. See supplement to the *Bahama Gazette,* 30 April 1815.

116. Craton and Saunders, *Islanders in the Stream,* 197–98.

117. Melish, *A Description,* 10.

118. Wylly to Zachary Macaulay, 15 April 1812. Enclosure in Charles Cameron to Earl Bathurst, 24 January 1816. C.O. 23/63. Wylly, a Loyalist, was at this point serving as the colony's attorney general. He was a cotton planter and slave owner who owned three plantations at the western end of New Providence.

119. Anderson and Gallman, "Slaves as Fixed Capital," 24.

120. For a valuable discussion of slave demography during this period, see Craton and Saunders, *Islanders in the Stream,* chapter 16. See chapter 4 of this volume for an examination of the impact of the liberated Africans on the colony's labor market.

121. See Johnson, "A Slow and Extended Abolition."

Chapter 2: The Self-Hire System and the Transition to Contractual Relations in Nassau

1. See Johnson, "A Slow and Extended Abolition."

2. Schoepf, *Travels in the Confederation,* 2:301.

3. Blum, *Lord and Peasant,* 203–4, 400; Kolchin, *Unfree Labor,* 45, 110; Kula, "Money and the Serfs," 40–41.

4. Schoepf, *Travels in the Confederation,* 2:273. Cf. Mingay, *A Social History,* 92.

5. *Bahama Gazette,* 22–25 January 1799.

6. See discussion in chapter 1.

7. Cf. Neville A. T. Hall, *Slave Society,* 88.

8. Craton, "Hope Town and Hard Bargain," 274.

9. "An Act to consolidate and bring into one Act the several Laws relating to Slaves . . ." in Manuscript Laws of the Bahamas, 29 September 1729–17 August 1792. Bahamas Archives.

10. For an interesting parallel, see Hahn, "Hunting, Fishing, and Foraging," 37–64.

11. For examples of proprietors dealing in wood and ballast, see advertisements by John Allen, Robert Weir, and James Gould in *Royal Gazette,* 22 February 1805.

12. *Bahama Gazette,* 30 October–6 November 1784, 20–24 May 1791.

13. See, for example, advertisements by Abraham Greenage, *Bahama Gazette,* 6–10 December 1799; John Ferguson, Senior, *Bahama Gazette,* 3–6 June 1800; Isaac Baillou, *Royal Gazette,* 29 January 1805; Samuel Moxey and George Saunders, *Bahama Gazette,* 16 March 1815.

14. Presentments of the Grand Jury for the November Term 1799, *Bahama Gazette,* 6–10 December 1799. Cf. Peter H. Wood, *Black Majority,* 210; Morgan, "Black Life," 194; Betty Wood, "'White Society,'" 317; John Hebron Moore, *Emergence of the Cotton Kingdom,* 279.

15. See notice by Peter Edwards, the Acting Magistrate, 2 June 1800 in *Bahama Gazette,* 3–6 June 1800.

16. Presentments of the Grand Jury for the November Term 1799, *Bahama Gazette,* 6–10 December 1799.

17. Betty Wood, *Slavery in Colonial Georgia,* 143–44.

18. See report by a select committee of the House of Assembly, December 1815. Enclosure in Charles Cameron to Earl Bathurst, 24 January 1816. C.O. 23/63.

19. Eltis, "The Traffic in Slaves," 58; Craton and Saunders, *Islanders in the Stream,* 225.

20. James Carmichael Smyth to Sir George Murray, 10 April 1830, no. 10. C.O. 23/82. Carmichael Smyth had also observed in 1831 that "many of the slaves in this colony, pay a monthly sum to their owners, & look out for work & employment as they please." See James Carmichael Smyth to Viscount Goderich, 2 May 1831, no. 93. C.O. 23/84.

21. Charles Penny to William Colebrooke, 9 November 1835. Enclosure in William Colebrooke to Baron Glenelg, 21 November 1835, no. 115. C.O. 23/94.

22. Alexander Murray to Earl Bathurst, 10 August 1816. C.O. 23/63. For a discussion of the terms of employment of the liberated Africans, see chapter 4.

23. See Karasch, *Slave Life in Rio de Janeiro,* 185–213; Mattoso, *To Be a Slave in Brazil,* 121–23. For an excellent overview of the operation of the self-hire system in the British Caribbean, see Higman, *Slave Populations,* 237–38, 242, 244–47, 258–59.

24. James Carmichael Smyth to Viscount Goderich, 2 August 1832, no. 163. C.O. 23/87.

25. Message to Governor Lewis Grant from the House of Assembly, 1 January 1823. *Votes of the House of Assembly of the Bahama Islands,* 31–32.

26. James Carmichael Smyth to Sir George Murray, 8 March 1830, no. 30. C.O. 23/82.

27. See statement by William Wylly to the select committee of the House of Assembly on a proposal for a general registry of slaves, December 1815. Enclosure in Charles Cameron to Earl Bathurst, 24 January 1816. C.O. 23/63.

28. "Report on the State and Condition of the Liberated Africans," 10 October 1828. Enclosure no. 7 in Lewis Grant to Sir George Murray, 10 October 1828, no. 19. C.O. 23/79.

29. *Bahama Gazette,* 29 November–3 December 1799.

30. See "An Act to consolidate and bring into one Act the several Laws relating to Slaves . . ." in Manuscript Laws of the Bahamas, 29 September 1729–17 August 1792. Bahamas Archives. Cf. Higman, *Slave Populations,* 237–38.

31. Presentments of the Grand Jury, February Term 1795, in *Bahama Gazette,* 27 February–3 March 1795. Cf. Morgan, "Black Life," 194.

32. See notice by John J. Smith, High Constable, 21 December 1804, in *Royal Gazette,* 25 December 1804.

33. "Report on the State and Condition of the Liberated Africans," 10 October 1828. Enclosure no. 7 in Lewis Grant to Sir George Murray, 10 October 1828, no. 19. C.O. 23/79. Cf. Neville A. T. Hall, *Slave Society,* 90–91.

34. "Report on the State and Condition of the Liberated Africans," 10 October 1828. Enclosure no. 7 in Lewis Grant to Sir George Murray, 10 October 1828, no. 19. C.O. 23/79, 88.

35. Stern, "Feudalism, Capitalism," 854.

36. Higman, *Slave Populations,* 237.

37. "Report on the State and Condition of the Liberated Africans," 10 October 1828. Enclosure no. 7 in Lewis Grant to Sir George Murray, 10 October 1828, no. 19. C.O. 23/79. The quotation of wage rates in both dollars and pounds sterling reflects the fact that British silver and Spanish and United States dollars circulated in the Bahamas at this point. See memorandum in *Bahama Argus,* 2 December 1835.

38. For an extended discussion of this point, see Johnson, "Slave Life and Leisure."

39. Craton, *History of the Bahamas,* 187–88.

40. James Carmichael Smyth to Sir George Murray, 8 March 1830, no. 30. C.O. 23/82.

41. Higman, *Slave Populations,* 380; see table 10.1 in this source.

42. Cf. Morris, "The Measure of Bondage," 234–35; Eaton, "Slave–Hiring," 672; Wade, *Slavery in the Cities,* 48–54; Goldin, *Urban Slavery,* 38–42; Schweninger, "The Free-Slave Phenomenon," 303–304; "The Underside of Slavery," 9–14; *Black Property Owners,* 36–44; Morgan, "Black Life," 191–94. By the closing years of the eighteenth century, slaves and free coloreds in Nassau lived in the Negro Town. See Craton and Saunders, *Islanders in the Stream,* 195.

43. *Bahama Gazette,* 15–18 December 1795; *Royal Gazette,* 30 June 1808; *Bahama Argus,* 21 September 1831. See also notices by Stephen Haven, 28 October 1800, in *Bahama Gazette,* 24–28 October 1800; and Robert Bell, 13 November 1813, in *Bahama Gazette,* 14 November 1813.

44. *Bahama Gazette,* 19–22 July 1796; 5–8 August 1800; 4–7 November 1800.

45. Presentments of the Grand Jury, February 1790, in *Bahama Gazette,* 5–9 March 1790.

46. *Bahama Gazette,* 17–21 May 1799. Cf. Eaton, "Slave–Hiring," 672; *Bahama Gazette,* 25–28 June 1799; *Bahama Gazette,* 17–21 January 1794. See also notice by S. A. Poitier, *Royal Gazette,* 27 June 1832.

47. James Carmichael Smyth to Viscount Goderich, 2 August 1832, no. 163. C.O. 23/86. In England, servants were punished as criminals for breaches of contract under the Masters and Servants Act until 1875.

48. Thomas Winder to William Colebrooke, 26 August 1836. Enclosure in William Colebrooke to Earl of Glenelg, 27 August 1836, no. 90. C.O. 23/97.

49. See "Extract from An Act for regulating the hire of Slaves, Carts, Waggons and Drays . . ." in *Bahama Gazette,* 19–23 December 1800. Cf. Goldin, *Urban Slavery,* 39; Betty Wood, *Slavery in Colonial Georgia,* 144.

50. See "Extract from An Act the more effectively to prevent desertion of Slaves . . ." in *Bahama Gazette,* 19–23 December 1800.

51. *Bahama Gazette,* 30 September–3 October 1800.

52. See the discussion by Turner, "Chattel Slaves into Wage Slaves," 14–31.

53. Mintz, "Slavery and the Rise of Peasantries," 240. See also Mintz, "Was the Plantation Slave a Proletarian?," 93–94.

Chapter 3: The Restructuring of Agrarian Relations After 1800

1. The term "protoproletarianization" is suggested by Bolland's "Proto–Proletarians?"

2. The phrase "peasant breach" originated with Tadeusz Lepkowski. See Cardoso, "Peasant Breach," 49.

3. Craton, "Hobbesian or Panglossian?," 355. Sidney W. Mintz has defined the term "protopeasantry" in this way: "A third category of peasantry I have referred to elsewhere as a "proto–peasantry" . . . by which I meant simply that the subsequent adaptation to a peasant style of life was worked out by people when they were still enslaved." Mintz, *Caribbean Transformations,* 151.

4. The term "peasantry" is used here as defined by Mintz: "rural cultivators with access to land who produce part of their subsistence, sell part of their product, and are economically and politically under the control of others, within a specific time period and region." See Mintz, "Slavery and the Rise of Peasantries," 218, note 9.

5. "An Act for the Governing of Negroes, Mulattoes and Indians" in Manuscript Laws of the Bahamas, 29 September 1729–17 August 1792. Bahamas Archives. For a parallel development in Belize, see Bolland, "Reply to William A. Green's," 121.

6. Schoepf, *Travels in the Confederation,* 2:301.

7. Bruce, *Bahamian Interlude,* 47.

8. Schoepf, *Travels in the Confederation,* 2:301.

9. Cf. Mintz, *Caribbean Transformations,* 194.

10. *Bahama Gazette,* 17–24 October 1789.

11. Letter from "A Planter," 13 March 1794, in *Bahama Gazette,* 18–21 March 1794.

12. *Bahama Gazette,* 6–13 June 1789.

13. Berlin, "Time, Space and the Evolution," 65; Morgan, "Work and Culture," 598, note 148.

14. "An Act to consolidate and bring into one Act the several Laws relating to Slaves. . . ." in Manuscript Laws of the Bahamas, 29 September 1729–17 August 1792. Bahamas Archives.

15. Goveia, *Slave Society;* see also chapter 1 of this book.

16. For the impact of the decline in the cotton industry on the work routine of slaves on the Rolle plantations in the Bahamas, see Craton, "Hobbesian or Panglossian?," 354–56.

17. In the last years of slavery, gang labor was used mainly in salt raking, in which the arduous and unpleasant nature of the work made direct supervision necessary. Blayney Balfour to Lord Stanley, 5 August 1833, no. 37. C.O. 23/89.

18. For a discussion of this feature of the task system in the lowcountry, see Strickland, "Traditional Culture and Moral Economy," 145. For the Bahamian context, see McKinnen, *Tour Through the British West Indies,* 172–73.

19. Gray, *History of Agriculture,* 1:552; Strickland, "Traditional Culture and Moral Economy," 145. For a description of the Bahamian arrangement, see William Wylly to Zachary Macaulay, 15 April 1812. Enclosure in Charles Cameron to Earl Bathurst, 24 January 1816. C.O. 23/63.

20. Cited in Higman, *Slave Populations,* 179.

21. Gaspar, "Slavery, Amelioration and Sunday Markets," 4. See also Neville A. T. Hall, *Slave Society,* 110. Cf. Morgan, "Work and Culture," 399–400; Berlin, "Time, Space and the Evolution," 65–66.

22. McKinnen, *Tour Through the British West Indies,* 172–73.

23. Alexander Murray to the Earl of Liverpool, 18 April 1812. C.O. 23/59.

24. Johnson, "Labour Systems in Postemancipation Bahamas," 181.

25. Morgan, "Work and Culture," 566. In the Bahamas, the basic task unit seems to have been established by the cotton industry, and it was set at a quarter of an acre. By 1828 the task unit in Out Island plantations, which specialized in the production of provisions for the Nassau market, was one acre.

26. William Wylly to Zachary Macaulay, 15 April 1812. Enclosure in Charles Cameron to Earl Bathurst, 24 January 1816. C.O. 23/63.

27. William Wylly to Zachary Macaulay, 15 April 1812. For comparable developments in divergent economies, see Usner, "The Frontier Exchange Economy," 184–85; Schwartz, *Slaves, Peasants, and Rebels,* chapter 2. See also the essays in Berlin and Morgan, eds., *Cultivation and Culture;* Tomich, *Slavery in the Circuit of Sugar,* chapter 8; McDonald, *The Economy and Material Culture.*

28. "Regulations for the Government of the Slaves at Clifton and Tusculum in New Providence, July 1815," 156. C.O. 23/67.

29. William Wylly to William Vesey Munnings, 31 August 1818. Enclosure in William Vesey Munnings to Earl Bathurst, 9 September 1818. C.O. 23/67.

30. Message to Governor Lewis Grant from the House of Assembly, 3 December 1823. *Votes of the House of Assembly of the Bahama Islands,* 1821–1824.

31. James Carmichael Smyth to Sir George Murray, 29 April 1830. C.O. 23/82.

32. See statement by William Wylly to a select committee of the House of Assembly on a proposal for a general registry of slaves, December 1815. Enclosure in Charles Cameron to Earl Bathurst, 24 January 1816. C.O. 23/63.

33. See report of James Moss's trial on a charge of providing his slaves with less than the legally stipulated rations, April 1815. Enclosure in William Vesey Munnings to Earl Bathurst, 10 August 1818. C.O. 23/67.

34. Cf. McDonald, *The Economy and Material Culture,* 69.

35. *Royal Gazette,* 1 March 1805; *Bahama Argus,* 16 July 1834.

36. For a valuable discussion of plantation slaves in Jamaica and Louisiana as consumers, see McDonald, *The Economy and Material Culture.* See also Walvin, "Slaves, Free Time."

37. *Royal Gazette,* 13 April 1807; *Bahama Gazette,* 21 July 1814.

38. "An Act to consolidate and bring into one Act the several Laws relating to Slaves" in Manuscript Laws of the Bahamas, 29 September 1729–17 August 1792. Bahamas Archives. See also Sheridan, *Doctors and Slaves,* 170–71.

39. Higman, *Slave Populations,* 223.

40. See Presentments of the Grand Jury, February Term, 1795, in *Bahama Gazette,* 27 February–3 March 1795.

41. See, for example, advertisement in *Bahama Gazette,* 3–10 January 1789.

42. 7 Geo. IV. c.1, clause xxxvi, *Laws of the Bahamas,* 1826. Cf. Mintz and Hall, "Jamaican Internal Marketing System," 21–22; McDonald, *The Economy and Material Culture,* 149; Schwartz, *Slaves, Peasants, and Rebels,* 46.

43. Goveia, *West Indian Slave Laws,* 26.

44. See estimates of Africans landed in the Bahamas by Canzoneri, "Early History of the Baptists," 9.

45. For a detailed discussion of the liberated Africans, see chapter 4.

46. "Report on the State and Condition of the Liberated Africans," 10 October 1828. Enclosure no. 7 in Lewis Grant to Sir George Murray, 10 October 1828, no. 19. C.O. 23/79.

47. David Galenson's comment on the status of the indentured European servant in British America is applicable to the African apprentice in the Bahamas: "The indenture did not make the servant a slave, for it was the servant's labor rather than his person, that was temporarily owned by the master." Galenson, *White Servitude in Colonial America,* 3.

48. Gray, *History of Agriculture,* 1:552; Morgan, "Work and Culture," 581. The area of land to which the term "task" referred on the plantations of the Out Islands can be gauged from the apprentice Ele's statement as reported by the committee on "the state and condition" of the liberated Africans: "That he has three pieces of Ground of his own; consisting of five fields, one of three tasks, another of one Task and the third of Six Tasks, equal to Ten Acres." C.O. 23/79.

49. C.O. 23/79.

50. See discussion in chapter 4.

51. "Report on the State and Condition of the Liberated Africans." C.O. 23/79.

52. See discussion in chapter 5. Cf. Morgan, "Work and Culture," 585.

53. "Report on the State and Condition of the Liberated Africans." C.O. 23/79.

54. Handler has identified these features as "simple technologies, limited capital, small land units, production of foodstuffs for household consumption and, most importantly, sale within a market economy; and in addition, the production of items specifically designed for market exchange and not necessarily for household consumption *per se.*" Handler, "The History of Arrowroot," 49.

55. "Report on the State and Condition of the Liberated Africans." C.O. 23/79. See also Mintz and Hall, "Jamaican Internal Marketing System," 15.

56. C. Poitier to Earl Bathurst, 8 February 1825. C.O. 23/74.

57. C. Poitier to Lewis Grant, 5 May 1825. Enclosure in Lewis Grant to R. W. Horton, 18 April 1826. C.O. 23/75.

58. Lewis Grant to R. W. Horton, 18 April 1826. C.O. 23/75.

59. James Carmichael Smyth to Viscount Goderich, 5 February 1832, no. 137. C.O. 23/86.

60. See, for example, Adamson, *Sugar Without Slaves,* 38; Frucht, "A Caribbean Social Type," 295–300.

61. "Report on the State and Condition of the Liberated Africans." C.O. 23/79.

62. *Laws of the Bahamas, in Force on the 14th March, 1842,* 183–84. The provisions of the law made it clear that the legislators were exempting the peasant sector: "That nothing herein contained shall be construed to prohibit the sale, without licence, of milk, poultry, eggs, vegetables, grass, cornblades, or the like; fruit, roots, firewood, fish, game, bread–cakes, corn grits, shells, sugar, coffee, mats, baskets, brooms or other articles of the growth and manufacture of the Bahama Islands, and sold by the maker thereof."

63. Tomich, *Slavery in the Circuit of Sugar,* 260.

64. The phrase "networks of exchange" is from Usner, "Food Marketing and Interethnic Exchange," 292. Cf. Schwartz, *Slaves, Peasants, and Rebels,* 83.

65. The phrase is from Mintz, "Slavery and the Rise of Peasantries," 219.

Chapter 4: Between Slavery and Freedom: The Liberated Africans and Unfree Labor

1. For a discussion of the experience of liberated Africans in Cuba and Brazil, respectively, see Murray, *Odious Commerce,* chapter 13; and Conrad, *World of Sorrow,* chapter 7. For examples of other slave societies in the Americas where slavery underwent a slow dissolution, see Scott, *Slave Emancipation in Cuba;* and Fields, *Slavery and Freedom.*

2. Historians of the Caribbean have traditionally discussed the liberated Africans exclusively in the context of the labor demands of the plantation economy after 1834. See, for example, Laurence, *Immigration into the West Indies,* 13–16; Schuler, *"Alas, Alas, Kongo"* and "Recruitment of African Indentured Labourers," 125–61. The exceptions are Dalleo, "Africans in the Caribbean," 15–24; Saunders, *Slavery in the Bahamas,* 193–204.

3. Bethell, "The Mixed Commissions," 79–93.

4. Curtin, *The Atlantic Slave Trade,* 234, table 67.

5. Schuler, "Recruitment of African Indentured Labourers," 128.

6. Laurence, *Immigration into the West Indies,* 13–16.

7. William Vesey Munnings to the Earl of Liverpool, 22 August 1811. C.O. 23/58. Munnings was chief justice of the colony and president of the council.

8. Enclosure in William Vesey Munnings to the Earl of Liverpool, 25 November 1811. C.O. 23/58.

9. For estimates of the number of Africans landed in the Bahamas, see Dalleo, "Africans in the Caribbean," 24; and Canzoneri, "Early History of the Baptists," 9.

10. Quoted in North, "Amelioration and Abolition of Slavery," 77.

11. Enclosure in William Vesey Munnings to the Earl of Liverpool, 22 August 1811. C.O. 23/58. The terms "liberated Africans" and "recaptives" are used interchangeably. For a discussion of this point, see Fyfe, "Freed Slave Colonies," 181. Cf. Murray, *Odious Commerce,* 272.

12. Enclosure in William Vesey Munnings to the Earl of Liverpool, 22 August 1811. C.O. 23/58.

13. Enclosure in William Vesey Munnings to the Earl of Liverpool, 25 November 1811. C.O. 23/58.

14. "An Account of the Population of the Island of New Providence taken in the month of December 1810." Enclosure in William Vesey Munnings to Robert Peel, 16 July 1812. C.O. 23/59. Cf. Berlin, *Slaves Without Masters,* 219.

15. John Richardson to William Colebrooke, 12 November 1836. Enclosure in William Colebrooke to Baron Glenelg, 15 November 1836, no. 120. C.O. 23/97. Richardson was the surgeon to the Second West India Regiment, which was stationed in Nassau.

16. "Report on the State and Condition of the Liberated Africans in the Bahamas," 10 October 1828. Enclosure no. 7 in Lewis Grant to Sir George Murray, no. 19, 10 October 1828. C.O. 23/79.

17. *Bahama Gazette,* 14 May 1812.

18. Enclosure in Charles Cameron to Earl Bathurst, 24 January 1816. C.O. 23/63.

19. Ibid.

20. Charles Cameron to Bathurst, 24 January 1816. C.O. 23/63.

21. Report of a committee of the House of Assembly, 9 January 1816. Enclosure in Charles Cameron to Earl Bathurst, 24 January 1816. C.O. 23/63.

22. Charles Cameron to Earl Bathurst, 24 January 1816. C.O. 23/63.

23. Enclosure in Charles Cameron to Earl Bathurst, 12 July 1816. C.O. 23/63.

24. *Royal Gazette,* 13 July 1816.

25. Craton, *History of the Bahamas,* 184–85.

26. Charles Cameron to Earl Bathurst, 12 February 1817, no. 10. C.O. 23/64.

27. Enclosure in Charles Cameron to Earl Bathurst, 12 July 1816. C.O. 23/63. Some of the holders of African apprentices were free nonwhites.

28. Alexander Murray to Earl Bathurst, 27 September 1816. C.O. 23/63.

29. Charles Poitier to Earl Bathurst, 8 February 1825. C.O. 23/74.

30. Charles Poitier to Earl Bathurst, 4 March 1824. C.O. 23/73.

31. Charles Poitier to Earl Bathurst, 8 February 1825. C.O. 23/74.

32. James Carmichael Smyth to Viscount Goderich, 5 February 1832, no. 137. C.O. 23/86.

33. Editorial in *Bahama Argus,* 7 April 1832.

34. Charles Poitier to Earl Bathurst, 8 February 1825. C.O. 23/74.

35. Lewis Kerr to Lewis Grant, 3 May 1823. Enclosure in Lewis Grant to Earl Bathurst, 3 May 1823, no. 16. C.O. 23/72. Kerr was a member of the House of Assembly.

36. Lewis Grant to Viscount Goderich, 26 September 1827, no. 9. C.O. 23/76.

37. Lovejoy, *Transformations in Slavery,* 139.

38. Higman, *Slave Populations,* 116. For a discussion of the diverse ethnic origins of the African recaptives in the Bahamas, see Dalleo, "Africans in the Caribbean," 17.

39. For an extended discussion of this point, see Patrice Williams, *A Guide to African Villages.*

40. *Bahama Argus,* 13 August 1831.

41. *Bahama Argus,* 14 September 1831.

42. For a parallel situation in Barbados, see Le Page and Tabouret–Keller, *Acts of Identity,* 41.

43. *Bahama Argus,* 22 August 1835.

44. William Colebrooke to James Stephen, 4 October 1835. C.O. 23/94. In 1815 the House of Assembly's select committee on slave registration had also contended that it was possible to distinguish between newly arrived African and creole slaves on the basis of their "appearance, carriage, habits and language." See *Votes of the House of Assembly of the Bahama Islands,* 31 October–18 December 1815, 107.

45. Shilling, "Non–Standard Features of Bahamian Dialect Syntax," 18.

46. 4 Wm.4.c.1. *Laws of the Bahamas,* 1833.

47. 5 Wm.2.c.9. *Laws of the Bahamas,* 1834.

48. See opinion by G. Birrell, attorney general. Enclosure in William Colebrooke to Glenelg, 12 March 1836, no. 23. C.O. 23/96.

49. James Walker to James Stephen, 12 April 1836. C.O. 23/98.

50. Ibid.

51. *Votes of the House of Assembly of the Bahama Islands,* 1835–36, 53.

52. William Colebrooke to Baron Glenelg, 2 June 1836, no. 52. C.O. 23/96.

53. James Carmichael Smyth to Sir George Murray, 20 February 1830, no. 36. C.O. 23/82.

54. William Colebrooke to Baron Glenelg, 3 February 1836, no. 10. C.O. 23/96.

55. William Colebrooke to James Stephen, 19 August 1835. C.O. 23/94.

56. James Stephen to Lord Fitzroy Somerset, 10 March 1836. Bound with Francis Cockburn to Lord John Russell, 27 February 1841, no. 92. C.O. 23/109. Somerset was then military secretary of the Horse Guards.

57. Cf. Asiegbu, *Slavery and the Politics of Liberation,* 27; Murray, *Odious Commerce,* 273; Martínez Vergne, "Allocation of Liberated African Labour," 204.

58. Temperley, "Anti–Slavery," 335–50.

59. James Stephen to the Earl of Liverpool, 14 July 1811. C.O. 23/58.

60. Enclosure in William Colebrooke to Baron Glenelg, 5 August 1835, no. 77. C.O. 23/94. For a discussion of the *encomienda* system, see Wallerstein, *The Modern World-System,* 1:92–93.

61. Cf. Berlin, *Slaves Without Masters,* 227.

62. Moreno Fraginals, *The Sugarmill,* 140; Murray, *Odious Commerce,* 273; Scott, *Slave Emancipation in Cuba,* 70; Conrad, *World of Sorrow,* 154–55.

63. Lewis Grant to Earl Bathurst, 5 May 1825, no. 13. C.O. 23/74.

64. "Report on the State and Condition of the Liberated Africans," 10 October 1828. Enclosure no. 7 in Lewis Grant to Sir George Murray, 10 October 1828, no. 19. C.O. 23/79. Cf. Conrad, *World of Sorrow,* 158.

65. "Report on the State and Condition of the Liberated Africans," 10 October 1828.

66. Lewis Grant to Viscount Goderich, 26 September 1827, no. 9. C.O. 23/76.

67. "Report on the State and Condition of the Liberated Africans," 10 October 1828. Cf. Galenson, *White Servitude in Colonial America,* 171–72.

68. See chapter 6. Cf. Conrad, *World of Sorrow,* 159.

69. "Report on the State and Condition of the Liberated Africans," 10 October 1828.

70. Ibid.

71. William Vesey Munnings to Earl Bathurst, 21 February 1826, no. 12. C.O. 23/75. Schedule B.

72. "Report on the State and Condition of the Liberated Africans," 10 October 1828.

73. J. Sullivan to Earl Bathurst, 31 December 1816. C.O. 23/63.

74. Lewis Grant to Earl Bathurst, 5 May 1825, no. 13. C.O. 23/74.

75. Blayney Balfour to Thomas Spring-Rice, 8 September 1834, no. 5. C.O. 23/91.

76. William Colebrooke to Earl of Aberdeen, 12 March 1835, no. 8. C.O. 23/93.

77. William Colebrooke to Baron Glenelg, 18 July 1836, no. 77. C.O. 23/97.

78. William Colebrooke to Baron Glenelg, 1 November 1836, no. 105. C.O. 23/97.

79. "Report to the committee appointed to inspect and report upon the condition and treatment of the Liberated Africans," 6 July 1835. Reprinted in *Bahama Argus,* 11 July 1835. For a discussion of the nature of the voluntary agreements between ex–slaves and their former masters, see chapter 5.

80. Instructions to the Members of the Board of Superintendence of Liberated Africans, 18 August 1836. Enclosure in William Colebrooke to Baron Glenelg, 9 September 1836, no. 92. C.O. 23/97.

81. Francis Cockburn to Baron Glenelg, 19 May 1838, no. 75. C.O. 23/102.

82. Baron Glenelg to West Indian Governors, 15 May 1838. C.O. 318/141.

83. Baron Glenelg to Francis Cockburn, 10 August 1838, no. 79 (draft). C.O. 23/102.

84. Francis Cockburn to Lord John Russell, 27 December 1839, no. 8. C.O. 23/105.

85. Lord John Russell to Francis Cockburn, 17 March 1840, no. 23 (draft). C.O. 23/105.

86. See discussion in chapter 6.

87. Francis Cockburn to Lord John Russell, 6 April 1840, no. 20. C.O. 23/107.

88. Lord John Russell to Francis Cockburn, 30 May 1840 (draft). C.O. 23/107.

89. Charles Bayley to the Duke of Newcastle, 22 August 1860, no. 82. C.O. 23/163.

90. See discussion in chapter 6.

91. Charles Bayley to the Duke of Newcastle, 16 November 1860, no. 107. C.O. 23/163.

92. For a discussion of changing Colonial Office policy on long–term labor contracts for immigrants, see Laurence, "Evolution of Long–Term Labour Contracts," 9–27.

93. Minute by Sir Frederic Rogers, 16 October 1860, on Charles Bayley to the Duke of Newcastle, 22 August 1860, no. 82. C.O. 23/163. Sir Frederic Rogers succeeded Herman Merivale as permanent undersecretary of state for the colonies in May 1860.

94. Chichester S. Fortescue to Charles Bayley, 23 October 1860, no. 111 (draft). C.O. 23/164.

95. 24 Vic.c.2. *Laws of the Bahamas,* 1861. Cf. Wiener, "Class Structure and Economic Development," 974; Woodman, "Post–Civil War Southern Agriculture," 335.

96. 25 Vic.c.5; 26 Vic.c.16. *Laws of the Bahamas,* 1862, 1863.

97. See chapter 6 for an extended discussion of the operation of the truck system in the Bahamas.

Chapter 5: The Establishment of a Dependent Tenantry

1. Letter by James C. Smith, *Nassau Guardian,* 29 September 1886.

2. The phrase is from Bloch, "Rise of Dependent Cultivation," 253.

3. Enclosure in William Colebrooke to Lord Glenelg, 27 August 1835, no. 86. For a detailed discussion of the arrangements made for apprentices, see Johnson, "Labour Systems in Postemancipation Bahamas," 182.

4. The term "sharecropping" is used here as defined by Ralph Shlomowitz: "a labor arrangement by which individual family units, in payment for their labor on a separate parcel of land, receive a share of the output produced on that parcel of land." Shlomowitz, "Origins of Southern Sharecropping," 557, note 2.

5. Report of Special Justice Thomas Winder on his visit to the district of Eleuthera and Harbour Island, 16 May–8 June 1835. Reprinted in *Bahama Argus,* 1 July 1835.

6. Editorial on "Resources of the Bahamas," *Bahama Argus,* 24 June 1835.

7. Report of Special Justice Thomas Winder, 6 July 1836. Enclosure in Joseph Hunter to Baron Glenelg, 12 August 1836, no. 51. C.O. 23/99.

8. Ibid. The term "family–labour form of production" is from Goodman and Redclift, *From Peasant to Proletarian,* 150.

9. Millar, "On the Cultivation of Cotton," 50–51. By 1835 the sharecropping system was already being used in pineapple production. On his visit to Eleuthera in May–June 1835, Thomas Winder noted that "the apprentices [were] being allowed by their masters to raise the same [pineapples]." See Report of Special Justice Thomas Winder on Eleuthera and Harbour Island, 16 May–8 June 1835. Reprinted in the *Bahama Argus,* July 1835.

10. Thomas Winder to William Colebrooke, 4 November 1836, no. 116. C.O. 23/97.

11. Report of Special Justice Thomas Winder on a visit to Southern Eleuthera, 6 July 1837. Enclosure in Joseph Hunter to Glenelg, 12 August 1837, no. 51. C.O. 23/99. By 1838 sharecropping had also been adopted on the island of New Providence. In August of that year, Winder wrote, "On the estate of James Moss, esq., the whole of the able–bodied labourers have entered into engagements for continuing the cultivation of the land upon equitable terms, sanctioned by myself, as a justice of the peace." Report by Thomas R. Winder on district of New Providence, 2 August 1838. Enclosure in Francis Cockburn to Glenelg, 2 August 1838, no. 92. C.O. 23/103.

12. Carmichael Smyth to Viscount Goderich, 17 September 1832, no. 178. C.O. 23/86.

13. Blayney Balfour to Lord Stanley, 19 February 1834, no. 78. C.O. 23/91.

14. C. R. Nesbitt to Lord Stanley, 12 July 1842, no. 18. C.O. 23/113.

15. Enclosure in C. R. Nesbitt to Earl Grey, 7 September 1847, no. 36. C.O. 23/126.

16. Rawson Rawson to Earl of Carnarvon, 17 October 1866, no. 161. C.O. 23/185.

17. Enclosure in C. R. Nesbitt to Earl Grey, 7 September 1847, no. 36. C.O. 23/126.

18. See discussion in chapter 4.

19. C. R. Nesbitt to Thomas R. Winder, 20 December 1838. Colonial Secretary's Letter Book, 29 December 1835–17 January 1839. Bahamas Archives.

20. Ibid.

21. Agreement between James Farquharson and Jacob, 22 April 1839. O'Brien Family Collection. Bahamas Archives.

22. Lenin, *Development of Capitalism,* 200.

23. For an extended discussion of this point, see chapter 2. See also Higman, *Slave Populations,* 84.

24. Henry Blake to Earl of Derby, 28 March 1885, no. 34. C.O. 23/226.

25. Report of Special Justice Thomas Winder, 6 July 1837. Enclosure in Joseph Hunter to Baron Glenelg, 12 August 1837, no. 51. C.O. 23/99.

26. *Bahama Argus,* 24 June 1835.

27. Francis Cockburn to Lord John Russell, 6 April 1840, no. 2. C.O. 23/107.

28. Curtin, *Two Jamaicas,* 137.

29. John J. Burnside to Francis Cockburn, 11 July 1838. Enclosure in Francis Cockburn to Baron Glenelg, 5 September 1838, no. 101. C.O. 23/103.

30. C. R. Nesbitt to Lord Stanley, 12 July 1842, no. 18. C.O. 23/113.

31. Henry Blake to Frederick Stanley, 27 August 1885, no. 89. C.O. 23/226.

32. William Colebrooke to Baron Glenelg, 8 August 1835, no. 79. C.O. 23/94.

33. Minutes of evidence taken before Commissioners of Crown Lands and Woods on 6 August 1835. Reprinted in *Bahama Argus,* 22 August 1835.

34. Extract from the *Observer,* 18 August 1838. Enclosure in Francis Cockburn to Baron Glenelg, 5 September 1838, no. 101. C.O. 23/103.

35. "Statistical Summary for the half year ending 30th June 1847," table C. Enclosure in C. R. Nesbitt to Earl Grey, 7 September 1847, no. 36. C.O. 23/126.

36. Henry Blake to Sir Henry Holland, 15 March 1887, no. 34. C.O. 23/229.

37. "Statistical Summary for the half year ending 30th June 1847," table C. Enclosure in C. R. Nesbitt to Earl Grey, 7 September 1847, no. 36. C.O. 23/126.

38. Records of the United Society for the Propagation of the Gospel. Records Relating to the Bahamas 1726–1858, Microfilm Reel 3. Table and Comments. Statistical Account from 1837 to 1840.

39. Rawson Rawson to Edward Cardwell, 20 January 1866, no. 33. C.O. 23/183.

40. See Address delivered to tenants at Prospect Hall, Watling's Island, 23 August 1865, by Alexander Forsyth. O'Brien Family Collection. Bahamas Archives.

41. "Alexander Forsyth to Henry Stevenson, Esq. Report on Prospect Hill Estate, Watling's Island, 25 September 1865." O'Brien Family Collection. Bahamas Archives.

42. Address delivered to tenants at Prospect Hall, Watling's Island, 23 August 1865, by Alexander Forsyth.

43. See duplicate of agreement made between Alexander Forsyth and tenants on William J. Hall and John Harrison tracts, 18 August 1865. O'Brien Family Collection. Bahamas Archives.

44. For a description of the slash and burn technique as practiced in the Bahamas, see Henry Blake to Earl of Derby, 12 August 1884, no. 108. C.O. 23/224.

45. See duplicate of agreement between Alexander Forsyth and tenants on William J. Hall and John Harrison tracts, 18 August 1865. O'Brien Family Collection. Bahamas Archives.

46. See duplicate of agreement between Alexander Forsyth and tenants on the lands of the Estate of the late Charles Farquharson, 29 August 1865. O'Brien Family Collection. Bahamas Archives.

47. See original of agreement between Alexander Forsyth and Jacob Deveaux, Senior, 14 August 1865. O'Brien Family Collection. Bahamas Archives.

48. Henry Blake to Earl Granville, 20 March 1886, no. 32. C.O. 23/228.

49. W. F. Haynes–Smith to Joseph Chamberlain, 7 July 1896, no. 76. C.O. 23/44.

50. For a discussion of the impact of the American Civil War on the Bahamian economy, see Craton, *History of the Bahamas,* 222–24.

51. Report on Blue Book for 1865. Enclosure in Rawson Rawson to the Earl of Carnarvon, 1 September 1866, no. 142. C.O. 23/185.

52. W. Arthur Lewis, "The Export Stimulus," 14.

53. E. B. A. Taylor to the Earl of Kimberley, 29 July 1881, no. 100. C.O. 23/221.

54. James Walker to the Earl of Kimberley, 30 November 1870, no. 489. C.O. 23/202.

55. Mooney, "Soils of the Bahama Islands," 75. For an example of the concentration of land ownership, see advertisement "Valuable Pineapple Land for Sale," *Nassau Guardian,* 1 February 1899.

56. See "New Life for Pineapple Industry," *Nassau Tribune,* 14 May 1924.

57. See advertisement for J. S. Johnson Company, *Nassau Guardian,* 7 January 1893.

58. Stolcke and Hall, "Introduction of Free Labour," 174. See also Stein, *Vassouras,* 272.

59. For an excellent discussion of indebtedness as a feature of the sharecropping relationship, see Adrienne Cooper, "Sharecroppers and Landlords," 240–43. See also Mandle, *Roots of Black Poverty,* 48–50.

60. Report on San Salvador for 1885 in Appendix to *Votes of the House of Assembly of the Bahama Islands,* 23 February–26 May 1886, 29.

61. Report on San Salvador for 1900 in Appendix to *Votes of the Legislative Council of the Bahama Islands,* 19 February–11 May 1901, 69. For the experiment with wage labor in the sisal industry, see Johnson, "Labour Systems in Postemancipation Bahamas," 193–94.

62. See discussion in chapter 9.

63. Memorandum by the Colonial Secretary. "Agriculture in the Bahamas 1930," 34.

64. Marshall, "Metayage in the Sugar Industry," 50–55.

65. The phrase is Edward E. Malefakis's. Quoted in Byres, "Historical Perspectives on Sharecropping," 22–23.

Chapter 6: The Credit and Truck Systems: The Control of Credit and Labor

1. Cf. Bergad, *Coffee and the Growth,* 198.

2. For a valuable overview of the historical literature on forms of labor control in the plantation colonies after slavery, see Bolland, "Systems of Domination," 593–600. Cf. Cardoso, "Formation of the Coffee Estate," 196.

3. Henry Blake to the Earl of Derby, 12 August 1884, no. 108. C.O. 23/224. The credit and truck systems are being dealt with separately here, although most contemporary commentators did not distinguish between them and referred to them simply as the truck system. Cf. Bolland, "Systems of Domination," 593–600.

4. Department of Archives, "The Loyalist Bi–Centennial," 5.

5. For an excellent discussion of the emergence of an agrocommercial bourgeoisie in Barbados, see Karch, "Growth of the Corporate Economy," 213–41.

6. See chapter 1; Peters, "The American Loyalists," 227.

7. See Craton and Saunders, *Islanders in the Stream,* 213–17.

8. James Carmichael Smyth to Earl Bathurst, 25 January 1832. C.O. 23/86.

9. William Colebrooke to Baron Glenelg, 3 February 1836, no. 10. C.O. 23/96.

10. Lewis Grant to Viscount Goderich, 26 September 1827, no. 9. C.O. 23/76.

11. For a parallel situation in the southern United States after the Civil War, see Higgs, *Competition and Coercion,* 55. Sir Ambrose Shea, governor of the colony between 1887 and 1895, recognized that the reliance on credit was due largely to the absence of regular wages. After an 1894 visit to the Chamberlain family's sisal plantation in Andros, he commented, "Credit is rigidly refused on this estate and is easily dispensed with when wages are paid weekly." Ambrose Shea to the Marquis of Ripon, 24 April 1894, no. 63. C.O. 23/239.

12. Stavenhagen, *Social Classes in Agrarian Societies,* 147.

13. Enclosure in C. R. Nesbitt to Earl Grey, 7 September 1847, no. 36. C.O. 23/126.

14. For an excellent discussion of nineteenth-century metropolitan perceptions of what constituted work in British Africa and the British Caribbean, see Frederick Cooper, *From Slaves to Squatters,* chapter 2. See also Davidson, *Africa in Modern History,* 108.

15. Charles Bayley to Henry Labouchere, 23 September 1857, no. 51. C.O. 23/154. For a similar view, see William Robinson to the Earl of Carnarvon, 24 June 1875, no. 137. C.O. 23/213. Cf. Bauer, "Rural Workers in Spanish America," 55.

16. It is most likely that the freeholders to whom Bayley referred were mainly squatters. See Henry Blake to Stanley, 27 August 1885, no. 89. C.O. 23/226.

17. For a discussion of the pineapple and sponge industries in the late nineteenth century, see Craton, *History of the Bahamas,* 233–41.

18. Henry Blake to the Earl of Derby, 12 August 1884, no. 108. C.O. 23/224. A system of advances was used as a method of labor recruitment in South Africa and Nigeria. See Bundy, *The Rise and Fall,* 130; Shenton and Lennihan, "Capital and Class," 56–62. For a general discussion, see Kloosterboer, *Involuntary Labour,* 199.

19. Francis Cockburn to Lord John Russell, 6 April 1840, no. 20. C.O. 23/107.

20. See also discussion in chapter 5.

21. Francis Cockburn to Lord Stanley, 19 May 1843, no. 18. C.O. 23/115.

22. Enclosure in C. R. Nesbitt to Earl Grey, 7 September 1847, no. 36. C.O. 23/126.

23. See also letter by Winfred W. Richardson, *Nassau Guardian,* 26 April 1889.

24. *Nassau Guardian,* 27 April 1889. For a description of the truck system as it operated in England, see Hammond and Hammond, *The Town Labourer,* 45–50; Hilton, *The Truck System.* The truck system was also used in Russia in the late nineteenth century. See Crisp, "Labour and Industrialization in Russia," 380. For an excellent discussion of the operation of a truck system in a colonial context, see Graves, "Truck and Gifts," 87–124.

25. *Nassau Guardian,* 8 May 1889.

26. *Nassau Guardian,* 7 January 1882.

27. Blayney Balfour to Thomas Spring-Rice, 15 January 1835, no. 39. C.O. 23/93.

28. John Gregory to Earl Grey, 7 January 1852, no. 3. C.O. 23/140. For the labor problems of the Salt Islands, see Harvey, *Official Reports,* 44–47.

29. *Nassau Guardian,* 20 March 1880.

30. Albury, *Story of the Bahamas,* 198. See also Dalleo, "'Making Pickle,'" 19.

31. Powles, *Land of the Pink Pearl,* 86. Powles served as stipendiary and circuit magistrate for the Bahamas in the mid-1880s. He alienated the white establishment by his outspoken views and was subsequently dismissed.

32. See discussion in chapter 5.

33. William F. Haynes Smith to Joseph Chamberlain, 7 July 1896, no. 76. C.O. 23/244.

34. *Annual Colonial Report for the Bahamas, 1897,* 10. Cf. Ransom and Sutch, *One Kind of Freedom,* chapter 7; Donald, *The Negro Freedman,* 17–19; Higgs, *Competition and Coercion,* 55–57.

35. William F. Haynes Smith to Joseph Chamberlain, 7 July 1896, no. 76. C.O. 23/244.

36. Report on the Parish of San Salvador for 1885 by Rev. F. B. Matthews, *Nassau Quarterly Mission Papers,* 1 September 1886, 56. Indebtedness was a problem faced primarily by tenants, but it also occurred among the peasant proprietors of the Out Islands. See, for example, Report on Rock Sound, Eleuthera, for 1886. Appendix to *Votes of the House of Assembly of the Bahama Islands,* 3 March–6 May 1887, 38–39. Freeholders in New Providence were also often in debt to Nassau merchants. John Gardiner, who was scientific advisor to the Board of Agriculture of the Bahamas in 1886, wrote, "It is difficult

to find a cultivator who is even free from debt to the Nassau tradesmen." Letter by John Gardiner, *Nassau Guardian,* 6 October 1886. See also Powles, *Land of the Pink Pearl,* 97.

37. Henry Blake to the Earl of Derby, 12 August 1884, no. 108. C.O. 23/224.

38. Report on Rock Sound, Eleuthera, for 1882. Appendix to *Votes of the House of Assembly of the Bahama Islands,* 6 February–5 May 1883, 89.

39. *Nassau Guardian,* 16 May 1894. Sands owned properties at Kemp's Bay, Mount Pleasant, Rainbow Harbour, Mutton Fish Point, and Hatchet Bay.

40. Letter by C. Tyldesley Sands of 30 July 1898. *Nassau Guardian,* 3 August 1898.

41. *Nassau Guardian,* 8 September 1906. For another description of this system of payment, see Report on Governor's Harbour, Eleuthera, for 1906. Appendix to *Votes of the Legislative Council of the Bahama Islands,* 5 February–8 July 1907, 134. Cf. Fernández, "British Nitrate Companies," 54–55; Moreno Fraginals, "Plantations in the Caribbean," 6–7; Bergquist, *Labor in Latin America,* 38.

42. Hilton, *The Truck System,* 1; cf. Graves, "Truck and Gifts," 119.

43. Report of speech by Sir William Grey-Wilson on the closing of the session of the legislature, *Nassau Guardian,* 10 July 1907. Grey-Wilson was governor between 1904 and 1911.

44. 7 Edw. VII, c.4. *Laws of the Bahamas,* 1907.

45. The American Consul in the Bahamas had commented in 1891, "The sponge industry is still the most valuable one in the Colony giving steady employment to 500 or 600 vessels of small size and to one–eighth of the entire population of the islands." "Report by Consul McLain on Trade and Industries of the Bahamas, 10 March 1891." Reprinted in *Nassau Guardian,* 24 October 1891.

46. Letter by W. C. Pritchard, 29 March 1892, in the *Nassau Guardian,* 30 March 1892.

47. Powles, *Land of the Pink Pearl,* 88.

48. Letter by Joseph Brown, *Nassau Guardian,* 7 January 1885.

49. Powles, *Land of the Pink Pearl,* 88.

50. Letter by Rev. F. B. Matthews, *Nassau Guardian,* 20 April 1898.

51. Henry Blake to Sir Henry Holland, 30 April 1887, no. 49. C.O. 23/229.

52. Powles, *Land of the Pink Pearl,* 90–91.

53. Henry Blake to Sir Henry Holland, 30 April 1887, no. 49. C.O. 23/229.

54. 49 Vic., c.19. *Laws of the Bahamas,* 1886.

55. Minute by Edward Wingfield, 22 June 1892, on Sir Ambrose Shea to Lord Knutsford, 12 May 1892, no. 72; and Minute by Edward Wingfield, 20 August 1892, on Sir Ambrose Shea to Lord Knutsford, 28 July 1892, no. 113. C.O. 23/234. See 4 and 5 Edw. VII, c.18. *Laws of the Bahamas,* 1905.

56. See Report on Andros for 1904. Appendix to *Votes of the House of Assembly of the Bahama Islands,* 11 January–18 April 1905, 34. It was not unusual for an outfitter in the 1920s to charge 12.5 percent on a loan for a three–month period. This is equivalent to an annual interest rate of 50 percent. Interview with Thomas Armaly, 17 March 1983.

57. Knight, "Mexican Peonage," 48.

58. Shedden, *Ups and Downs,* 111–12.

59. Rev. F. B. Matthews noted in a letter to the *Nassau Guardian,* "Notwithstanding that the compulsory Education Act is in force, boys from 9 to 12 years old are now being sent to sea, in shiploads." *Nassau Guardian,* 19 March 1898. See also Commissioner's Report on Mangrove Cay, Andros, for 1912. Bahamas Archives.

60. Commissioner's Report on Nicoll's Town, Andros, for 1907. Bahamas Archives.

61. Letter by W. E. Pritchard, 29 March 1892, in *Nassau Guardian,* 30 March 1892. For a comparable situation, see Mandle, *Roots of Black Poverty,* 50.

62. See, for example, Commissioner's Report on Nicoll's Town, Andros, for 1918 and Commissioner's Report on Mangrove Cay, Andros, for 1919. Bahamas Archives. See also chapter 9.

63. Commissioner's Report on Mangrove Cay, Andros, for 1922. Bahamas Archives.

64. Letter by John Gardiner in *Nassau Guardian,* 16 October 1886.

65. Powles, *Land of the Pink Pearl,* 98.

66. William F. Haynes Smith to Joseph Chamberlain, 7 July 1896, no. 76. C.O. 23/224.

67. Powles, *Land of the Pink Pearl,* 59.

68. Report on the Biminis for 1897. Appendix to *Votes of the House of Assembly of the Bahama Islands,* 15 March–26 August 1898, 52.

69. *Nassau Guardian,* 11 February 1882, 18 March 1882.

70. *Nassau Guardian,* 20 March 1880.

71. Report on Long Cay District for 1884. Appendix to *Votes of the House of Assembly of the Bahama Islands,* 24 February–22 August 1885, 17. The earlier example of a foreign company using the truck system in the Bahamas is the case in which the United States firm had the monopoly for the export of guano in the early 1870s. As Governor William Robinson remarked in 1875, "The [guano] trade has certainly been the means of putting rather more money into circulation and thus it indirectly benefits to a small extent the Colonial Revenue. The benefit would probably be greater if it was not the practice to pay a large proportion of the wages in kind, that is, in that class of food consumed by the natives which is not liable to import duties." William Robinson to the Earl of Carnarvon, 9 April 1875, no. 73. C.O. 23/213.

72. Eric, "*Buckra Land,*" 5. The name Allan Eric was a pseudonym for C. W. Willis.

73. Report on Long Cay for 1897. Appendix to *Votes of the House of Assembly of the Bahama Islands,* 15 March–26 August 1898, 62. See also William F. Haynes Smith to Joseph Chamberlain, 7 July 1896, no. 76. C.O. 23/244.

74. "Report on certain questions that have arisen between the Government and Messrs. Cohen & Co. of New York with reference to the wages of labourers shipped from Inagua," by Anton Bertram, Attorney General, 12 June 1906. Enclosure in William Grey-Wilson to the Earl of Elgin, 11 June 1906, no. 62. C.O. 22/261.

75. William Grey-Wilson to the Earl of Elgin, 17 July 1907, no. 70. C.O. 23/262.

76. William Grey-Wilson to the Earl of Elgin, 11 June 1906, no. 62. C.O. 23/261.

77. 7 Edw. VII, c.3. *Laws of the Bahamas,* 1907.

78. William Grey-Wilson to Lewis Harcourt, 7 June 1911, no. 94. C.O. 23/267.

79. The phrase is from Lewis, *Growth of the Modern,* 312.

80. William Grey-Wilson to the Earl of Crewe, 31 August 1908, Confidential. C.O. 23/263. See also Colonel K. M. Foss to the Under Secretary of State, 27 July 1908. C.O. 23/264.

81. Letter by Cyril Stevenson, 11 September 1935, in *Nassau Tribune,* 18 September 1935.

82. Bolland, "Systems of Domination," 611; Green, "The Perils of Comparative History," 114.

83. Adamson, *Sugar Without Slaves,* 123.

84. *San Fernando Gazette,* 8 May 1875.

85. *San Fernando Gazette,* 1 May 1875.

86. *San Fernando Gazette,* 4 May 1875.

87. Eric Williams, *History of the People,* 124.

88. Douglas Hall, *Free Jamaica,* 208–9. Cf. Nwulia, *History of Slavery in Mauritius,* 191.

89. Bolland, "Reply to William A. Green's," 122.

90. The phrase is from Roseberry, *Coffee and Capitalism,* 109.

Chapter 7: Race, Class, and Urban Policing

1. The term "social control" is here used as defined by John A. Mayer: "'coercive' controls, which either use or imply force, legal or extra–legal." Mayer, "Notes Towards a Working Definition," 24.

2. For an important discussion of the state and social control in the metropolitan context, see Cohen and Scull, eds., *Social Control and the State.* For a valuable collection of essays on policing in the British Empire, see Anderson and Killingray, eds., *Policing the Empire.*

3. The phrase is from Gatrell, "Crime, Authority," 254.

4. For a discussion of policing activities in the Bahamas during slavery, see Johnson, "Patterns of Policing," 73–74.

5. Goveia, *West Indian Slave Laws,* 20.

6. Johnson, "Patterns of Policing," 71–91. For a discussion of the role of the police in present–day Guyana, see Danns, *Domination and Power in Guyana.*

7. Ambrose Shea to Lord Knutsford, 22 November 1888, Confidential. C.O. 23/230. This was not the first occasion on which it had been suggested that a strengthened police force might replace the troops. See Henry Blake to Frederick Stanley, 8 August 1885, Confidential. C.O. 23/226.

8. Joseph, "The Strategic Importance," 25–26.

9. Ambrose Shea to Lord Knutsford, 22 November 1888, Confidential. C.O. 23/230.

10. Charles Lees to the Earl of Kimberley, 29 December 1882, no. 155. C.O. 23/222; Henry Blake to Frederick Stanley, 8 August 1885, Confidential. C.O. 23/226.

11. For the persistence of this racial stereotype into the twentieth century, see Spackman, "Official Attitudes and Official Violence," 327.

12. Charles Lees to the Earl of Kimberley, 29 December 1882, no. 155. C.O. 23/222.

13. See discussion in chapter 6.

14. Ignatieff, "State, Civil Society," 94.

15. Powles, *Land of the Pink Pearl,* 41.

16. Ambrose Shea to Lord Knutsford, 22 November 1888, Confidential. C.O. 23/230.

17. Enclosure, undated, in Henry Blake to Frederick Stanley, 19 September 1885, Confidential. C.O. 23/226.

18. Henry Blake to Frederick Stanley, 8 August 1888, Confidential. C.O. 23/226.

19. Sir Ambrose Shea to Lord Knutsford, 22 November 1888, Confidential. C.O. 23/230.

20. Powles, *Land of the Pink Pearl,* 114. In this period, creole whites were referred to as Conchs. The attitude of the whites to the black majority can be gauged from another comment by Powles on this incident: "About two years ago a white man called Sands shot a black policeman. Sands was undoubtedly mad and was acquitted on that ground. The way the whites talked of this habitually was, 'that the man was only a nigger, and that it was a pity that a few more were not shot.'" Powles, 113.

21. For a discussion of the Bahamian sisal industry, see Craton, *History of the Bahamas,*

236–38. Joseph Chamberlain was a major investor in sisal plantations in the colony in this period. See Kubicek, *The Administration of Imperialism,* 10–11.

22. Ambrose Shea to Lord Knutsford, 20 June 1892, no. 94. C.O. 23/234.

23. Ambrose Shea to Lord Knutsford, 22 November 1888, Confidential. C.O. 23/230.

24. Ibid. Minute of 19 December 1888 by Edward Wingfield.

25. Ibid. Minute of 26 December 1888 by George S. Clarke.

26. Buckley, *Slaves in Red Coats,* 117.

27. Charles Bayley to the Duke of Newcastle, 11 February 1861, no. 19. C.O. 23/165.

28. Ibid. Minute of 16 March 1861 by the Duke of Newcastle. For an extended discussion of the policing role of imperial troops in the Caribbean, see Johnson, "Patterns of Policing," 77–79.

29. Rawson Rawson to Edward Cardwell, 6 March 1866, Confidential. C.O. 23/184.

30. Lord Knutsford to Sir Ambrose Shea, 19 January 1888, Confidential (draft). C.O. 23/230.

31. Ambrose Shea to Lord Knutsford, 7 November 1890, Confidential. C.O. 23/232.

32. Metcalf, *The Aftermath of Revolt,* 297–98.

33. For an example of the use of Sikhs in Asia, see Kannangara, "The Riots of 1915," 158.

34. Gutteridge, "Military and Police Forces," 289. For a discussion of the "martial races" idea in Africa, see Kirk–Greene, "'Damnosa Hereditas,'" 392–414.

35. Governor Bayley had suggested in 1861 that soldiers from Madras might be recruited for the West India Regiments: "They might, I think, be enlisted along with liberated Africans; & the union of both, in my opinion would present a strong bulwark against any local sympathies or personal insubordination evinced by the Creole soldiers." Charles Bayley to the Duke of Newcastle, 11 February 1861, no. 19. C.O. 23/165.

36. Lord Knutsford to Ambrose Shea, 16 December 1890, Confidential (draft). C.O. 23/232.

37. 54 Vic., c.14. *Laws of the Bahamas,* 1891.

38. Report of Attorney General, 4 July 1891. Enclosure in H. M. Jackson to Lord Knutsford, 6 July 1891, no. 80. C.O. 23/233.

39. Minute of 27 July 1891 by John Hales on H. M. Jackson to Lord Knutsford, 6 July 1891, no. 80. C.O. 23/233.

40. Report of Attorney General, 4 July 1891. Enclosure in Jackson to Lord Knutsford, 6 July 1891, no. 80. C.O. 23/233.

41. Isolation from the civilian population was a distinguishing feature of the army in nineteenth–century Europe. According to Geoffrey Parker, "The larger countries of nineteenth century Europe . . . began to build up a large professional army which was kept separate from society in general (mainly by means of the barracks)." Parker, "Warfare," 211.

42. "Rule for the General Government of the Bahamas Constabulary framed by the Governor in Council under Section XII of Act 54 Victoria, Cap. 14, 189," 24. Enclosure in H. M. Jackson to Lord Knutsford, 15 August 1891, no. 94. C.O. 23/233.

43. Report of Attorney General, 4 July 1891. Enclosure in H. M. Jackson to Lord Knutsford, 6 July 1891, no. 6. C.O. 23/233.

44. Gutteridge, "Military and Police Forces," 312.

45. Ambrose Shea to Lord Knutsford, 8 January 1891, no. 6. C.O. 23/233.

46. See entry on H. M. Jackson in *Colonial Office List,* 1887.

47. Gutteridge, "Military and Police Forces," 312.

48. Fyfe, *History of Sierra Leone,* 487. See Minute of 8 December 1890 by C. A. Harris on Sir Ambrose Shea to Lord Knutsford, 17 November 1890, Confidential. C.O. 23/232. The original model for paramilitary police forces in the colonial context was the Royal Irish Constabulary; see Hawkins, "The 'Irish Model,'" 18–32.

49. H. M. Jackson to Lord Knutsford, 6 July 1891, no. 81. C.O. 23/233.

50. "Memorandum on the causes leading to the late disturbances and on the general organization of the Police," 18 May 1893. Enclosure no. 2 in H. M. Jackson to the Marquis of Ripon, 8 July 1893, no. 94. C.O. 23/237. For a discussion of the relations between Barbadian policemen and the creole population in Trinidad, see Johnson, "Barbadian Immigrants in Trinidad," 19–20.

51. "Report of the Select Committee of the House of Assembly on the Progress of the Colony during the Past Five Years," 9. Enclosure in Ambrose Shea to the Marquis of Ripon, 3 April 1893, no. 39. C.O. 23/236.

52. H. M. Jackson to the Marquis of Ripon, 20 September 1892, no. 128. C.O. 23/234.

53. "Memorandum on the causes leading to the late disturbances and on the general organization of the Police," 18 May 1893. Enclosure no. 2 in H. M. Jackson to the Marquis of Ripon, 8 July 1893, no. 94. C.O. 23/237.

54. H. M. Jackson to the Marquis of Ripon, 8 July 1893, no. 94. C.O. 23/237.

55. "Report of the Committee of the Executive Council appointed to enquire into the causes of the disturbances in Grant's Town on the evening of the 15th April last; and to make recommendations with regard to the reorganization and control of the Police and Constabulary Forces of the Colony," 30 June 1893. Enclosure no. 1 in Jackson to the Marquis of Ripon, 8 July 1893, no. 94. C.O. 23/237.

56. Stavrianos, *Global Rift,* 291. See also Enloe, *Ethnic Soldiers,* chapter 1.

57. Rodney, *How Europe Underdeveloped Africa,* 186–87.

58. Ibid. See also Davidson, *Africa in Modern History,* 84–89; Buckley, *Slaves in Red Coats,* 189, note 44.

Chapter 8: Merchant Hegemony and the Making of Immigration Policy

1. A "trading minority" may be defined as an ethnic minority with a dominant position in some aspect of trade. See Wertheim, "Trading Minorities in Southeast Asia."

2. Report of meeting of the House of Assembly, 30 April 1925, in *Nassau Guardian,* 2 May 1925.

3. *Nassau Guardian,* 8 December 1926. For Jamaican immigration to the Bahamas, see Johnson, "Labour on the Move," 85–98.

4. Blalock, *Toward a Theory,* 79–84. For a useful discussion of "middleman minorities," see Bonacich, "Theory of Middleman Minorities," 583–94.

5. Report of meeting of the House of Assembly, 30 April 1925, in *Nassau Guardian,* 2 May 1925.

6. Report of meeting of the House of Assembly, 7 May 1925, in *Nassau Guardian,* 9 May 1925.

7. Report of meeting of the House of Assembly, 11 May 1925, in *Nassau Guardian,* 12 May 1925.

8. For a discussion of this point, see Johnson, "Friendly Societies in the Bahamas," 188–89.

9. William Allardyce to T. C. MacNaghten, 4 July 1917. Enclosure in William Allardyce to Walter Long, 19 September 1917, Confidential. C.O. 23/280.

10. For a discussion of the system of government in the Bahamas and especially the

extent of local autonomy in matters of policy making, see "Notes on the System of Government in the Bahamas," 1 September 1927, by C. W. J. Orr. Enclosure in C. W. J. Orr to L. S. Amery, 21 September 1927, Confidential. C.O. 23/368.

11. Burns, *Colonial Civil Servant,* 80.

12. Craton, *History of the Bahamas,* chapter 16.

13. Letter of "J. B.," *Nassau Guardian,* 28 December 1887.

14. Department of Archives, "The Sponging Industry," 14.

15. *Nassau Guardian,* 28 December 1887.

16. Ibid.

17. Petition reprinted in *Nassau Guardian,* 3 March 1888.

18. Report reprinted in *Nassau Guardian,* 5 October 1889.

19. "The Greek Connection," *Tribune,* 26 March 1981.

20. See advertisement for Geo. Damianos & Son, *Tribune Handbook* (Nassau, 1924), lxvii.

21. "The Greek Connection," *Tribune,* 26 March 1981.

22. *Nassau Tribune,* 2 August 1924. See Editorial, "Hoodlumism Needs Iron Hand." During the 1920s the *Nassau Tribune* became a daily newspaper and was referred to as the *Nassau Daily Tribune.* It will, however, be cited throughout this chapter as the *Nassau Tribune.*

23. "The Greek Connection," *Tribune,* 26 March 1981.

24. *Nassau Tribune,* 17 December 1927, "Here and There."

25. "The Greek Connection," *Tribune,* 26 March 1981.

26. See advertisements in *Nassau Tribune,* 17 December 1927, 10 December 1930.

27. *Nassau Tribune,* 21 August 1926, "Here and There."

28. See advertisements, *Nassau Guardian,* 1 September 1928; *Nassau Tribune,* 8 January 1930.

29. "The Greek Connection," *Tribune,* 26 March 1981.

30. *Report on the Census of the Bahama Islands, Taken on 24 April 1921,* 3.

31. Ibid.

32. *Report on the Census of the Bahama Islands, Taken on 26 April 1931,* 4. The Greek community might have been larger; this figure does not include children born to Greek parents in the Bahamas.

33. "Nassau's Incomparable Greeks," *Bahamas Handbook,* 1970–71 (Nassau, 1970), 57.

34. Jones, *American Immigration,* 203.

35. Nicholls, "No Hawkers and Pedlars," 416.

36. *Nassau Tribune,* 10 February 1926, "Death of Mr. Joseph Kalil Amoury."

37. The phrase is R. Bayly Winder's in "Lebanese in West Africa," 307. For similar experiences in the Caribbean, see Nicholls, "No Hawkers and Pedlars," 415–31; Lowenthal, *West Indian Societies,* 208.

38. *Nassau Guardian,* 15 May 1897.

39. *Nassau Guardian,* 11 May 1902.

40. Interview with Irwin Bowen, February 1984.

41. Interview with Rowena Eldon, February 1984.

42. The exception was W. J. Armaly, who arrived in the colony in 1905 and became involved in the sponging industry. Interview with Thomas Armaly, March 1984.

43. For an interesting comment on K. S. Moses's use of advertising, see *Nassau Tribune,* 27 August 1930, "Here and There."

44. *Nassau Tribune,* 1 November 1924, "Here and There."
45. See advertisement in *Nassau Tribune,* 22 December 1923.
46. *Tribune Handbook* (Nassau, 1924), lxxix.
47. *Nassau Tribune,* 5 January 1924.
48. See advertisement, *Nassau Tribune,* 4 July 1925.
49. See advertisement, *Nassau Tribune,* 22 December 1923.
50. Leuchtenburg, *The Perils of Prosperity,* 196.
51. According to Thomas Armaly, there were only six Lebanese families in Nassau at that time: The Amourys, the Armalys, the Bakers, the Moseses, the Ageebs, and the Farahs. Interview with Thomas Armaly, March 1984. The censuses did not list the Lebanese separately.
52. *Nassau Tribune,* 10 February 1926, "Death of Mr. Joseph Kalil Amoury."
53. *Nassau Tribune,* 10 February 1923.
54. *Nassau Tribune,* 7 June 1924, "Jewish Customs Strange to Nassau."
55. *Nassau Guardian,* 3 and 15 December 1879.
56. See advertisement in *Nassau Guardian,* 2 June 1923. Chea's Christian name was later anglicized as "Louis."
57. See advertisement in *Nassau Guardian,* 27 December 1923.
58. *Nassau Guardian,* 24 July 1924.
59. The advertisement for the Oriental Laundry, owned by John Chea, mentioned that he had "10 years experience of laundry work in Havana," *Nassau Tribune,* 2 January 1929.
60. See Johnson, "The Anti–Chinese Riots," 55.
61. *Nassau Tribune,* 12 July 1924, "Here and There."
62. *Nassau Tribune,* 6 December 1924.
63. *Nassau Tribune,* 19 November 1924; 27 May 1925.
64. *Nassau Tribune,* 25 July 1925, 1 September 1926.
65. Bonacich, "Theory of Middleman Minorities," 586.
66. *Nassau Guardian,* 8 December 1925.
67. Letter by R. J. Bowe, *Nassau Tribune,* 22 July 1925.
68. Report of the meeting of the House of Assembly, 13 August 1928, in *Nassau Guardian,* 15 August 1928. Kenneth Solomon was one of the colony's leading lawyers, a member of the Executive Council, and part of the ruling elite of "white Bahamian merchants and lawyers." See Colin A. Hughes, *Race and Politics,* 29.
69. See report of Bowe's comments in *Nassau Guardian,* 15 August 1928.
70. *Nassau Guardian,* 15 August 1928.
71. Ibid.
72. See advertisement, *Nassau Tribune,* 20 January 1926.
73. See advertisement, *Nassau Tribune,* 6 February 1926.
74. See advertisement, *Nassau Tribune,* 17 March 1926.
75. *Nassau Tribune,* 1 January 1927.
76. *Nassau Tribune,* 17 December 1927, "Here and There."
77. See advertisement, *Nassau Tribune,* 19 May 1926.
78. See advertisement, *Nassau Tribune,* 2 February 1927.
79. See advertisement, *Nassau Tribune,* 12 January 1927.
80. See advertisement, *Nassau Tribune,* 27 October 1926. William Yanowitz, one of the partners in this business, was a Polish Jew who came to the Bahamas via Cuba.
81. See advertisement, *Nassau Tribune,* 27 November 1926.
82. See advertisement, *Nassau Tribune,* 6 November 1926.

83. See *Nassau Guardian,* 15 August 1928, Editorial, "Safeguarding Our Traders."

84. Executive Council Minutes, 18 January 1927–19 December 1928. Gov. 1/39, Bahamas Archives.

85. Ibid., meeting of 20 April 1927.

86. Ibid., meeting of 15 June 1927.

87. Ibid., meeting of 2 November 1927; meeting of 25 April 1928.

88. Ibid., meeting of 5 June 1928. The minutes of that meeting read in part, "Council authorised the issue of a landing permit to . . . two Chinamen who are to be employed by Hatchet Bay Ltd., on condition that the Company enters into an agreement with the men to leave at the end of a year if required to do so, and gives a bond to the Government to repay cost of repatriation if necessary."

89. Ibid., meeting of 6 April 1927; Executive Council Minutes, 2 January 1929–20 December 1933. Gov. 1/40. Meeting of 16 January 1929.

90. Executive Council Minutes, 2 January 1929–20 December 1933. Gov. 1/40. Meetings of 23 October 1929 and 1 February 1932. By October 1930 there were approximately 32 Chinese in the Bahamas. See *Nassau Tribune,* 11 October 1930, "Chinese in Chinatown."

91. See *Nassau Tribune,* 15 August 1928, Editorial, "Foreigners."

92. See, for example, the article "Alien Problem in Jamaica," reprinted from Jamaica's *Daily Gleaner* in *Nassau Tribune,* 22 July 1925.

93. Eitzen, "Two Minorities," 136.

94. *Nassau Guardian,* 15 August 1928, Editorial, "Safeguarding Our Traders."

95. *Nassau Tribune,* 15 August 1928, Editorial, "Foreigners."

96. As the editor of the *Nassau Tribune* commented in 1930, "It is clearly evident that this Bill is defective: or was it designed only to keep labourers from other West Indian Islands from flocking to this island?" *Nassau Tribune,* 14 June 1930.

97. 19 George 5.c.24. *Laws of the Bahamas,* 1928.

98. Report of meeting of the House of Assembly, 5 September 1928. *Nassau Guardian,* 8 September 1928.

99. *Nassau Guardian,* 15 September 1928. A recent comment by Michael Pye about the significance of "Bay Street" in the year 1940 also holds true for 1928: "Bay Street had already been an abstract noun, a description of a ruling class and a government." Pye, *The King over the Water,* 67.

100. 20 and 21 George 5.c.8. *Laws of the Bahamas,* 1930.

101. 20 and 21 George 5.c.10. *Laws of the Bahamas,* 1930. For the use of discriminatory legislation against middleman minorities, see Bonacich, "Theory of Middleman Minorities," 590. For an example of discriminatory measures directed at the Chinese, see Hu–De Hart, "Immigrants to a Developing Society," 49–86.

102. See *Nassau Tribune,* 12 and 29 June 1929.

103. *Nassau Tribune,* 29 June 1929, Editorial, "No Need for Panic."

104. *Nassau Tribune,* 1 March 1930, Editorial, "Legislative Problems."

105. See, for example, letter on "The Invasion of Aliens" by "Bay Street," *Nassau Guardian,* 1 November 1930; letter on "Undesirable Aliens" by "Citizen," *Nassau Tribune,* 1 November 1930. A comment by "Bay Street" suggests that many of these later immigrants were Jewish: "The fine class of tourists which our extensive advertising is inducing to visit Nassau in increasing numbers, does not look with approval on the type of merchants found on 6th Avenue or the Bowery of New York."

106. *Nassau Guardian,* 26 November 1930.

107. *Nassau Tribune,* 15 November 1930, "The Alien Invasion." The other spokesman

of this delegation was A. F. Adderley, a successful black lawyer and son of W. P. Adderley, one of the leading black merchants on Bay Street.

108. For the text of the proclamation issued by Sir Charles Orr restricting immigration, see *Nassau Guardian,* 6 December 1930.

109. See report of discussion at meeting of the House of Assembly, 7 May 1931, *Nassau Guardian,* 9 May 1931.

110. Typical of the "nativist" sentiment of this period was a statement made by Eric Solomon, a leading commission merchant and member of the House, which was recorded by the *Nassau Guardian:* "When he was overseas during the War he was frequently asked about the Colony and he had always been proud to say that there were no foreigners there and people had said that there must be no money there or the Jews or Chinamen would be there."

111. *Nassau Tribune,* 9 and 23 May 1931, Editorials on "The Shopkeeper's Bill."

112. *Nassau Guardian,* 20 May 1931.

113. 23 and 23 George 5.c.8. *Laws of the Bahamas,* 1933. This act also made it compulsory for traveling salesmen to have licenses. This was probably aimed at Jewish salesmen who traveled to the colony in this period. Interview with Rowena Eldon, February 1984.

Chapter 9: Labor Migration as Protest and Survival Strategy

1. Alpers, "'To Seek a Better Life,'" 384.

2. The term "labor migration" is used here as defined by Alejandro Portes and John Walton: that is, migration for which "the specific intent is to sell human work in an established market." Portes and Walton, *Labor, Class,* 22.

3. Albury, *Story of the Bahamas,* 143.

4. *Bahama Herald,* 30 November 1849.

5. Charles Bayley to the Duke of Newcastle, 25 April 1860, no. 38. C.O. 23/162.

6. Craton, *History of the Bahamas,* 239.

7. Letter from J. H. Webb to Sir Charles Lees, 29 April 1881. *Votes of the House of Assembly of the Bahama Islands,* 14 February–29 March 1882, 40.

8. Windhorn and Langley, *Yesterday's Key West.*

9. Henry Blake to Frederick Stanley, 8 August 1885, Confidential. C.O. 23/226.

10. "Report on the Agricultural Condition and Prospects of the Bahamas," 27 April 1886, by John Gardiner. *Votes of the House of Assembly of the Bahama Islands,* 23 February–26 May 1886, 221–22.

11. Appendix to *Votes of the House of Assembly of the Bahama Islands,* 24 February–22 August 1885, 10.

12. Report on Rock Sound, Eleuthera, for 1907. Appendix to *Votes of the House of Assembly of the Bahama Islands,* 3 January–8 June 1908, 40.

13. Appendix to *Votes of the House of Assembly of the Bahama Islands,* 3 March–6 May 1887, 42.

14. Ibid., 43.

15. Report on Harbour Island for 1885. Appendix to *Votes of the House of Assembly of the Bahama Islands,* 23 February–26 May 1886, 23.

16. Dodge, *Abaco,* 80.

17. Report on Cherokee Sound, Abaco. Appendix to *Votes of the House of Assembly of the Bahama Islands,* 24 February–5 June 1891, 2.

18. *Nassau Quarterly Mission Papers,* ix, 1894, 26.

19. Report on the Biminis for 1890. Appendix to *Votes of the House of Assembly of the Bahama Islands,* 24 February–5 June 1891, 5; Northcroft, *Sketches of Summerland,* 211.

20. "Letter from the Bishop," *Nassau Quarterly Mission Papers,* v, 1890, 14.

21. "Bimini and Grand Bahama," *Nassau Quarterly Mission Papers,* iii, 1888, 63; Report on the Biminis for 1897. Appendix to *Votes of the House of Assembly of the Bahama Islands,* 15 March–26 August 1898, 52.

22. For a detailed discussion of this point, see chapter 6.

23. Powles, *Land of the Pink Pearl,* 88.

24. William F. Haynes Smith to Joseph Chamberlain, 7 July 1896, no. 76. C.O. 23/244.

25. Ibid.

26. *Nassau Quarterly Mission Papers,* vi, 1891, 42; *Report on the Bahamas Blue Book,* 1901–02, 32.

27. William F. Haynes Smith to Joseph Chamberlain, 7 July 1896, no. 76. C.O. 23/244.

28. Craton, *History of the Bahamas,* 239.

29. Albury, *Story of the Bahamas,* 166.

30. Erickson, "Why Did Contract Labour," 54.

31. Parks, *Miami,* 88; see speech by Sir William Grey-Wilson, 5 February 1907. *Votes of the Legislative Council of the Bahama Islands,* 5 February–8 July 1907, 2; Report on the Biminis for 1906. Appendix to *Votes of the House of Assembly of the Bahama Islands,* 8 February–8 July 1907, 120.

32. Parks, *Miami,* 87.

33. "Bahamians in Florida, United States," *Nassau Quarterly Mission Papers,* xxx, 1915, 13.

34. "Florida—Impressions of a Visitor," *Nassau Tribune,* 2 December 1911.

35. Windhorn and Langley, *Yesterday's Key West,* 17; Interview with Oscar Johnson, February 1987.

36. See letter by "Twist Back," *Nassau Tribune,* 19 January 1911.

37. *Report on the Bahamas Blue Book,* 1903–4, 39.

38. Report on Long Cay, Fortune Island, for 1919. *Votes of the Legislative Council of the Bahama Islands,* 3 February–26 August 1920, 167.

39. Speech of Sir William Allardyce, 18 December 1919. *Votes of the Legislative Council of the Bahama Islands,* 18 February–18 December 1919, 140.

40. Memorandum by the Colonial Secretary, "Agriculture in the Bahamas, 1930," 8.

41. Craton, *History of the Bahamas,* 234.

42. *Votes of the House of Assembly of the Bahama Islands,* 10 January–13 July 1911, 53–54.

43. Commissioner's Report on Arthur's Town, San Salvador, for 1912. Bahamas Archives.

44. Albury, *Story of the Bahamas,* 168.

45. See, for example, Report on Watling's Island for 1907. Appendix to *Votes of the Legislative Council of the Bahama Islands,* 3 January–8 June 1908, 206.

46. See Ambrose Shea to Lord Knutsford, 21 May 1888, no. 51. C.O. 23/230; William F. Haynes Smith to Joseph Chamberlain, 7 July 1896, no. 76. C.O. 23/244; Gilbert Carter to Joseph Chamberlain, 23 December 1899, no. 123. C.O. 23/253; Speech of Sir William Grey-Wilson, 4 December 1911. *Votes of the Legislative Council of the Bahama Islands,* 4 December 1911–22 May 1912, 5; William Allardyce to Viscount Milner, 16 January 1920, Confidential. C.O. 23/286.

47. "Second Interim Report of the Commission appointed to make Diligent and Full Enquiry into and Report on the General Administration of the Out Islands," 22 June 1920.

Votes of the Legislative Council of the Bahama Islands, 15 February 1921–16 January 1922, 238.

48. See, for example, Commissioner's Report on Fresh Creek, Andros, for 1912. Bahamas Archives; Report on Grand Bahama for 1923. Appendix to *Votes of the House of Assembly of the Bahama Islands,* 19 February–15 May 1924, 418.

49. Letter by "Twist Back," *Nassau Tribune,* 19 January 1911.

50. See "Florida—Impressions of a Visitor," *Nassau Tribune,* 2 December 1911.

51. Interview with Oscar Johnson, May 1985.

52. "Florida—Impressions of a Visitor," *Nassau Tribune,* 2 December 1911.

53. Commissioner's Report on the Biminis for 1918. Bahamas Archives.

54. Appendix to *Votes of the Legislative Council of the Bahama Islands,* 4 December 1911–22 May 1912, 96A.

55. Commissioner's Report on Long Cay, Fortune Island, for 1916. Bahamas Archives.

56. Appendix to *Votes of the House of Assembly of the Bahama Islands,* 15 February 1921–16 January 1922, 275.

57. Speech of Sir William Grey-Wilson, 10 January 1911. *Votes of the House of Assembly of the Bahama Islands,* 10 January–13 July 1911, 14.

58. Petition from Bahamians in Florida, 27 October 1911. Enclosure in Grey-Wilson to Lewis Harcourt, 17 November 1911, no. 188. C.O. 23/268.

59. "Florida—Impressions of a Visitor," *Nassau Tribune,* 16 December 1911.

60. "Bahamians in Florida, United States," *Nassau Quarterly Mission Papers,* xxx, 1915, 13.

61. Petition from Bahamians in Florida, 21 October 1911. Enclosure in Grey-Wilson to Lewis Harcourt, 17 November 1911, no. 188. C.O. 23/268.

62. "Florida—Impressions of a Visitor," *Nassau Tribune,* 14 December 1911.

63. Interview with Oscar Johnson, May 1985; interview with Sir Etienne Dupuch, April 1985.

64. *Nassau Tribune,* 12 December 1911.

65. See chapter 6. See also Williams, "The Emigrant Labour Business," 9–14.

66. *Nassau Guardian,* 14 January 1920. There is extensive evidence indicating that the introduction of a literary test checked migration to Florida from the Bahamas. See, for example, letter from Dr. J. G. Long to Walter Long, 6 March 1918. C.O. 23/283; Report on Governor's Harbour, Eleuthera, for 1917. Appendix to *Votes of the Legislative Council of the Bahama Islands,* 26 November 1917–4 July 1918; Report on Watling's Island for 1923. Appendix to *Votes of the House of Assembly of the Bahama Islands,* 19 February–15 May 1924, 493; Report on Exuma for 1920. Appendix to *Votes of the Legislative Council of the Bahama Islands,* 15 February 1921–16 January 1922, 206; Report on Exuma for 1921. Appendix to *Votes of the Legislative Council of the Bahama Islands,* 23 March–23 May 1922, 96.

67. *Nassau Guardian,* 21 April 1920. For an authoritative discussion of United States immigration policy in the early twentieth century, see Jones, *American Immigration.*

68. Greenberg, "The Contract, 'The Project,'" 170.

69. See, for example, the editorial in *Nassau Guardian,* 8 October 1911.

70. "Second Interim Report of the Commission Appointed . . . to Report on the General Administration of the Out Islands," 22 June 1890. *Votes of the Legislative Council of the Bahama Islands,* 15 February 1921–16 January 1922, 284.

71. Speech of William Hart Bennett, 18 November 1912. *Votes of the Legislative Council of the Bahama Islands,* 18 November 1912–7 July 1913, 5.

72. William Allardyce to Walter Long, 31 July 1918, no. 107. C.O. 23/283.

73. *Report on the Bahamas Blue Book,* 1917–18, 16.

74. Letter by "Cat Island," *Nassau Guardian,* 28 January 1920; Report on Long Cay for 1905. Appendix to *Votes of the Legislative Council of the Bahama Islands,* 18 January–29 May 1906, 72; Commissioner's Report on Arthur's Town, San Salvador, for 1916. Bahamas Archives.

75. See, for example, Commissioner's Report on Arthur's Town, San Salvador, for 1912. Bahamas Archives.

76. See, for example, Commissioner's Report on the Bight, San Salvador, for 1912; Commissioner's Report on Rock Sound and Tarpum Bay, Eleuthera, for 1922. Bahamas Archives.

77. Commissioner's Report on Rock Sound and Tarpum Bay, Eleuthera, for 1920. Appendix to *Votes of the Legislative Council of the Bahama Islands,* 15 February 1921–16 January 1922, 194.

78. Memorandum by the Colonial Secretary, "Agriculture in the Bahamas, 1930" (Nassau, 1938), 2. See also editorial, *Nassau Tribune,* 29 June 1929. For a discussion of the effects of emigration in a later period on peasant agricultural production in other Caribbean territories, see Rubenstein, "Remittances and Rural Underdevelopment," 298.

79. Appendix to *Votes of the Legislative Council of the Bahama Islands,* 11 January–6 June 1910, 86.

80. See, for example, Report on Governor's Harbour, Eleuthera, for 1909. Appendix to *Votes of the Legislative Council of the Bahama Islands,* 11 January–6 June 1910, 87; Report on Nicoll's Town, Andros, for 1911. Appendix to *Votes of the Legislative Council of the Bahama Islands,* 4 December 1911–22 May 1922; 97; Report on Long Island for 1914. Appendix to *Votes of the Legislative Council of the Bahama Islands,* 8 February–31 May 1915, 168; Report on the Bight, San Salvador, for 1914. Appendix to *Votes of the Legislative Council of the Bahama Islands,* 8 February–31 May 1915, 202.

81. For a valuable study of the effects of "Panama Money" on Barbadian economy and society, see Richardson, *Panama Money in Barbados.*

82. Appendix to *Votes of the Legislative Council of the Bahama Islands,* 15 February 1921–16 January 1922, 206.

83. Commissioner's Report on Clarence Town, Long Island, for 1912. Bahamas Archives.

84. Commissioner's Report on the Bight, San Salvador, for 1912. Bahamas Archives.

85. Letter by R. J. Bowe, *Nassau Tribune,* 12 January 1929.

86. Myers, "'I love my home bad,'" 140.

87. *Nassau Tribune,* 16 October 1929, "Here and There."

88. Commissioner's Report on Rock Island and Tarpum Bay for 1920. Appendix to *Votes of the Legislative Council of the Bahama Islands,* 15 February 1921–16 January 1922, 194. See also Report on Arthur's Town, San Salvador, for 1916. Bahamas Archives.

89. Report on Ragged Island for 1911. Appendix to *Votes of the Legislative Council of the Bahama Islands,* 4 December 1911–22 May 1912, 173–74.

90. Report on Mangrove Cay, Andros, for 1921. Appendix to *Votes of the Legislative Council of the Bahama Islands,* 23 March–23 May 1922, 64.

91. Cf. Amin, ed., *Modern Migrations,* 111.

Conclusion

1. Mörner, De Viñuela, French, "Comparative Approaches," 57.

2. Scott, "Explaining Abolition," 34; Turner, "Chattel Slaves into Wage Slaves," 14–31.

3. Mintz and Hall, "Jamaican Internal Marketing System," 24.
4. McDonald, *The Economy and Material Culture.*
5. Emmer, ed., *Colonialism and Migration.*
6. Engerman, "Servants to Slaves to Servants," 263–94.
7. Stolcke, "Labors of Coffee," 71.
8. Marshall, "Metayage in the Sugar Industry," 54.
9. See Bolland, "Politics of Freedom," 123.
10. Johnson, "Origins and Early Development," 73.
11. Johnson, "Merchant Credit and the Dispossession," 28.
12. Trotman, *Crime in Trinidad,* 90–97; Brian L. Moore, *Race, Power and Social Segmentation,* 203–11.
13. Johnson, "Patterns of Policing," 87.
14. Petras, *Jamaican Labor Migration,* 1.
15. Newton, *The Silver Men;* Richardson, *Caribbean Migrants;* Petras, *Jamaican Labor Migration.*
16. Schoepf, *Travels in the Confederation,* 2:273.
17. Letter by James C. Smith, *Nassau Guardian,* 13 October 1886. Brecht wrote:

> Who built Thebes of the seven Gates?
> In the books stand the names of Kings
> Did they then drag up the rock-slabs?
> And Babylon so often destroyed,
> Who kept rebuilding it?

BIBLIOGRAPHY

Manuscript Sources

Records of the Colonial Office, Public Records Office, London

C.O. 23/58–368. Original Correspondence, Bahamas, 1811–1923.
C.O. 318/141. Original Correspondence, West Indies, 1838.

Bahamas Archives, Public Records Office, Nassau

Abstracts from Supreme Court Wills, 1769–1824.
Colonial Secretary's Letter Book, 29 December 1835–17 January 1839.
Executive Council Minutes, 18 January 1927–19 December 1928.
Gov. 1/39; 2 January 1929–20 December 1933. Gov. 1/40.
Manuscript Laws of the Bahamas, 29 September 1729–17 August 1792; 1795–99.
Out Island Commissioners' Reports, 1907–22.
O'Brien Family Collection.
Records of the United Society for the Propagation of the Gospel. Records Relating to the Bahamas, 1726–1859. Microfilm Reel 3.

Printed Official Sources

Annual Colonial Reports for the Bahamas, 1897–1920.
Bahamas *Blue Books,* 1921–29.
Colonial Office List, 1887.
Laws of the Bahamas, 1826–36, 1860–63, 1886, 1905–7, 1928–33.
Laws of the Bahamas, in Force on the 14th March, 1842.
Memorandum by the Colonial Secretary, "Agriculture in the Bahamas, 1930." Nassau: Nassau Guardian, 1938.
Report on the Census of the Bahama Islands, Taken on 27 June 1891. Nassau: Nassau Guardian, 1891.
Report on the Census of the Bahama Islands, Taken on 14 April 1901. Nassau: Nassau Guardian, 1901.
Report on the Census of the Bahama Islands, Taken on 2 April 1911. Nassau: Nassau Guardian, 1911.
Report on the Census of the Bahama Islands, Taken on 24 April 1921. Nassau: Nassau Guardian, 1921.
Report on the Census of the Bahama Islands, Taken on 26 April 1931. Nassau: Nassau Guardian, 1931.

Report on the Bahamas Blue Books, 1901–2, 1903–4, 1917–18.
Votes of the House of Assembly of the Bahama Islands, 1815, 1821–24, 1835–36, 1882–1924.
Votes of the Legislative Council of the Bahama Islands, 1891–1922.

Newspapers

Bahama Argus, 1831–35.
Bahama Gazette, 1784–1819.
Bahama Herald, 1849.
Nassau Guardian, 1849–1931.
Nassau Quarterly Mission Papers, 1886–1915.
Nassau Tribune, 1911–31.
Royal Gazette and Bahama Advertiser, 1804–34.
Tribune, 1981.
San Fernando Gazette, 1875, 1889.

Interviews by the Author, Nassau, Bahamas

Armaly, Thomas, March 1983, March 1984.
Bowen, Irwin, February 1984.
Dupuch, Sir Etienne, April 1985.
Eldon, Rowena, February 1984.
Johnson, Oscar, May 1985, February 1987.

Books and Articles

Adamson, Alan. *Sugar Without Slaves: The Political Economy of British Guiana, 1838–1904.* New Haven: Yale University Press, 1972.

Albury, Paul. *The Story of the Bahamas.* London: Macmillan Caribbean, 1975.

Alpers, Edward A. "'To Seek a Better Life': The Implications of Migration from Mozambique to Tanganyika for Class Formation and Political Behavior." *Canadian Journal of African Studies* 18, no. 2 (1984): 367–88.

Amin, Samir, ed. *Modern Migrations in Western Africa.* London: Oxford University Press, 1974.

Anderson, David M., and David Killingray, eds. *Policing the Empire: Government, Authority and Control, 1830–1940.* Manchester: Manchester University Press, 1991.

Anderson, Ralph V., and Robert E. Gallman. "Slaves as Fixed Capital: Slave Labor and Southern Economic Development." *Journal of American History* 64, no. 1 (June 1977): 24–46.

Aptheker, Herbert. "Slave Resistance in the United States." In *Key Issues in the Afro-American Experience,* edited by Nathan I. Huggins, Martin Kilson, and Daniel M. Fox, vol. 1, 161–73. New York: Harcourt Brace Jovanovich, 1971.

Asiegbu, Johnson U. J. *Slavery and the Politics of Liberation, 1787–1861: A Study of Liberated African Emigration and British Anti-Slavery Policy.* London: Longmans, Green, 1969.

The Bahamas Handbook and Businessman's Annual, 1970–71. Nassau: Dupuch Jr. Publications, 1970.

Bauer, Arnold J. "Rural Workers in Spanish America: Problems of Peonage and Oppression." *Hispanic American Historical Review* 59, no. 1 (February 1979): 34–63.

Bergad, Laird W. *Coffee and the Growth of Agrarian Capitalism in Nineteenth-Century Puerto Rico.* Princeton: Princeton University Press, 1983.

Bergquist, Charles. *Labor in Latin America: Comparative Essays on Chile, Argentina, Venezuela, and Colombia*. Stanford: Stanford University Press, 1986.

Berlin, Ira. *Slaves Without Masters: The Free Negro in the Antebellum South*. New York: Pantheon, 1974.

———. "Time, Space, and the Evolution of Afro-American Society on British Mainland North America." *American Historical Review* 85, no. 1 (February 1980): 44–78.

Berlin, Ira, and Philip D. Morgan, eds. *Cultivation and Culture: Labor and the Shaping of Slave Life in the Americas*. Charlottesville: University Press of Virginia, 1993.

Best, Lloyd. "Outlines of a Model of Pure Plantation Economy." *Social and Economic Studies* 17, no. 3 (September 1968): 283–326.

Bethell, A. Talbot. *The Early Settlers of the Bahamas with a Brief Account of the American Revolution*. Nassau: privately published, 1914.

Bethell, Leslie. "The Mixed Commissions for the Suppression of the Transatlantic Slave Trade in the Nineteenth Century." *Journal of African History* 7, no. 1 (1966): 79–93.

Blalock, Hubert M., Jr. *Toward a Theory of Minority Group Relations*. New York: John Wiley & Sons, 1967.

Bloch, Marc. "The Rise of Dependent Cultivation and Seignorial Institutions." In *The Cambridge Economic History of Europe,* 2d ed., edited by M. M. Postan, vol. 1, 235–90. Cambridge: Cambridge University Press, 1966.

Blum, Jerome. *Lord and Peasant in Russia from the Ninth to the Nineteenth Century.* Princeton: Princeton University Press, 1961.

Bolland, O. Nigel. "The Politics of Freedom in the British Caribbean." In *The Meaning of Freedom: Economics, Politics and Culture After Slavery,* edited by Frank McGlynn and Seymour Drescher, 113–46. Pittsburgh: University of Pittsburgh Press, 1992.

———. "Proto-Proletarians? Slave Wages in the Americas: Between Slave Labour and Wage Labour." In *From Chattel to Wage Slavery: The Dynamics of Labour Bargaining in the Americas,* edited by Mary Turner, 123–47. London: James Currey, 1995.

———. "Reply to William A. Green's 'The Perils of Comparative History.'" *Comparative Studies in Society and History* 26, no. 1 (January 1984): 120–25.

———. "Systems of Domination After Slavery: the Control of Land and Labor in the British West Indies After 1838." *Comparative Studies in Society and History* 23, no. 4 (October 1981): 591–619.

Bonacich, Edna. "A Theory of Middleman Minorities." *American Sociological Review* 38, no. 5 (October 1973): 583–94.

Bruce, Peter Henry. *Bahamian Interlude.* 1782. Rpt. with an introduction by Richard Kent. London: John Culmer, 1949.

Bryan, Patrick. *The Jamaican People 1880–1902: Race, Class and Social Control.* London: Macmillan Education, 1991.

Buckley, Roger Norman. *Slaves in Red Coats: The British West India Regiments, 1795–1815.* New Haven: Yale University Press, 1979.

Bundy, Colin. *The Rise and Fall of the South African Peasantry.* London: Heinemann, 1978.

Burns, Sir Alan. *Colonial Civil Servant.* London: Allen & Unwin, 1949.

Byres, T. J. "Historical Perspectives on Sharecropping." In his *Sharecropping and Sharecroppers,* 7–40. London: Frank Cass, 1983.

Campbell, Randolph B. *An Empire for Slavery: The Peculiar Institution in Texas, 1821–1865.* Baton Rouge: Louisiana State University Press, 1989.

Canzoneri, Antonia. "Early History of the Baptists in the Bahamas." *Journal of the Bahamas Historical Society* 4, no. 1 (October 1982): 9–16.

Cardoso, Ciro Flamarion S. "The Formation of the Coffee Estate in Nineteenth-Century

Costa Rica." In *Land and Labour in Latin America: Essays in the Development of Agrarian Capitalism in the Nineteenth and Twentieth Centuries,* edited by Kenneth Duncan and Ian Rutledge, 165–202. Cambridge: Cambridge University Press, 1977.

———. "The Peasant Breach in the Slave System: New Developments in Brazil." *Luso-Brazilian Review* 25, no. 1 (Summer 1988): 49–57.

Chaplin, Joyce E. *An Anxious Pursuit: Agricultural Innovation and Modernity in the Lower South, 1730–1815.* Chapel Hill: University of North Carolina Press, 1993.

———. "Creating a Cotton South in Georgia and South Carolina, 1760–1815." *Journal of Southern History* 57, no. 2 (May 1991): 171–200.

Cohen, Stanley, and Andrew Scull, eds. *Social Control and the State: Historical and Comparative Essays.* Oxford: Martin Robertson, 1983.

Conrad, Robert Edgar. *World of Sorrow: The African Slave Trade to Brazil.* Baton Rouge: Louisiana State University Press, 1986.

Cooper, Adrienne. "Sharecroppers and Landlords in Bengal, 1930–50: The Dependency Web and Its Implications." In *Sharecropping and Sharecroppers,* edited by T. J. Byres, 226–55. London: Frank Cass, 1983.

Cooper, Frederick. *From Slaves to Squatters: Plantation Labor and Agriculture in Zanzibar and Coastal Kenya, 1890–1925.* New Haven: Yale University Press, 1980.

Craton, Michael. *A History of the Bahamas.* 3d ed. Waterloo, Ont.: San Salvador Press, 1986.

———. "Hobbesian or Panglossian? The Two Extremes of Slave Conditions in the British Caribbean, 1783 to 1834." *William and Mary Quarterly,* 3d series, 35, no. 2 (April 1978): 324–56.

———. "Hope Town and Hard Bargain: The Loyalist Transformation in the Bahamas." In *Settlements in the Americas: Cross-Cultural Perspectives,* edited by Ralph Bennett, 252–82. Newark: University of Delaware Press, 1993.

———. "We Shall Not Be Moved: Pompey's Slave Revolt in Exuma Island, 1830." *Nieuwe West-Indische Gids/New West Indian Guide* 57, nos. 1 and 2 (1983): 19–36.

Craton, Michael, and Gail Saunders. *Islanders in the Stream: A History of the Bahamian People.* Vol. 2: *From Aboriginal Times to the End of Slavery.* Athens: University of Georgia Press, 1992.

Crisp, Olga. "Labour and Industrialization in Russia." In *The Cambridge Economic History of Europe,* edited by Peter Mathias and M. M. Postan, vol. 7, part 2, 308–415. Cambridge: Cambridge University Press, 1978.

Curtin, Philip D. *The Atlantic Slave Trade: A Census.* Madison: University of Wisconsin Press, 1969.

———. *Two Jamaicas: The Role of Ideas in a Tropical Colony, 1830–1865.* Cambridge, Mass.: Harvard University Press, 1955.

Dalleo, Peter D. "Africans in the Caribbean: A Preliminary Assessment of Recaptives in the Bahamas 1811–1860." *Journal of the Bahamas Historical Society* 6, no. 1 (October 1984): 15–24.

———. "'Making Pickle': Salt-Raking in the Bahamas in the Nineteenth Century." Unpublished Paper, 22d Conference of the Association of Caribbean Historians, Nassau, Bahamas, March 1992.

Danns, George K. *Domination and Power in Guyana: A Study of the Police in a Third World Context.* New Brunswick, N.J.: Transaction Books, 1982.

Davidson, Basil. *Africa in Modern History; The Search for a New Society.* London: Allen Lane, 1978.

Department of Archives. "The Loyalist Bi-Centennial." Nassau, 1983.

———. "The Sponging Industry." Nassau, 1974.

Dodge, Steve. *Abaco: The History of an Out Island and Its Cays.* Decatur, Ill.: White Sound Press, 1983.

Donald, Henderson H. *The Negro Freedman: Life Conditions of the American Negro in the Early Years After Emancipation.* New York: H. Schuman, 1952.

Duncan, Kenneth, and Ian Rutledge, eds. *Land and Labour in Latin America: Essays on the Development of Agrarian Capitalism in the Nineteenth and Twentieth Centuries.* Cambridge: Cambridge University Press, 1977.

Eaton, Clement. "Slave-Hiring in the Upper South: A Step Toward Freedom." *Mississippi Valley Historical Review* 46, no. 4 (March 1960): 663–78.

Eitzen, D. Stanley. "Two Minorities: The Jews of Poland and the Chinese of the Philippines." In *Majority and Minority: The Dynamics of Racial and Ethnic Relations,* edited by Norman R. Yetman and C. Hoy Steele, 117–37. Boston: Allyn & Bacon, 1971.

Eltis, David. "The Traffic in Slaves Between the British West Indian Colonies, 1807–1833." *Economic History Review,* 2d series, 25, no. 1 (February 1972): 55–64.

Emmer, P. C., ed. *Colonialism and Migration; Indentured Labour Before and After Slavery.* Dordrecht: Martinus Nijhoff, 1986.

Engerman, Stanley L. "Servants to Slaves to Servants: Contract Labour and European Expansion." In *Colonialism and Migration; Indentured Labour Before and After Slavery,* edited by P. C. Emmer, 263–94. Dordrecht: Martinus Nijhoff, 1986.

Enloe, Cynthia. *Ethnic Soldiers: State Security in Divided Societies.* Athens: University of Georgia Press, 1980.

Eric, Allan. *"Buckra Land" Land: Two Weeks in Jamaica: Details of a Voyage to the West Indies, Day by Day, and a Tour of Jamaica, Step by Step.* 2d ed. Boston: Boston Fruit Company, 1897.

Erickson, Charlotte. "Why Did Contract Labour Not Work in the Nineteenth Century United States?" In *International Labour Migration: Historical Perspective,* edited by Shula Marks and Peter Richardson, 34–56. London: Maurice Temple Smith, 1984.

Feduccia, Alan, ed. *Catesby's Birds of Colonial America.* Chapel Hill: University of North Carolina Press, 1985.

Fernández, Manuel. "British Nitrate Companies and the Emergence of Chile's Proletariat, 1800–1914." In *Proletarianisation in the Third World: Studies in the Creation of a Labour Force Under Dependent Capitalism,* edited by B. Munslow and H. Finch, 42–76. London: Croom Helm, 1984.

Fields, Barbara Jeanne. *Slavery and Freedom on the Middle Ground: Maryland During the Nineteenth Century.* New Haven: Yale University Press, 1985.

Frucht, Richard. "A Caribbean Social Type: Neither 'Peasant' Nor 'Proletarian.'" *Social and Economic Studies* 16, no. 3 (September 1967): 295–301.

Fyfe, Christopher. "Freed Slave Colonies in West Africa." In *The Cambridge History of Africa,* edited by John E. Flint, vol. 5, 171–99. Cambridge: Cambridge University Press, 1976.

———. *A History of Sierra Leone.* London: Oxford University Press, 1962.

Galenson, David W. *White Servitude in Colonial America: An Economic Analysis.* Cambridge: Cambridge University Press, 1981.

Gaspar, David Barry. "Slavery, Amelioration, and Sunday Markets in Antigua, 1823–1831." *Slavery and Abolition* 9, no. 1 (May 1988): 1–28.

Gatrell, V. A. C. "Crime, Authority and the Policeman-State." In *The Cambridge Social History of Britain, 1750–1950,* edited by F. M. L. Thompson, vol. 3, 243–310. Cambridge: Cambridge University Press, 1991.

Genovese, Eugene. *The Political Economy of Slavery: Studies in the Economy and Society of the Slave South.* New York: Vintage Books, 1965.

Goldfield, David R. "Pursuing the American Urban Dream: Cities in the Old South." In *The City in Southern History: The Growth of Urban Civilization in the South,* edited by Blaine A. Brownell and David R. Goldfield, 52–91. Port Washington, N.Y.: Kennikat Press, 1977.

Goldin, Claudia Dale. *Urban Slavery in the American South, 1820–1860: A Quantitative History.* Chicago: University of Chicago Press, 1976.

Goodman, David, and Michael Redclift. *From Peasant to Proletarian: Capitalist Development and Agrarian Transitions.* Oxford: Basil Blackwell, 1981.

Goveia, Elsa V. *Slave Society in the British Leeward Islands at the End of the Eighteenth Century.* New Haven: Yale University Press, 1965.

———. *The West Indian Slave Laws of the Eighteenth Century.* Barbados: Caribbean Universities Press, 1970.

Graves, Adrian. "Truck and Gifts: Melanesian Immigrants and the Trade Box System in Colonial Queensland." *Past and Present,* no. 101 (November 1983): 87–124.

Gray, Lewis Cecil. *History of Agriculture in the Southern United States to 1860.* 2 vols. Washington, D.C.: Carnegie Institution of Washington, 1933.

Green, William A. "The Perils of Comparative History: Belize and the British Sugar Colonies After Slavery." *Comparative Studies in Society and History* 26, no. 1 (January 1984): 112–19.

Greenberg, David. "The Contract, 'The Project' and Work Experiences." In *Strangers No More,* edited by Joel S. Savishinsky, 170–207. Ithaca, N.Y.: Ithaca College, Department of Anthropology, 1978.

Gutteridge, William F. "Military and Police Forces in Colonial Africa." In *Colonialism in Africa 1870–1960,* edited by L. H. Gann and Peter Duignan, vol. 2, 286–319. Cambridge: Cambridge University Press, 1970.

Hahn, Steven. "Hunting, Fishing, and Foraging: Common Rights and Class Relations in the Postbellum South." *Radical History Review* 26 (1982): 37–64.

Hall, Douglas. *Free Jamaica, 1838–1865.* New Haven: Yale University Press, 1959.

Hall, Neville A. T. *Slave Society in the Danish West Indies,* edited by B. W. Higman. Mona, Jamaica: University of the West Indies Press, 1992.

Hammond, J. L., and Barbara Hammond. *The Town Labourer.* New ed. London: Longman, 1978.

Handler, J. S. "The History of Arrowroot and the Origins of Peasantries in the British West Indies." *Journal of Caribbean History* 2 (May 1971): 46–93.

Hart, Richard. *Black Jamaicans' Struggle Against Slavery.* Kingston, Jamaica: Institute of Jamaica for the African-Caribbean Institute, 1977.

Harvey, Thomas C. *Official Reports of the Out Islands of the Bahamas.* Nassau: Nassau Guardian, 1858.

Hawkins, Richard. "The 'Irish Model' and the Empire: A Case for Reassessment." In *Policing the Empire: Government, Authority and Control, 1830–1940,* edited by David M. Anderson and David Killingray, 18–32. Manchester: Manchester University Press, 1991.

Higgs, Robert. *Competition and Coercion: Blacks in the American Economy 1865–1914.* New York: Cambridge University Press, 1977.

Higman, B. W. *Slave Populations of the British Caribbean 1807–1834.* Baltimore: Johns Hopkins University Press, 1984.

Hilton, George W. *The Truck System Including a History of the British Truck Acts 1465–1960.* Rpt. Westport, Conn.: Greenwood Press, 1975.

Hu-DeHart, Evelyn. "Immigrants to a Developing Society: The Chinese in Northern Mexico, 1875–1932." In *The Chinese Experience in Arizona and Northern Mexico,* 49–86. Tucson: Arizona Historical Society, 1980.

Hughes, Colin A. *Race and Politics in the Bahamas.* New York: St. Martin's Press, 1981.

Hughes, Sarah S. "Slaves for Hire: The Allocation of Black Labor in Elizabeth City County, Virginia, 1782 to 1810." *William and Mary Quarterly,* 3d series, 35, no. 2 (April 1978): 260–86.

Hurt, R. Douglas. *Agriculture and Slavery in Missouri's Little Dixie.* Columbia, Mo.: University of Missouri Press, 1992.

Ignatieff, Michael. "State, Civil Society and Total Institutions: A Critique of Recent Social Histories of Punishment." In *Social Control and the State: Historical and Comparative Essays,* edited by Stanley Cohen and Andrew Scull, 75–105. Oxford: Martin Robertson, 1983.

Johnson, Howard. "The Anti-Chinese Riots of 1918 in Jamaica." *Immigrants and Minorities* 3, no. 1 (March 1983): 50–63.

———. *The Bahamas in Slavery and Freedom.* Kingston: Ian Randle, 1991.

———. "Barbadian Immigrants in Trinidad 1870–1897." *Caribbean Studies* 13, no. 3 (October 1973): 5–30.

———. "Friendly Societies in the Bahamas, 1834–1910." *Slavery and Abolition* 12, no. 3 (December 1991): 183–99.

———. "Labour on the Move: West Indian Migration to the Bahamas, 1922–1930." *Revista/Review Interamericana* 13, nos. 1–4 (Winter 1983): 85–98.

———. "Labour Systems in Postemancipation Bahamas." In "Caribbean Economic History," edited by B. W. Higman. *Social and Economic Studies* 37, nos. 1 and 2 (March-June 1988): 181–201.

———. "Merchant Credit and the Dispossession of the Cocoa Peasantry in Trinidad in the Late Nineteenth Century." *Peasant Studies* 15, no. 1 (Fall 1987): 27–38.

———. "The Origins and Early Development of Cane Farming in Trinidad, 1882–1906." *Journal of Caribbean History* 5 (November 1972): 46–74.

———. "Patterns of Policing in the Post-Emancipation British Caribbean, 1835–95." In *Policing the Empire: Government, Authority and Control, 1830–1940,* edited by David M. Anderson and David Killingray, 72–91. Manchester: Manchester University Press, 1991.

———. "Slave Life and Leisure in Nassau, Bahamas, 1783–1838." *Slavery and Abolition* 16, no. 1 (April 1995): 45–64.

———. "A Slow and Extended Abolition: The Case of the Bahamas, 1800–1838. In *From Chattel to Wage Slaves: The Dynamics of Labour Bargaining in the Americas,* edited by Mary Turner, 165–81. London: James Currey, 1995.

Jones, Maldwyn Allen. *American Immigration.* Chicago: University of Chicago Press, 1960.

Joseph, Cedric L. "The Strategic Importance of the British West Indies, 1882–1932." *Journal of Caribbean History* 7 (November 1973): 23–67.

Kannangara, A. P. "The Riots of 1915 in Sri Lanka: A Study in the Roots of Communal Violence." *Past and Present,* no. 102 (February 1984): 130–65.

Karasch, Mary. *Slave Life in Rio de Janeiro 1808–1856.* Princeton: Princeton University Press, 1987.

Karch, Cecilia. "The Growth of the Corporate Economy in Barbados: Class/Race Factors, 1890–1977." In *Contemporary Caribbean: A Sociological Reader,* edited by Susan Craig, 1:213–42. Maracas, Trinidad, and Tobago: Susan Craig, 1981.

Keegan, William F. *The People Who Discovered Columbus: The Prehistory of the Bahamas.* Gainesville: University Press of Florida, 1992.

Kirk-Greene, A. H. M. "'Damnosa Hereditas': Ethnic Ranking and the Martial Races Imperative in Africa." *Ethnic and Racial Studies* 3, no. 4 (October 1980): 392–414.

Kloosterboer, W. *Involuntary Labour Since the Abolition of Slavery.* Leiden: E. J. Brill, 1960.

Knight, Alan. "Mexican Peonage: What Was It and Why Was It?" *Journal of Latin American Studies* 18, part 1 (May 1986): 41–74.

Koger, Larry. *Black Slaveowners: Free Black Slave Masters in South Carolina, 1790–1860.* Jefferson, N.C.: McFarland, 1985.

Kolchin, Peter. *Unfree Labor: American Slavery and Russian Serfdom.* Cambridge, Mass.: Harvard University Press, 1987.

Kubicek, Robert V. *The Administration of Imperialism: Joseph Chamberlain at the Colonial Office.* Durham, N.C.: Duke University Press, 1969.

Kula, Witold. "Money and the Serfs in Eighteenth Century Poland." In *Peasants in History: Essays in Honour of Daniel Thomer,* edited by E. J. Hobsbawm, Witold Kula, Ashok Mitra, K. N. Raj, and Ignacy Sachs, 30–41. Calcutta: Oxford University Press, 1980.

Laurence, K. O. "The Evolution of Long-Term Labour Contracts in Trinidad and British Guiana, 1834–1863." *Jamaican Historical Review* 5 (May 1965): 9–27.

———. *Immigration into the West Indies in the Nineteenth Century.* Barbados: Caribbean Universities Press, 1971.

Lenin, V. I. *The Development of Capitalism in Russia.* Rpt. Moscow: Progress, 1977.

Le Page, R. B., and Andrée Tabouret-Keller. *Acts of Identity: Creole-Based Approaches to Language and Ethnicity.* Cambridge: Cambridge University Press, 1985.

Leuchtenburg, William E. *The Perils of Prosperity, 1914–32.* Chicago: University of Chicago Press, 1958.

Lewis, Gordon K. *The Growth of the Modern West Indies.* New York: Monthly Review Press, 1968.

Lewis, Ronald L. *Coal, Iron, and Slaves: Industrial Slavery in Maryland and Virginia, 1715–1865.* Westport, Conn.: Greenwood Press, 1979.

Lewis, W. Arthur. "The Export Stimulus." In *Tropical Development 1880–1913: Studies in Economic Progress,* edited by W. Arthur Lewis, 13–45. London: Allen & Unwin, 1970.

Lovejoy, Paul E. *Transformations in Slavery: A History of Slavery in Africa.* Cambridge: Cambridge University Press, 1983.

Lowenthal, David. *West Indian Societies.* London: Oxford University Press, 1972.

Mandle, Jay. *The Roots of Black Poverty: The Southern Plantation Economy After the Civil War.* Durham, N.C.: Duke University Press, 1978.

Marshall, W. K. "Metayage in the Sugar Industry of the British Windward Islands, 1838–1865." *Jamaican Historical Review* 5 (May 1965): 28–55.

Martínez Vergne, Teresita. "The Allocation of Liberated African Labour Through the Case da Beneficiencia: San Juan, Puerto Rico, 1859–1864." *Slavery and Abolition* 12, no. 3 (December 1991): 200–216.

Mattoso, Katia M. De Queirós. *To Be a Slave in Brazil 1500–1888.* New Brunswick, N.J.: Rutgers University Press, 1986.

Mayer, John A. "Notes Toward a Working Definition of Social Control in Historical Analysis." In *Social Control and the State: Historical and Comparative Essays,* edited by Stanley Cohen and Andrew Scull, 17–32. Oxford: Martin Robertson, 1983.

McCusker, John J. *Money and Exchange in Europe and America, 1600–1775: A Handbook.* Chapel Hill: University of North Carolina Press, 1978.

McCusker, John J., and Russell R. Menard. *The Economy of British America, 1607–1789.* Chapel Hill: University of North Carolina Press, 1985.

McDonald, Roderick A. *The Economy and Material Culture of Slaves: Goods and Chattels on the Sugar Plantation of Jamaica and Louisiana.* Baton Rouge: Louisiana State University Press, 1993.

McKinnen, Daniel. *A Tour Through the British West Indies, in the Years, 1802 and 1803, Giving a Particular Account of the Bahama Islands.* London: J. White, 1804.

Melish, John. *A Description of East and West Florida and the Bahama Islands.* Philadelphia: Palmers, 1813.

Metcalf, Thomas R. *The Aftermath of Revolt: India, 1857–1870.* Princeton: Princeton University Press, 1964.

Millar, Robert. "On the Cultivation of Cotton in the Bahamas." *Journal of the Bahama Society for the Diffusion of Knowledge,* no. 6 (November 1835): 48–51.

Mingay, G. E. *A Social History of the English Countryside.* London: Routledge, 1990.

Mintz, Sidney W. *Caribbean Transformation.* Chicago: Aldine, 1974.

———. "Slavery and the Rise of Peasantries." *Historical Reflections/Réflexions Historiques* 6, no. 1 (Summer 1979): 213–42.

———. "Was the Plantation Slave a Proletarian?" *Review* 2, no. 1 (Summer 1978): 81–98.

Mintz, Sidney W., and Douglas Hall. "The Origins of the Jamaican Internal Marketing System." *Yale University Publications in Anthropology,* no. 57 (1960): 1–26.

Mitchell, Robert D. "The Formation of Early American Cultural Regions: An Interpretation." In *European Settlement and Development in North America: Essays on Geographical Change in Honour and Memory of Andrew Hill Clark,* edited by James R. Gibson, 66–90. Toronto: University of Toronto Press, 1978.

Mooney, Charles N. "Soils of the Bahama Islands." In *The Bahama Islands,* edited by George Burbank Shattuck, 147–81. New York: Macmillan, 1905.

Moore, Brian L. *Race, Power and Social Segmentation in Colonial Society: Guyana After Slavery, 1839–1891.* New York: Gordon and Breach, 1991.

Moore, John Hebron. *The Emergence of the Cotton Kingdom in the Old Southwest, Mississippi, 1770–1860.* Baton Rouge: Louisiana State University Press, 1988.

Moreno Fraginals, Manuel. "Plantations in the Caribbean: Cuba, Puerto Rico, and the Dominican Republic in the Late Nineteenth Century." In *Between Slavery and Free Labor: The Spanish-Speaking Caribbean in the Nineteenth Century,* edited by Manuel Moreno Fraginals, Frank Moya Pons, and Stanley L. Engerman, 3–24. Baltimore: Johns Hopkins University Press, 1985.

———. *The Sugarmill: The Socioeconomic Complex of Sugar in Cuba, 1760–1860.* New York: Monthly Review Press, 1976.

Morgan, Philip. "Black Life in Eighteenth Century Charleston." *Perspectives in American History,* new series, 1 (1984): 187–232.

———. "Black Society in the Lowcountry, 1760–1810." In *Slavery and Freedom in the Age of the American Revolution,* edited by Ira Berlin and Ronald Hoffman, 83–142. Charlottesville: University Press of Virginia, 1983.

———. "Work and Culture: The Task System and the World of Lowcountry Blacks, 1700–1880." *William and Mary Quarterly,* 3d series, no. 4 (October 1982): 563–93.

Mörner, Magnus, Julia Fawaz De Viñuela, and John D. French. "Comparative Approaches to Latin American History." *Latin American Research Review* 17, no. 3 (1982): 55–90.

Morris, Richard. "The Measure of Bondage in the Slave South." *Mississippi Valley Historical Review* 41, no. 2 (September 1954): 219–40.

Mullin, Gerald W. *Flight and Rebellion: Slave Resistance in Eighteenth Century Virginia.* New York: Oxford University Press, 1972.

Murray, David R. *Odious Commerce: Britain, Spain and the Abolition of the Cuban Slave Trade.* Cambridge: Cambridge University Press, 1980.

Myers, Robert A. "'I love my home bad, but. . . .': The Historical and Contemporary Context of Migration on Dominica, West Indies." Ph.D. diss., University of North Carolina, 1976.

Nash, Gary B., and Jean R. Soderlund. *Freedom by Degrees: Emancipation in Pennsylvania and Its Aftermath.* New York: Oxford University Press, 1991.

Newton, Velma. *The Silver Men: West Indian Labour Migration to Panama, 1850–1914.* Mona, Jamaica: Institute of Social and Economic Research, 1984.

Nicholls, David. "No Hawkers and Pedlars: Levantines in the Caribbean." *Ethnic and Racial Studies* 4, no. 4 (October 1981): 415–31.

North, D. Gail. "The Amelioration and Abolition of Slavery in the Bahamas, 1808–1838." B.A. diss., Modern History, University of Newcastle-upon-Tyne, 1966.

Northcroft, G. H. J. *Sketches of Summerland. Giving Some Account of Nassau and the Bahama Islands.* Nassau: Nassau Guardian, 1900.

Nwulia, Moses D. *The History of Slavery in Mauritius and the Seychelles, 1810–1875.* East Brunswick, N.J.: Fairleigh Dickinson University Press, 1981.

Oldmixon, John. *The History of the Isle of Providence.* Rpt. from *The British Empire in America,* 2 vols., 1741, with an introduction by Jack Culmer. Nassau: Providence Press, 1949.

Parker, Geoffrey. "Warfare." In *The New Cambridge Modern History,* edited by Peter Burke, vol. 13, 201–19. Cambridge: Cambridge University Press.

Parks, Arva Moore. *Miami: The Magic City.* Tulsa: Larry P. Silver and Douglas S. Drown, 1981.

Pearce, R. "Sharecropping: Towards a Marxist View." In *Sharecropping and Sharecroppers,* edited by T. J. Byres, 42–70. London: Frank Cass, 1983.

Peggs, A. Deans. *A Short History of the Bahamas.* 3d ed. Nassau: Tribune, 1959.

Peters, Thelma P. "The American Loyalists and the Plantation Period in the Bahama Islands." Ph.D. diss., University of Florida, 1960.

———. "The American Loyalists in the Bahama Islands: Who Were They." *Florida Historical Quarterly* 40, no. 3 (January 1962): 226–40.

Petras, Elizabeth McLean. "The Global Labor Market in the Modern World-Economy." In *Global Trends in Migration: Theory and Research on International Population Movements,* edited by Mary M. Kritz, Charles B. Keely, and Silvano M. Tomasi, 44–63. Staten Island: Center for Migration Studies, 1981.

———. *Jamaican Labor Migration: White Capital and Black Labor, 1850–1930.* Boulder: Westview Press, 1988.

Portes, Alejandro, and John Walton. *Labor, Class, and the International System.* Orlando: Academic Press, 1981.

Powles, L. D. *Land of the Pink Pearl.* London: S. Low, Marston, Searle and Rivington, 1888.

Pye, Michael. *The King over the Water.* London: Hutchinson, 1981.

Ransom, Roger L., and Richard Sutch. *One Kind of Freedom: The Economic Consequences of Emancipation.* New York: Cambridge University Press, 1977.

Richardson, Bonham C. *Caribbean Migrants: Environment and Human Survival on St. Kitts and Nevis.* Knoxville: University of Tennessee Press, 1983.

———. *Panama Money in Barbados, 1900–20.* Knoxville: University of Tennessee Press, 1985.

Riley, Sandra. *Homeward Bound: A History of the Bahama Islands to 1950, with a Definitive Study of Abaco in the American Loyalist Period.* Miami: Island Research, 1983.

Rodney, Walter. *How Europe Underdeveloped Africa.* Washington: Howard University Press, 1974.

Roseberry, William. *Coffee and Capitalism in the Venezuelan Andes.* Austin: University of Texas Press, 1983.

Rubenstein, Hymie. "Remittances and Rural Underdevelopment in the English-Speaking Caribbean." *Human Organization* 46, no. 4 (Winter 1983): 295–306.

Russell-Wood, A. J. R. *The Black Man in Slavery and Freedom in Colonial Brazil.* New York: St. Martin's Press, 1982.

Saunders, Gail. *Bahamian Loyalists and Their Slaves.* London: Macmillan Caribbean, 1983.

———. "Slave Life, Slave Society and Cotton Production in the Bahamas." *Slavery and Abolition* 11, no. 3 (December 1990): 332–50.

———. *Slavery in the Bahamas 1648–1838.* Nassau: privately published, 1985.

Schoepf, Johann David. *Travels in the Confederation, 1783–1784.* 2 vols. Translated and edited by Alfred J. Morrison. Philadelphia: William J. Campbell, 1911.

Schuler, Monica. *"Alas, Alas, Kongo": A Social History of Indentured African Immigration into Jamaica.* Baltimore: Johns Hopkins University Press, 1980.

———. "The Recruitment of African Indentured Labourers for European Colonies in the Nineteenth Century." In *Colonialism and Migration; Indentured Labour Before and After Slavery,* edited by P. C. Emmer, 125–161. Dordrecht: Martinus Nijhoff, 1986.

Schwartz, Stuart B. *Slaves, Peasants, and Rebels: Reconsidering Brazilian Slavery.* Urbana: University of Illinois Press, 1992.

Schweninger, Loren. *Black Property Owners in the South 1790–1915.* Urbana: University of Illinois Press, 1990.

———. "The Free-Slave Phenomenon: James P. Thomas and the Black Community in Ante-Bellum Nashville." *Civil War History* 22, no. 4 (December 1976): 293–307.

———. "The Underside of Slavery: The Internal Economy, Self-Hire, and Quasi-Freedom in Virginia." *Slavery and Abolition* 12, no. 2 (September 1991): 1–22.

Scott, Rebecca J. "Explaining Abolition: Contradiction, Adaptation, and Challenge in Cuban Slave Society, 1860–1886." In *Between Slavery and Free Labor: The Spanish-Speaking Caribbean in the Nineteenth Century,* edited by Manuel Moreno Fraginals, Frank Moya Pons, and Stanley L. Engerman, 25–53. Baltimore: Johns Hopkins University Press, 1985.

———. *Slave Emancipation in Cuba: The Transition to Free Labor, 1860–1899.* Princeton: Princeton University Press, 1985.

Scott, Rebecca J., et al., eds. *The Abolition of Slavery and the Aftermath of Emancipation in Brazil.* Durham, N.C.: Duke University Press, 1988.

Sealey, Neil E. *The Bahamas Today: An Introduction to the Human and Economic Geography of the Bahamas.* London: Macmillan Caribbean, 1990.

Shedden, Roscow. *Ups and Downs in a West Indian Diocese.* Milwaukee: Morehouse, 1927.

Shenton, R. W., and Louise Lennihan. "Capital and Class: Peasant Differentiation in Northern Nigeria." *Journal of Peasant Studies* 9, no. 1 (October 1981): 47–70.

Sheridan, Richard B. *Doctors and Slaves: A Medical and Demographic History of Slavery in the British West Indies, 1680–1834.* New York: Cambridge University Press, 1985.

Shilling, Alison Watt. "Some Non-Standard Features of Bahamian Dialect Syntax." Ph.D. diss., University of Hawaii, 1978.

Shlomowitz, Ralph. "The Origins of Southern Sharecropping." *Agricultural History* 53, no. 3 (July 1979): 557–75.

Siebert, Wilbur H. *The Legacy of the American Revolution to the British West Indies and Bahamas: A Chapter Out of the History of the American Loyalists.* 1913. Rpt. with a new introduction and preface by George Athan Billias. Boston: Gregg Press, 1972.

———. *Loyalists in East Florida 1774 to 1785.* 2 vols. DeLand: Florida State Historical Society, 1929.

Smith, Julia Floyd. *Slavery and Plantation Growth in Antebellum Florida, 1821–1860.* Gainesville: University of Florida Press, 1973.

Spackman, Ann. "Official Attitudes and Official Violence: The Ruimveldt Massacre, Guyana 1924." *Social and Economic Studies* 22, no. 3 (September 1973): 315–34.

Starobin, Robert S. *Industrial Slavery in the Old South.* New York: Oxford University Press, 1970.

Stavenhagen, Rodolfo. *Social Classes in Agrarian Societies.* Garden City, N.Y.: Anchor Press, 1975.

Stavrianos, L. S. *Global Rift.* New York: William Morrow, 1981.

Stein, Stanley J. *Vassouras: A Brazilian Coffee County, 1850–1900.* Cambridge, Mass.: Harvard University Press, 1957.

Stern, Steve J. "Feudalism, Capitalism and the World-System in the Perspective of Latin America and the Caribbean." *American Historical Review* 93, no. 4 (October 1988): 829–72.

Stolcke, Verena. "The Labors of Coffee in Latin America: The Hidden Charm of Family Labor and Self-Provisioning." In *Coffee, Society, and Power in Latin America,* edited by William Roseberry, Lowell Gudmundson, and Mario Samper Kutschbach, 65–93. Baltimore: Johns Hopkins University Press, 1995.

Stolcke, Verena, and Michael M. Hall. "The Introduction of Free Labour on São Paulo Coffee Plantations." In *Sharecropping and Sharecroppers,* edited by T. J. Byres, 170–200. London: Frank Cass, 1983.

Strickland, John Scott. "Traditional Culture and Moral Economy: Social and Economic Change in the South Carolina Low Country 1865–1910." In *The Countryside in the Age of Capitalist Transformation: Essays in the Social History of Rural America,* edited by Steven Hahn and Jonathan Prude, 141–78. Chapel Hill: University of North Carolina Press, 1985.

Temperley, Howard. "Anti-Slavery as a Form of Cultural Imperialism." In *Anti-Slavery, Religion and Reform: Essays in Memory of Roger Ansley,* edited by Christine Bolt and Seymour Drescher, 335–50. Folkestone, Kent: W. Dawson, 1980.

Tomich, Dale W. *Slavery in the Circuit of Sugar: Martinique and the World Economy, 1830–1848.* Baltimore: Johns Hopkins University Press, 1990.

The Tribune Handbook. Nassau: Nassau Daily Tribune, 1924.

Trotman, David Vincent. *Crime in Trinidad: Conflict and Control in a Plantation Society, 1838–1900.* Knoxville: University of Tennessee Press, 1986.

Turner, Mary. "Chattel Slaves into Wage Slaves: A Jamaican Case Study." In *Labour in the*

Caribbean from Emancipation to Independence, edited by Malcolm Cross and Gad Heuman, 14–31. London: Macmillan Caribbean, 1988.

Usner, Daniel H. Jr. "Food Marketing and Interethnic Exchange in the 18th Century Lower Mississippi Valley." *Food and Foodways* 1, no. 3 (1986): 279–310.

———. "The Frontier Exchange Economy of the Lower Mississippi Valley in the Eighteenth Century." *William and Mary Quarterly,* 3d series, 44, no. 2 (April 1987): 165–92.

Wade, Richard C. *Slavery in the Cities: The South, 1820–1860.* New York: Oxford University Press, 1964.

Wallerstein, Immanuel. *The Modern World-System.* 2 vols. New York: Academic Press, 1974.

Walvin, James. "Slaves, Free Time, and the Question of Leisure." *Slavery and Abolition* 16, no. 1 (April 1995): 1–13.

Watts, David. *The West Indies: Patterns of Development, Culture, and Environmental Change Since 1492.* Cambridge: Cambridge University Press, 1987.

Wertheim, W. F. "The Trading Minorities in Southeast Asia." In *East-West Parallels: Sociological Approaches to Modern Asia,* edited by W. F. Wertheim, 39–82. The Hague: N. V. Uitgeverij W. van Hoeve, 1964.

Whayne, Jeannie. "Creation of a Plantation System in the Arkansas Delta in the Twentieth Century." *Agricultural History* 66, no. 1 (Winter 1992): 63–84.

Wiener, Jonathan W. "Class Structure and Economic Development in the American South, 1865–1955." *American Historical Review* 84, no. 4 (October 1979): 970–92.

Williams, Eric. *History of the People of Trinidad and Tobago.* London: Andre Deutsch, 1970.

Williams, Patrice. "The Emigrant Labour Business: An Important Industry in the Late Nineteenth and Early Twentieth Centuries?" *Journal of the Bahamas Historical Society* 6, no. 1 (October 1985): 9–14.

———. *A Guide to African Villages in the Bahamas.* Nassau: Department of Archives, 1979.

Winder, R. Bayley. "The Lebanese in West Africa." *Comparative Studies in Society and History* 4, no. 3 (April 1962): 296–333.

Windhorn, Stan, and Wright Langley. *Yesterday's Key West.* Miami: Seeman, 1973.

Wood, Betty. *Slavery in Colonial Georgia, 1730–1775.* Athens: University of Georgia Press, 1984.

———. "'White Society' and the 'Informal' Slave Economies of Lowcountry Georgia c. 1763–1830." *Slavery and Abolition* 11, no. 3 (December 1990): 313–31.

Wood, Peter H. *Black Majority: Negroes in Colonial South Carolina from 1670 Through the Stono Rebellion.* New York: Knopf, 1974.

Woodman, Harold D. "Post-Civil War Southern Agriculture and the Law." *Agricultural History* 53, no. 1 (January 1979): 319–37.

Wright, James M. "History of the Bahama Islands, with a Special Study of the Abolition of Slavery in the Colony." In *The Bahama Islands,* edited by George Burbank Shattuck, 419–583. New York: Macmillan, 1905.

———. "The Wrecking System of the Bahama Islands." *Political Science Quarterly* 30, no. 4 (December 1915): 618–44.

Index

Page numbers in italics refer to tables.